SINGER
The Complete Photo Guide to Sewing

CREATIVE PUBLISHING international

MINNETONKA, MINNESOTA

www.creativepub.com

SINGER
The Complete Photo
Guide to Sewing

Contents

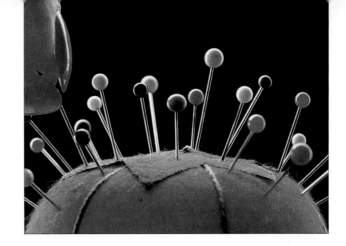

Library of Congress Cataloging-in-Publication Data

Singer : the complete photo guide to sewing.
    p.   cm.
   ISBN 0-86573-173-X (hardcover)
   1. Machine sewing. I. Singer Company. Dept. of Sewing
Education. II. Creative Publishing international. III. Title:
Complete photo guide to sewing.
TT713.S57 1999
646.2--dc21   99-29394

President/CEO: Michael Eleftheriou
Vice President/Publisher: Linda Ball

Copyright © 1999
Creative Publishing international, Inc.
5900 Green Oak Drive
Minnetonka, Minnesota 55343
1-800-328-3895

Created by: The Editors of Creative Publishing
international, Inc., in cooperation with the
Sewing Education Department, Singer
Sewing Company. Singer is a trademark of
The Singer Company Limited and is used
under license.

Printed on American paper by:
R. R. Donnelley & Sons Co.
10 9 8 7 6 5

The Complete Photo Guide to Sewing draws pages from the individual titles of the Singer Sewing Reference Library. Individual titles are also available from the publisher and in book stores and fabric stores:
Sewing Essentials, Sewing for the Home, Clothing Care & Repair, Sewing for Style, Sewing Specialty Fabrics, Sewing Activewear,

The Perfect Fit, Timesaving Sewing, More Sewing for the Home, Tailoring, Sewing for Children, 101 Sewing Secrets, Sewing Pants That Fit, Decorative Machine Stitching, Creative Sewing Ideas, Sewing Lingerie, Sewing Projects for the Home, Sewing with Knits, More Creative Sewing Ideas, Quilt Projects by Machine, Creating Fashion Accessories, Quick & Easy Sewing Projects,

Sewing for Special Occasions, Sewing for the Holidays, Quick & Easy Decorating Projects, Quilted Projects & Garments, Embellished Quilted Projects, Window Treatments, Holiday Projects, Halloween Costumes, Upholstery Basics, Fabric Artistry, The New Sewing with a Serger, The New Quilting by Machine

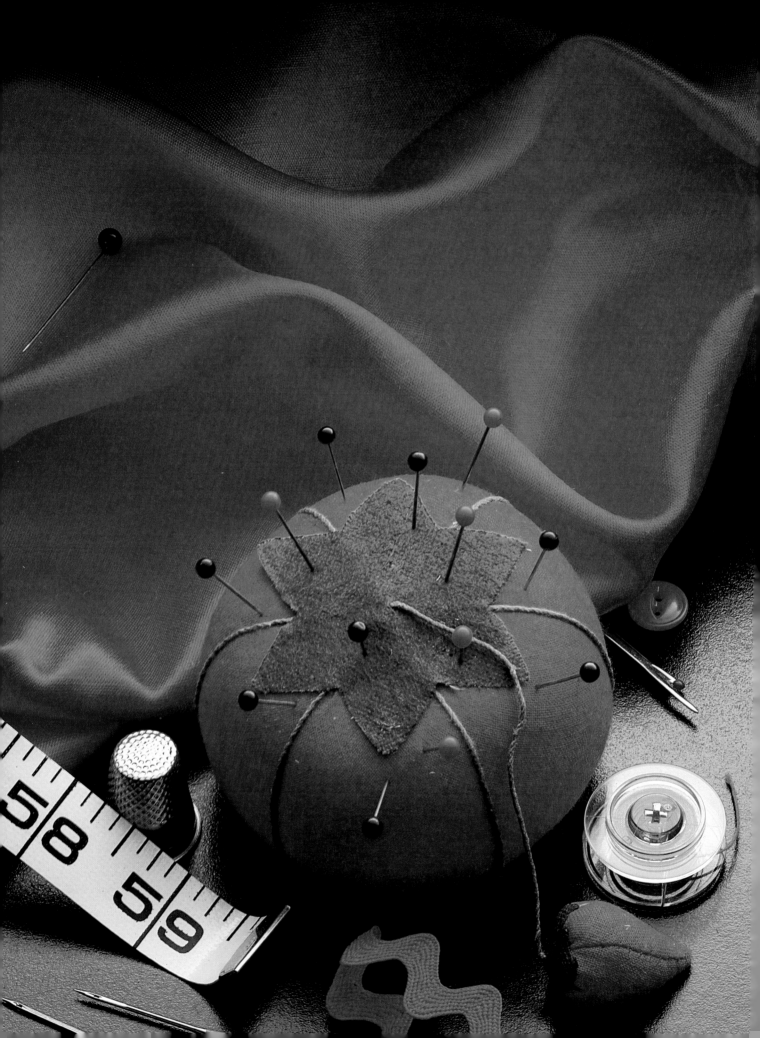

How to Use This Book

Like any other art or craft, sewing begins with basic techniques. *The Complete Photo Guide to Sewing* gives you the essential information you need for sewing garments and for sewing for the home. In addition to basic techniques, specialty sewing topics, such as tailoring, sewing activewear, and sewing for children, are also included.

Getting Started

This section gives you information on the sewing machine and the serger. We show you how to get the perfect stitch and tell you about special features and accessories for both machines. We also tell you about the equipment and notions you will need for all of your sewing, plus some timesaving equipment that will make your sewing easier.

Also covered in the first section is the pattern. You will learn how to take your measurements and select the correct size. A comprehensive guide to fabric selection is included as well as cutting and sewing tips. There is also information on how to choose and apply interfacing.

Sewing Techniques

The first part of this section features the basic techniques you will use for nearly everything you sew: garments and home decorating projects. The basic sewing techniques include fitting, seams, darts, gathering, sleeves, collars, waistbands, cuffs, and closures. Each is given an overview, followed by a step-by-step description of how to achieve the best results. Often several methods are presented with guidance as to when and where to use each one.

The remainder of this section concentrates on specific sewing techniques for tailored garments, children's clothing, and activewear. "Tailoring" introduces you to using fusible interfacing for timesaving and professional results. "Sewing for Children" includes projects for infants, fun ideas for adding durability and grow room, as well as appliqués.

Home Decorating Projects

We start with the basics of fabric and color selection and other tips on planning a project. Instructions for many of the projects include alternate sewing methods and suggest timesaving techniques.

The Home Decorating section is divided into four project categories: windows, pillows, beds, and tables. For windows, we give instructions for standard favorites, such as pinch-pleated draperies, and many others. Pillows range from simple knife-edge styles to ones with flanged edges. Make a comforter cover for your bed, and add pillow shams and a dust ruffle to match. For tables, learn how to make a ruffled table-cloth and many variations of placemats and napkins.

Each category includes an overview and how to take measurements for the projects. For easy reference, fabric and notions required to complete a project are included in a box labeled YOU WILL NEED. The step-by-step instructions are complete: you do not have to purchase additional patterns. The photographs show you how each project should look each step of the way.

Step-by-Step Guidance

The photos add depth and dimension to the instructions, giving you a close-up look at each step. In some cases, the stitches are shown in heavier thread or a contrasting color to make them more visible. Some marking lines have also been exaggerated to show a crucial matching point.

If you are learning to sew or getting back to sewing, you may want to practice your skills on an easy project before starting a larger one. Try sewing simple placemats and napkins to practice a new edge finish. When you sew a first garment, choose a simple style that is easy to fit, with few details.

Whether you are a new sewer, an experienced sewer, or a returning sewer, this book is designed to be a help and an inspiration. Use it as your step-by-step guide to the satisfaction and fun of successful sewing.

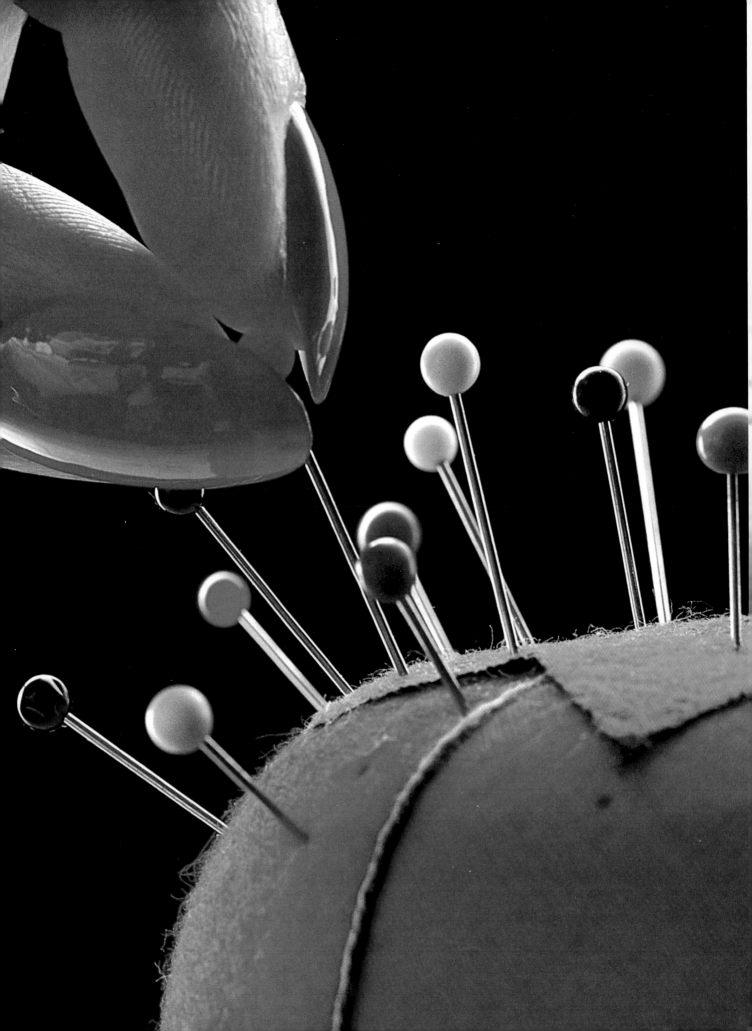

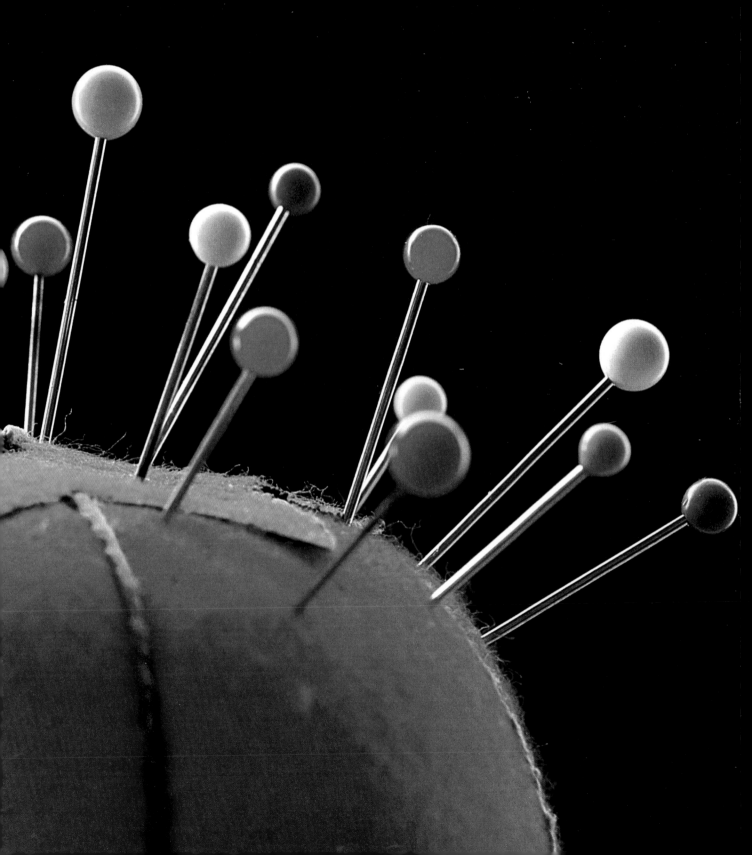

Getting Started

The Sewing Machine

A sewing machine is your most important piece of sewing equipment, so select one with care. A sturdy, well-built machine will give you many years of sewing enjoyment.

If you are buying a new machine, there are a variety of models available to fit any budget or sewing need. Types range from a basic zigzag with one or two built-in stitches, to the electronic machine that uses advanced computer technology to control and select the stitching.

Available features include built-in buttonholer, color-coded stitch selection, instant reverse, snap-on presser foot, free arm for stitching small round areas (such as pants legs), built-in bobbin winder, automatic tension and pressure adjustment, and automatic stitch length adjustment. Each feature usually adds to the cost of the machine, so look for a machine to match your sewing projects. Buy a machine that satisfies your sewing needs, but don't pay for features you will rarely use. Also consider the amount and difficulty of the sewing you do, and the number of people you sew for. Talk to fabric store personnel and friends who sew. Ask for demonstrations, and try out and compare several models. Look for quality workmanship and ease of operation as well as stitching options.

The machine's cabinetry is another factor to consider. Portable machines offer the flexibility of moving to various work surfaces. Machines built into cabinets are designed to be the right height for sewing. They also help you stay organized by providing a convenient place to store sewing equipment and keep it handy.

Although sewing machines vary in capabilities and accessories, each has the same basic parts and controls. The equipment you will need for your machine is described on pages 14 and 15.

The principal parts of the sewing machine (opposite) are shown on a free-arm portable, but its basic parts are representative of all machines. Check your manual for specific location of these parts on your machine.

Machine Essentials

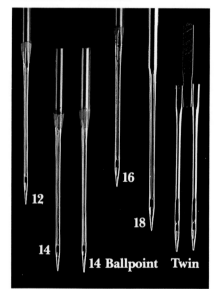

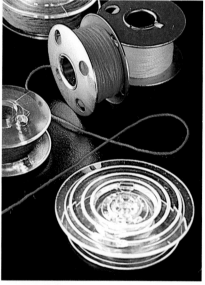

Needles are available in four basic types: *general-purpose* for a wide range of fabrics, in sizes 9/65 (finest) to 18/110; *ballpoint* for knits and stretch fabrics (size 9/65 to 16/100); *twin needle* for decorative stitching; and *wedge-point* (not shown) for leather and vinyl. Change the needle after sewing two to three garments or after hitting a pin. Damaged fabric is often caused by a bent, blunt or burred needle.

Thread for machine sewing comes in three weights: *extra fine* for lightweight fabrics and machine embroidery, *all-purpose* for general-purpose sewing, and *topstitching and buttonhole twist* for decorative and accent stitching. Thread should match the weight of the fabric and the size of the needle. For perfect tension, use the same size and type thread in the bobbin as you use in the needle.

Bobbins may be built-in or removable for winding. Bobbins with a built-in case are wound in the case. Removable bobbins have a removable bobbin case with a tension adjustment screw. They may be wound on the top or side of the machine. Start with an empty bobbin-so the thread will wind evenly. Do not wind it too full or the bobbin thread will break.

Principal Parts of the Sewing Machine

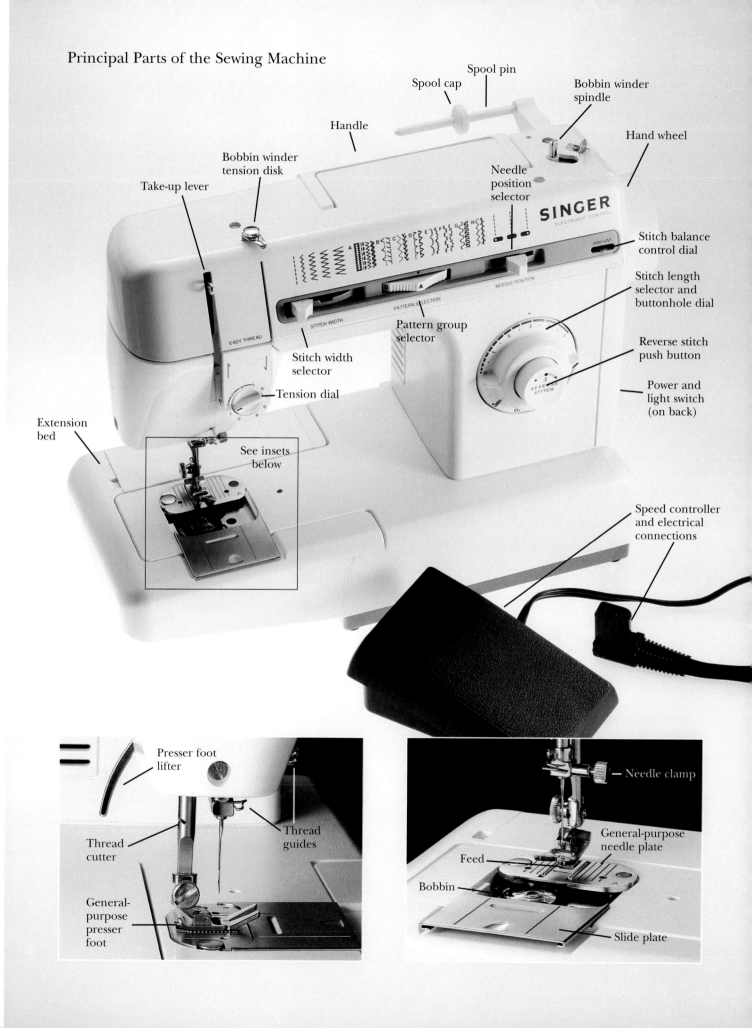

Spool cap

Spool pin

Bobbin winder spindle

Handle

Bobbin winder tension disk

Take-up lever

Needle position selector

Hand wheel

SINGER
ELECTRONIC CONTROL

Stitch balance control dial

Stitch length selector and buttonhole dial

Reverse stitch push button

Power and light switch (on back)

Stitch width selector

Pattern group selector

Tension dial

EASY THREAD

STITCH WIDTH

PATTERN SELECTION

NEEDLE POSITION

REVERSE STITCH

Extension bed

See insets below

Speed controller and electrical connections

Presser foot lifter

Thread cutter

Thread guides

General-purpose presser foot

Needle clamp

General-purpose needle plate

Feed

Bobbin

Slide plate

Creating the Perfect Stitch

Perfect machine stitching is easy to achieve if you thread the machine properly and make the right adjustments in the stitch length, tension and pressure. These adjustments depend on your fabric and the kind of stitch desired. Consult your machine manual for threading procedures and location of controls.

The *stitch length regulator* is on either an inch scale from 0 to 20, a metric scale from 0 to 4, or a numerical scale from 0 to 9. For normal stitching, set the regulator at 10 to 12 stitches per inch, or at the number 3 for metric scale machines. On the numerical scale, higher numbers form a longer stitch; if a shorter stitch is desired, dial a lower number. An average stitch length is at number 5.

A perfect stitch depends on the delicate balance of pressure on the fabric, action of the feed, and tension on the stitch formation. In the ideal stitch, both top and bobbin thread are drawn equally into the fabric, and the link is formed midway between fabric layers.

The *stitch tension control* determines the amount of pressure on the threads as they pass through the machine. Too much pressure results in too little thread fed into the stitch. This causes the fabric to pucker. Too little pressure produces too much thread and a weak, loose stitch.

Adjust the *pressure regulator* for light pressure on lightweight fabrics, more pressure on heavy fabrics. Correct pressure ensures even feeding of the fabric layers during stitching. Some machines automatically adjust tension and pressure to the fabric.

Always check tension and pressure on a scrap of fabric before starting to sew. When experimenting with pressure and tension, thread the machine with different colors for top and bobbin thread to make the stitch links easier to see.

Straight Stitch Tension and Pressure

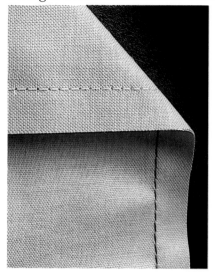

Correct tension and pressure makes stitches that are linked midway between the fabric layers. The stitches look even in length and tension on both sides. Fabric layers are fed evenly through the feed and fabric is not marred.

Too tight tension results in stitch links that are near the top layer of fabric. Fabric is puckered, and stitches are easily broken. Turn tension dial to a lower number. If pressure is too heavy, the bottom layer gathers up and may be damaged. Stitches may be uneven in length and tension. Dial pressure regulator to a lower number.

Too loose tension results in stitch links that are toward the bottom fabric layer. Seam is weak. Correct the problem by turning tension dial to a higher number. Too light pressure causes skipped and uneven stitches, and may pull fabric into the feed. Dial pressure regulator to a higher number.

Zigzag Stitch Tension and Pressure

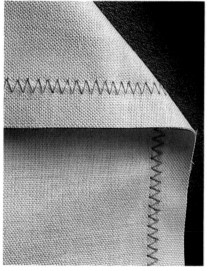

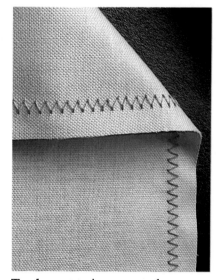

Correct tension and pressure in zigzag stitching produces stitches in which the interlocking link of threads falls at the corner of each stitch, midway between fabric layers. Stitches lie flat and fabric does not pucker.

Too tight tension causes fabric to pucker. The thread link falls near the top fabric layer. To correct, decrease the tension. Incorrect pressure is not as apparent in zigzag as in straight stitching. But if the pressure is not accurate, stitches will not be of even length.

Too loose tension causes the bottom layer to pucker and the thread link to fall near the bottom fabric layer. Increase tension to balance stitch. The zigzag stitch should be properly balanced in normal sewing. Loosen tension slightly for decorative stitches, and the top stitch pattern will become more rounded.

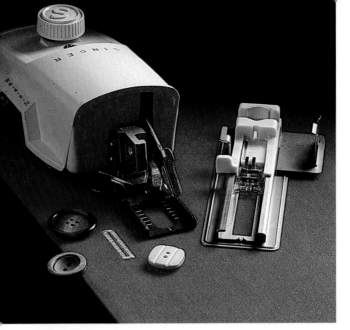

Machine Accessories for Special Tasks

Every sewing machine has accessories that allow it to perform a variety of special tasks. There are universal accessories that fit any machine, such as the zipper foot, buttonhole attachment and various hemming feet. Other accessories, such as a ruffler attachment, are designed to save time and effort for special types of sewing.

When adding a special accessory or foot to a machine you must know if your machine has a high shank, low shank or slanted shank. The *shank* is the distance from the bottom of the presser foot to the attachment screw. Attachments are specifically designed to fit one of these three styles.

The zigzag plate and the general-purpose foot usually come with the machine. Other accessories often included are the straight-stitch plate and foot, buttonhole foot or attachment, zipper foot, seam guide, various hemming feet, and Even Feed™ or roller foot. The machine manual explains how to attach the various accessories and achieve the best results with each.

Buttonhole attachments allow you to stitch complete buttonholes in a single step. One type stitches and adjusts the buttonhole length to fit the button placed in a carrier behind the foot. When the button is larger than 1½" (3.8 cm), or of an unusual shape or thickness, the gauge lines can be used instead of the carrier. Another type of buttonholer for straight-stitch machines makes buttonholes automatically using templates of various sizes. Keyhole buttonholes can be made with this accessory.

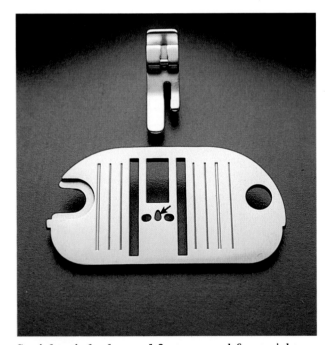

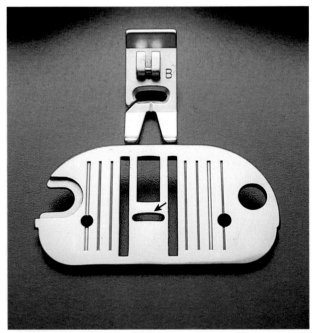

Straight-stitch plate and foot are used for straight stitching only. The needle hole (arrow) in the plate is small and round. The straight-stitch plate and foot do not allow for any sideways needle movement. Use these features when your fabric or sewing procedure requires close control, such as edgestitching or making collar points. They are also good for sheers and delicate fabrics, because the small needle hole helps keep fragile fabrics from being drawn into the feed.

Zigzag plate and foot are the general-purpose plate and foot on a zigzag machine at time of purchase. They are used for zigzag and multi-needle work as well as plain straight stitching on firm fabrics. The needle hole (arrow) in the plate is wider, and the foot has a wider area for the needle to pass through, allowing for side-to-side needle motion. Use this plate and foot for general-purpose sewing.

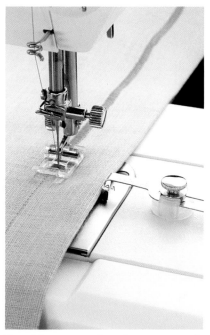

Zipper foot is used to stitch cording, insert zippers or stitch any seam that has more bulk on one side than the other. It adjusts to either side of the needle.

Special purpose foot has a grooved bottom that allows for thread build-up in decorative stitches. Seam guide attaches to machine and helps keep seam allowances and hems even.

Blindstitch hem foot positions the hem for blindstitch hemming on the machine. This is a fast alternative to hemming by hand.

Even Feed™ foot feeds top and bottom layers together so seams start and end evenly. Use it for vinyl, pile fabrics, bulky knits or other fabrics that tend to stick, slip or stretch. This foot is also useful for topstitching and stitching plaids.

Button foot holds flat buttons in position for attaching with machine zigzag stitch. This foot saves time when sewing several buttons on a garment.

Overedge foot helps keep stitches at full width and prevents curling of flat edges when sewing overedge stitches. Stitches are formed over a hook on the inside edge of the foot.

The Serger

A serger is a special-purpose sewing machine that supplements a conventional machine. It is similar to the speed-sewing equipment used by garment manufacturers. A serger cuts sewing time considerably, because it trims and overcasts raw fabric edges as it sews the seam. In addition, it performs this three-in-one operation at high speed. Sergers form 1,500 or more stitches a minute — about twice the rate of conventional sewing machines. As another benefit, all fabrics feed evenly so that even traditionally difficult-to-handle fabrics, such as slippery silks and thin sheers, will not take any extra sewing time.

Because of its unique capabilities, a serger streamlines garment construction. It eliminates time-consuming steps and encourages efficient sewing habits such as flat construction, pinless sewing, and continuous seaming. It also dispenses with routines such as raising and lowering the presser foot, backstitching, and filling bobbins.

Functions & Parts

A serger excels at making self-finished narrow seams, rolled hems, blindstitched hems, and overcast edge finishes. It is also the machine to choose for applying elastic, ribbing, ribbons, and lace. Use a conventional machine whenever straight or zigzag stitching is necessary, such as for topstitching, inserting a zipper, or making buttonholes.

Many different models of sergers are available, each offering different types of stitches. Sergers sew with two, three, four, or five threads. The name of each machine tells which stitches it offers; for example, a 4/3-thread serger can sew either a 4-thread mock safety stitch or a 3-thread overlock stitch. Each stitch type is unique and serves a special purpose.

Needles may be an industrial type with short or long shaft, or a standard type used on a conventional sewing machine. Use the needle specified for your machine. Industrial needles are stronger and last longer than conventional needles, but may be more expensive and less widely available. Change conventional needles frequently. Use the finest needle possible to avoid damaging the fabric. Size 11/80 works for most fabric weights.

Knives work like blades of scissors to trim the fabric for the stitch width selected. One knife is high-carbon steel and may last several years. The other knife is less durable and may require replacement three or four times annually. When knives seem dull, first clean them with alcohol; then reposition and tighten the screw. Test by sewing slowly. If a problem remains, replace the less durable knife and test again. As a last resort, replace the other knife.

Care & Maintenance

Because a serger trims fabric as it sews, it creates more lint than a conventional machine and needs to be cleaned inside and out frequently. Use a lint brush or canned air to remove lint from the looper and throat plate area. Wipe off tension discs, needles, knives, and feed dog with alcohol.

To keep a serger running smoothly and quietly, oil it often. Sergers are lubricated by a wick system and can lose oil by gravity even when idle.

Serger Thread

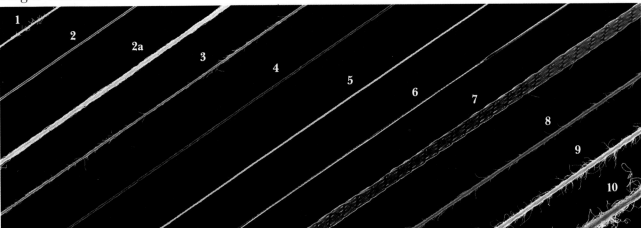

Thread that is fine and strong will perform best. Long-staple polyester (1) is a good, all-purpose choice; texturized nylon (2 and 2a) has exceptional strength and resilience. Cotton and cotton/polyester thread (3) also give satisfactory results but create more lint and may break with tighter tension adjustments and high speed. Decorative rayon (4), silk (5), and metallic (6) threads can be used for special effects, as can narrow ribbon (7), buttonhole twist (8), pearl cotton (9), and lightweight yarn (10).

Principal Parts of the Serger

Many different models of sergers are available, each offering different types of stitches. Sergers sew with two, three, four, or five threads. The name of each machine tells which stitches it offers; for example, a 4/3-thread serger can sew either a 4-thread mock safety stitch or a 3-thread overlock stitch. Each stitch type is unique and serves a special purpose.

A serger can be identified by type at a glance. Each type has a certain number of needles and loopers, and the shape of the loopers is easily recognized. For an overview of the sergers available and the stitches they sew, see pages 18 and 19.

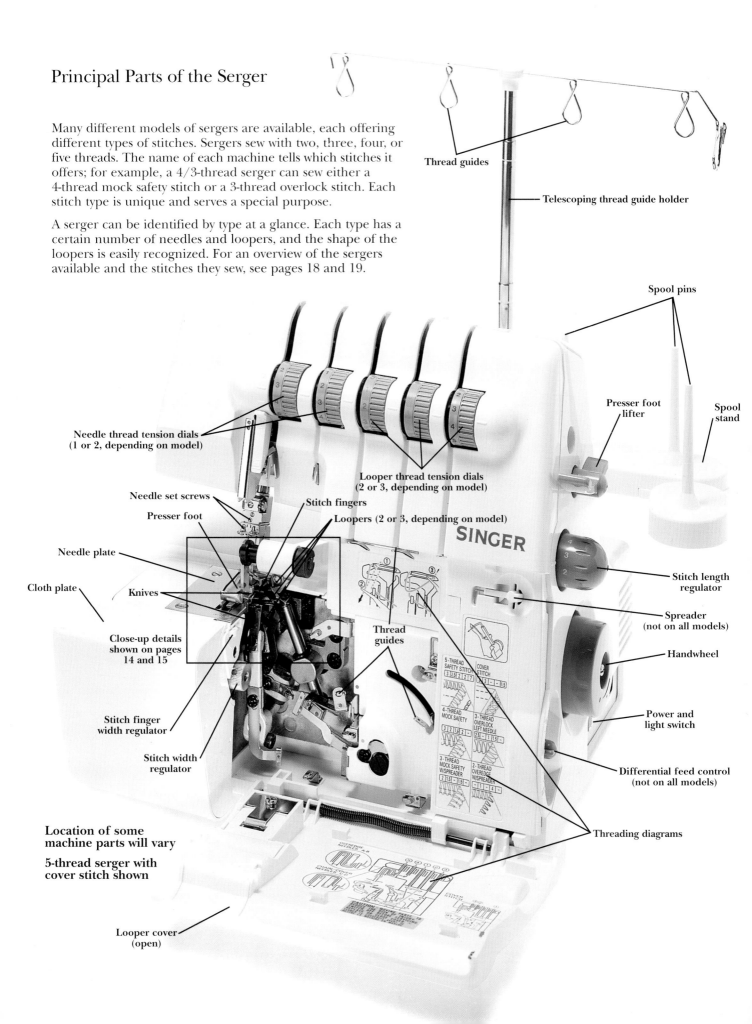

Thread guides

Telescoping thread guide holder

Spool pins

Presser foot lifter

Spool stand

Needle thread tension dials (1 or 2, depending on model)

Looper thread tension dials (2 or 3, depending on model)

Needle set screws

Stitch fingers

Presser foot

Loopers (2 or 3, depending on model)

SINGER

Needle plate

Knives

Cloth plate

Stitch length regulator

Spreader (not on all models)

Thread guides

Handwheel

Close-up details shown on pages 14 and 15

Power and light switch

Stitch finger width regulator

Threading diagrams

Stitch width regulator

Differential feed control (not on all models)

Location of some machine parts will vary

5-thread serger with cover stitch shown

Looper cover (open)

The Stitches
& Their Uses

Types of Stitches

Types of Sergers	2-Thread Overedge Stitch	3-Thread Overlock Stitch	2-Thread Chainstitch	4-Thread Safety Stitch	
	• lightweight seam finishes • used for wovens	• stretch seams • durable seams or seam finishes • used for knits and wovens	• stable basting stitch • decorative topstitching • used primarily for wovens	• stable seams with lightweight seam finishes • used primarily for wovens	
2/3 or 3-Thread Serger	on some models				
4/2-Thread Serger					
4/3/2 or 4/3-Thread Serger	on some models				
5/4/3/2-Thread Serger	on some models			on some models	

18

5-Thread Safety Stitch	3-Thread Mock Safety Stitch	4-Thread Mock Safety Stitch	Flatlock Stitch	Rolled Hem Stitch	Cover Stitch
• stable seams with durable seam finishes • used primarily for wovens	• durable ultra-stretch seams • used for super-stretch knits like Lycra® or spandex	• durable stretch seams • used for knits and wovens	• flat, nonbulky stretch seams • decorative stitching • used primarily for knits	• narrow hems and seams • decorative stitching • used for knits and wovens	• stretch hems and seams • decorative stitching, trims • used primarily for knits
	on some models				
		on some models			on some models

19

Creating the Perfect Stitch

The tension controls on a serger are actually stitch selectors. Each thread has its own tension control. Changing one or more tension settings affects the character of the stitch, because it changes how the threads loop together. With tension adjustments, the serger can stitch a wide range of threads, fabrics, seams, hems, and decorative treatments.

A good way to become comfortable with serger tension adjustments is to thread each looper and needle with a contrasting thread color. Copy the color code used for the machine's threading diagram. Make several stitch samples, tightening and loosening the tensions in sequence. You will see the effect of each tension adjustment and learn how to use the tension controls to create a balanced stitch. Most of the stitch samples shown below and opposite were made on a 3-thread serger; stitch samples made on other models look similar and are adjusted in the same way.

Correctly Balanced Tensions

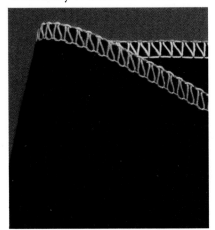

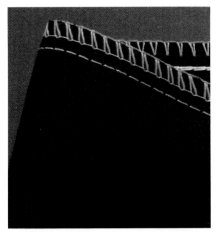

3-thread stitch is formed by two loopers and one needle. Upper (orange) and lower (yellow) looper threads form neat, smooth chain at raw edge. Needle thread (green) forms flat stitches without puckers.

4/3-thread stitch is formed by two loopers and two needles. Upper (orange) and lower (yellow) looper threads chain neatly at raw edge. Both needle threads (blue, green) form flat stitches that interlock with looper threads.

4/2-thread stitch makes double row of stitches with two loopers and two needles. Left needle thread (blue) interlocks with lower looper thread (yellow) to make neat, pucker-free chainstitch. Upper looper thread (orange) and right needle thread (green) interlock over raw edge.

Common Tension Adjustments

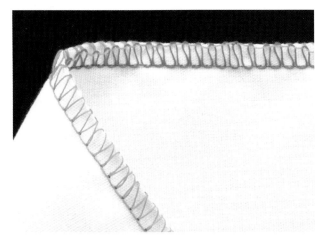

Upper looper too tight. Upper looper thread (orange) pulls lower looper thread (yellow) to top side of fabric. Loosen upper looper tension so threads interlock at raw edge.

Lower looper too loose. Lower looper thread (yellow) rides loosely on top of fabric. Tighten lower looper tension until stitches lie flat and smooth on fabric.

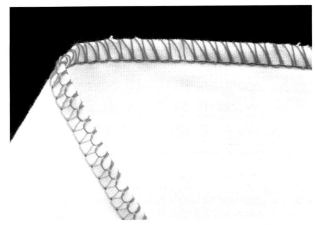

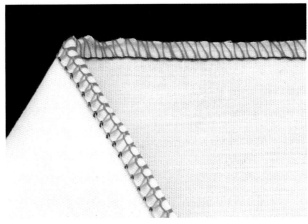

Upper looper too loose. Upper looper thread (orange) interlocks with lower looper thread (yellow) underneath fabric. Tighten upper looper tension so threads interlock at raw edge.

Lower looper too tight. Lower looper thread (yellow) pulls upper looper thread (orange), causing stitches to interlock under fabric. Loosen lower looper tension so threads interlock at raw edge.

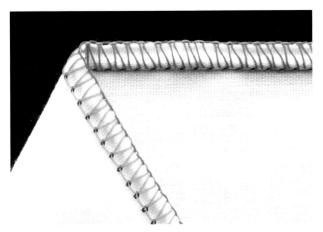

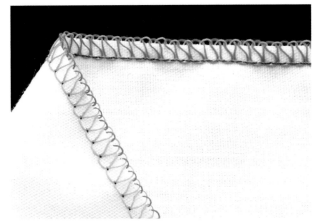

Upper and lower loopers too tight. Fabric bunches and puckers within stitches. Loosen upper and lower tensions until fabric relaxes.

Upper and lower loopers too loose. Lower (yellow) and upper (orange) looper threads interlock beyond raw edge and form loose loops. Tighten both looper tensions so stitches hug raw edge.

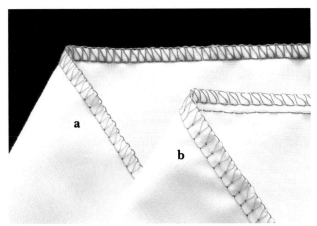

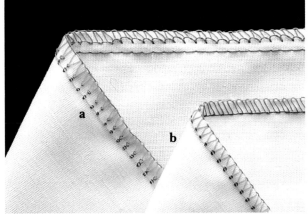

Needle too tight. Fabric puckers or draws up lengthwise when needle thread (green) is too tight **(a)**. Loosen needle tension until fabric relaxes. Test knits for thread breakage, loosening needle thread if necessary. On 4/3-thread machine **(b)**, adjust each needle thread (blue, green) individually.

Needle too loose. Needle thread (green) forms loose loops underneath fabric **(a)**. Tighten needle tension for flat, smooth stitches. On 4/3-thread serger **(b)**, adjust each needle thread (blue, green) individually.

Serger Basics

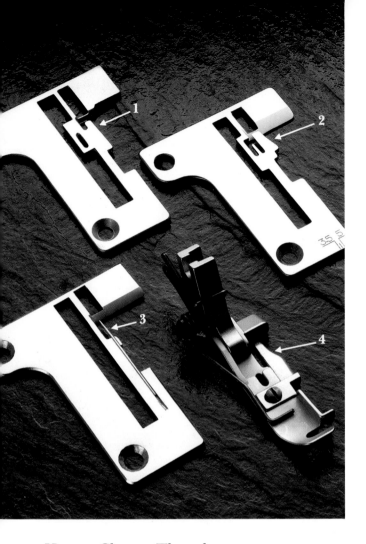

To begin stitching, run the serger without fabric under the presser foot to create a chain of stitches about 2" (5 cm) long. A thread chain at the start and end of seams prevents stitches from raveling. Operating a serger without fabric does not damage the machine or break threads, because stitches are formed on the stitch fingers (prongs).

The throat plate on most sergers has one (1) or two (2) stitch fingers. Stitches are formed around the stitch finger so that, with the correct tension, the width of the stitch finger determines the width of the stitch. A special throat plate with a narrow stitch finger (3) is used to sew a rolled hem or seam.

The presser foot may also contain a stitch finger (4). Machines with this type of presser foot use a special presser foot for a rolled hem or seam.

How to Change Thread

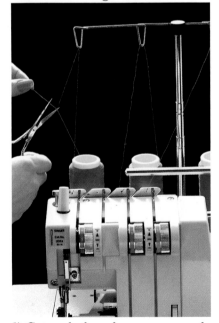

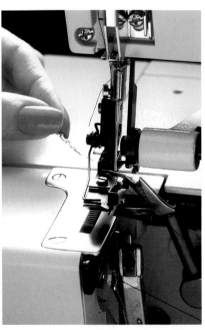

1) Cut each thread near cone, and remove cone. Tie new thread onto each thread in machine, using small overhand knot. Clip thread ends ½" (1.3 cm) from knot.

2) Release tensions, or set tension controls on 0. Cut needle thread in front of needle. Pull on tail chain to separate threads.

3) Pull threads one at a time through thread guides, upper looper, and lower looper. Pull needle thread until knot reaches needle eye. Cut off knot; thread needle with tweezers.

How to Clear the Stitch Fingers

1) Raise presser foot. Turn flywheel to raise needle. Place left hand on thread chain behind presser foot. To slacken needle thread, pull it gently above last thread guide before needle. (Presser foot has been removed to show detail.)

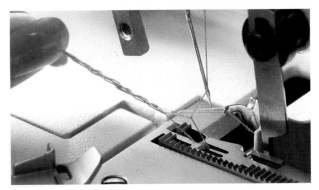

2) Pull straight back on thread chain behind presser foot until threads separate and stitch fingers (prongs) of throat plate or presser foot are empty.

How to Start a Seam

1) Make thread chain. Stitch seam for one or two stitches. Raise presser foot; turn flywheel to lift needle. Clear stitch fingers. Run your fingers along thread chain to make it smooth. (Presser foot has been removed to show detail.)

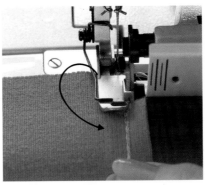

2) Bring thread chain to the left, around and under presser foot. Place thread chain between needle and knife. Hold thread chain in position, and lower presser foot.

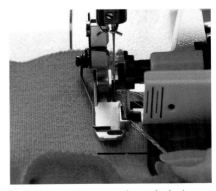

3) Stitch seam over thread chain for about 1" (2.5 cm); then swing thread chain to the right so it is trimmed off as you continue to stitch seam.

How to End a Seam

1) Stitch past end of seam by one stitch, and stop. Raise presser foot and needle to clear stitch fingers. (Presser foot has been removed to show detail.)

2) Turn seam over, and rotate it to align edge of seam with edge of knife. Lower presser foot. Turn flywheel to insert needle at end of seam and at left of edge the width of stitch.

3) Stitch over previous stitches for about 1" (2.5 cm). Stitch off edge, leaving thread chain. With scissors or serger knife, trim thread chain close to edge of seam.

How to Stitch Inside Corners and Slits

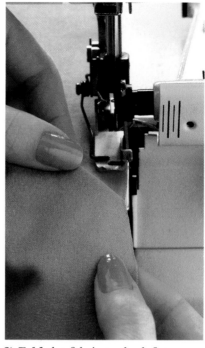

1) Finish seams of inside corners by aligning raw edge of fabric with knife of serger. Stitch, stopping before corner.

2) Fold the fabric to the left to straighten edge. This may create a tuck, which will not be stitched.

3) Resume stitching, holding fabric in straight line. Once past corner, fabric can be relaxed.

How to Stitch Curved Edges

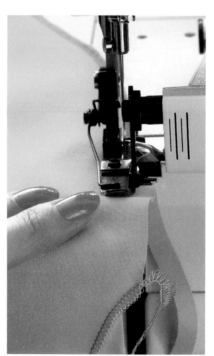

1) Begin cutting at an angle, until you reach the desired cutting or stitching line.

2) Guide fabric in front of presser foot so knives trim raw edge to curved shape. While stitching, watch knife, not needle.

3) Stop when stitches overlap previous stitches. Lift presser foot. Shift fabric so it is behind needle; stitch off edge to prevent gradual looping over edge of fabric. (Presser foot has been removed to show needle position.)

How to Stitch Outside Corners

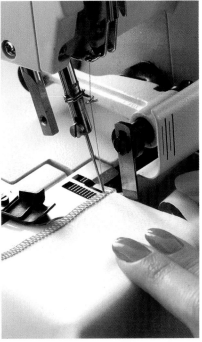

1) Trim off seam allowance past corner for about 2" (5 cm). If making napkins, placemats, or similar projects, you can cut fabric to finished size and omit this step.

2) Sew one stitch past end of the corner, and stop. Raise presser foot and needle to clear stitch fingers and slacken needle thread slightly. (Presser foot has been removed to show needle position.)

3) Pivot fabric to align raw edge of trimmed seam allowance with knife. Insert needle at serged edge. Lower presser foot, and continue stitching.

How to Remove Stitches

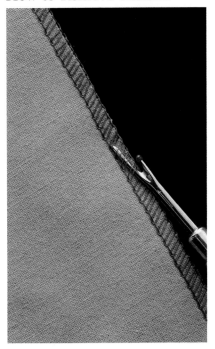

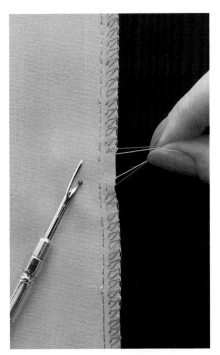

2-thread stitch. Cut threads by sliding seam ripper or blade of scissors under the stitches. Remove cut threads.

3-thread or 4/3-thread stitch. Clip needle threads every three or four stitches, working from upper side. Pull both looper threads straight out at edge. Remove cut threads.

4/2-thread stitch. Working from under side, pull on looper thread to remove chainstitching. Remove overedging as described for 2-thread stitch, left.

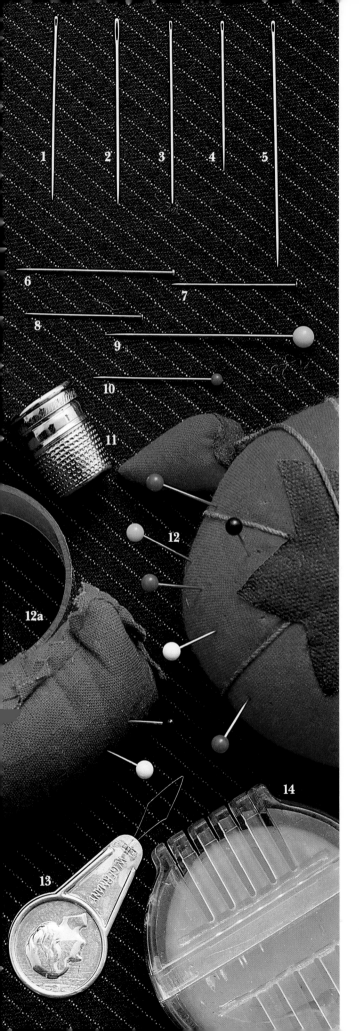

Essential Equipment & Supplies

Basic sewing is divided into five processes: measuring, cutting, marking, stitching by hand or machine, and pressing. For each of these tasks, there are essential tools to make the steps easier and the results superior. Build an equipment inventory as you add to your sewing skills.

Hand Sewing Equipment

Needles and pins are available in a variety of sizes and styles for different uses. Look for rustproof needles and pins made of brass, nickel-plated steel or stainless steel. Pins with colored ball heads rather than flat heads are easier to see in fabric and less likely to get lost.

1) Sharps are all-purpose, medium length needles used for general sewing.

2) Crewels are generally used for embroidery. They are sharp and of medium length.

3) Ballpoint needles are used on knits. Instead of a sharp point which may pierce the fabric, the rounded end pushes the knit loops apart.

4) Betweens are very short and round-eyed. They help make fine stitches in heavy fabric or quilting.

5) Milliner's needles are long with round eyes, used for making long basting or gathering stitches.

6) Silk pins are used for light to mediumweight fabrics. Size #17 is 1 1/16" (2.6 cm) long; #20 is 1 1/4" (3.2 cm). Both are also available with glass or plastic heads. Extra fine 1 3/4" (4.5 cm) silk pins are easier to see in fabric because of their length.

7) Straight pins in brass, steel or stainless steel are used for general sewing. They are usually 1 1/16" (2.6 cm) long.

8) Pleating pins are only 1" (2.5 cm) long, for pinning delicate fabrics in the seam allowance.

9) Quilting pins are 1 1/4" (3.2 cm) long, used for heavy materials because of their length.

10) Ballpoint pins are used for knits.

11) Thimble protects your middle finger while hand sewing. It is available in sizes 6 (small) to 12 (large) for individual, snug fit.

12) Pin cushion provides a safe place to store pins. Some pin cushions have an emery pack (an abrasive material) attached for cleaning pins and needles. A wrist pin cushion (**12a**) keeps pins handy.

13) Needle threader eases threading of hand or machine needles.

14) Beeswax with holder strengthens thread and prevents tangling for hand sewing.

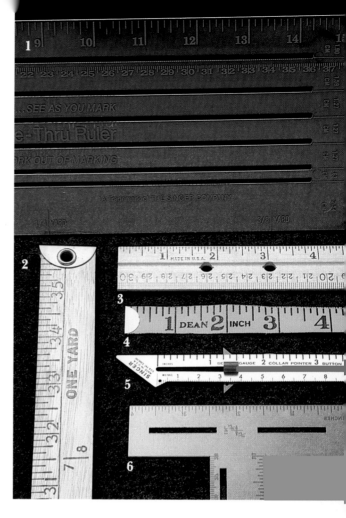

Marking Tools

The symbols on a pattern piece are guides for the accurate construction of the garment. Transferring these symbols from pattern to fabric is essential to fitting and sewing. Because you will be working with several types of fabrics, you will need a variety of marking tools.

1) Tracing wheels come in two types: serrated or smooth edge. The serrated edge makes a dotted line marking. It is suitable for most fabrics but may pierce delicate ones. The smooth-edge tracing wheel protects delicate, smooth fabrics such as silk and chiffon. It makes a solid line marking.

2) Dressmaker's tracing paper is a special waxed carbon paper which transfers the tracing wheel's line to the fabric. Choose a color close to that of the fabric, making sure it can be seen easily.

3) Tailor's chalk or marking pencil marks quickly and easily, directly on the fabric. Chalk rubs off quickly, so use it only when you plan to sew immediately. A tailor tacker **(3a)** holds two pieces of chalk and marks from both sides.

4) Liquid marking pencils make quick work of marking tucks, darts, pleats and pocket locations. One type disappears within 48 hours. The other washes off with water but should not be used on fabrics that show water marks. Pressing may set the marks permanently, so remove marking before pressing the area.

Measuring Tools

Body and pattern measurements both require measuring tools. To ensure a good fit, measure often and accurately with the best tool for the job.

1) See-through ruler lets you see what you measure or mark. This ruler is used to check fabric grainline and to mark buttonholes, tucks, and pleats.

2) Yardstick is for general marking and for measuring fabric grainline when laying out the pattern. It should be made of smooth, shellacked hardwood or metal.

3) Ruler is for general marking. The most useful sizes are 12" or 18" (30.5 or 46 cm) long.

4) Tape measure has the flexibility required to take body measurements. Select a 60" (152.5 cm) long tape with metal tips, made of a material that will not stretch. It should be reversible, with numbers and markings printed on both sides.

5) Seam gauge helps make quick, accurate measurements for hems, buttonholes, scallops, and pleats. It is a small, 6" (15 cm) metal or plastic ruler with a sliding marker.

6) See-through T-square is used to locate cross grains, alter patterns, and square off straight edges.

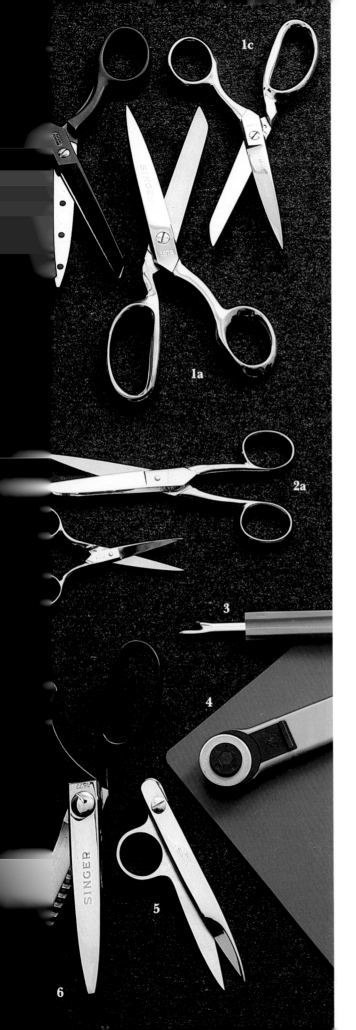

Cutting Tools

Buy quality cutting tools and keep them at their best with periodic sharpening by a qualified professional. Scissors have both handles the same size; shears have one handle larger than the other. The best quality scissors and shears are hot-forged, high-grade steel, honed to a fine cutting edge. Blades should be joined with an adjustable screw (not a rivet) to ensure even pressure along the length of the blade. Sharp shears make clean cuts and well-defined notches. More important, they do not damage fabric. Dull shears slow the cutting process, and make your hand and wrist tire easily. Sewing shears should not be used for other household tasks such as cutting paper or twine. Scissors and shears last longer if you occasionally put a drop of oil on the screw assembly, wipe them clean with a soft dry cloth after use, and store them in a box or pouch.

1) **Bent-handled dressmaker's shears** are best for pattern cutting because the angle of the lower blade lets fabric lie flat on the cutting surface. Blade lengths of 7" or 8" (18 or 20.5 cm) are most popular, but lengths up to 12" (30.5 cm) are available. Select a blade length appropriate to the size of your hand — shorter lengths for small hands, longer lengths for large hands. Left-handed models are also available. If you sew a great deal, invest in a pair of all-steel, chrome-plated shears (**1a**) for heavy-duty cutting. The lighter models with stainless steel blades and plastic handles (**1b**) are fine for less-frequent sewing or lightweight fabrics. For synthetic fabrics and slippery knits, a serrated-edge shears (**1c**) gives maximum cutting control.

2) **Sewing scissors** (**2a**) have one pointed and one rounded tip for trimming and clipping seams and facings. The 6" (15 cm) blade is most practical. Embroidery scissors (**2b**) have 4" or 5" (10 or 12.5 cm) finely-tapered blades. Both points are sharp for use in hand work and precision cutting.

3) **Seam ripper** quickly rips seams, opens buttonholes and removes stitches. Use carefully to avoid piercing the fabric.

4) **Rotary cutter** is an adaptation of the giant rotary cutters used by the garment industry. It works like a pizza cutter and can be used by left or right-handed sewers. Use the rotary cutter with a special plastic mat available in different sizes. The mat protects both the cutting surface and the blade. A special locking mechanism retracts the blade for safety.

5) **Thread clipper** with spring-action blades is more convenient than shears and safer than a seam ripper.

6) **Pinking shears or scalloping shears** cut a zigzag or scalloped edge instead of a straight one. Used to finish seams and raw edges on many types of fabric, they cut a ravel-resistant edge.

Pressing Tools

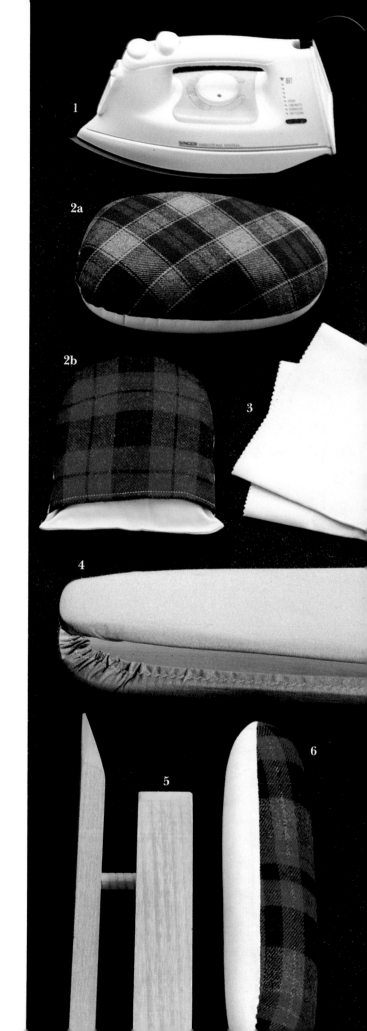

Pressing as you sew is one important procedure that is often neglected. It may seem like a needless interruption, but pressing at each stage of construction is the secret to a perfectly finished garment.

If you need help getting into the pressing habit, locate your pressing equipment near your sewing area. It also helps to press in batches. Do this by stitching as much as possible at the machine. Then press all the stitched areas at one time.

Pressing does not mean ironing. In ironing, you glide the iron over the fabric. In pressing, you move the iron very little while it is in contact with the fabric. Use minimum pressure on the iron, and press in the direction of the fabric grain. Lift the iron to move to another section.

Your pattern directions usually tell when to press, but the general rule is: Press each stitched seam before crossing with another. Press on the wrong side to prevent iron shine, and protect the iron's soleplate by removing pins before pressing.

1) Steam/spray iron should have a wide temperature range to accommodate all fabrics. Buy a dependable, name-brand iron. An iron that steams and sprays at any setting, not just the higher heat settings, is helpful for synthetic fabrics.

2) Tailor's ham or pressing mitt is used when pressing shaped areas such as curved seams, darts, collars or sleeve caps. The ham **(2a)** is a firmly-packed cushion with rounded curves. One side is cotton; the other side is covered with wool to retain more steam. The mitt **(2b)** is similar to the ham but is especially handy for small, hard-to-reach areas. It fits over the hand or a sleeve board.

3) Press cloth helps prevent iron shine and is always used when applying fusible interfacing. The transparent variety allows you to see if the fabric is smooth and the interfacing properly aligned.

4) Sleeve board looks like two small ironing boards attached one on top of the other. It is used when pressing seams and details of small or narrow areas such as sleeves, pants legs or necklines.

5) Point presser/clapper is made of hardwood and used for pressing seams open in corners and points. The clapper flattens seams by holding steam and heat in the fabric. This tool is used in tailoring to achieve a flat finish and sharp edges on hard-surfaced fabrics.

6) Seam roll is a firmly packed cylindrical cushion for pressing seams. The bulk of the fabric falls to the sides and never touches the iron, preventing the seam from making an imprint on the right side of the fabric.

Special Equipment

Many kinds of special equipment are designed to save time in layout, construction and pressing. The more you sew, the more these aids will become necessities. Just as you would invest in timesaving devices for cooking and cleaning, invest in sewing equipment to make your wardrobe and home decorating projects go faster.

Before using a new product, read all instructions carefully. Learn what special handling or care is required, and what fabrics or techniques it is suited for. Here is an overview of some of these specialized sewing products.

Table-top ironing board is portable and saves space. It is easy to set up near your sewing machine. This ironing board keeps large pieces of fabric on the table so they do not stretch out or drag on the floor. It also helps cultivate the habit of detail pressing while you sew.

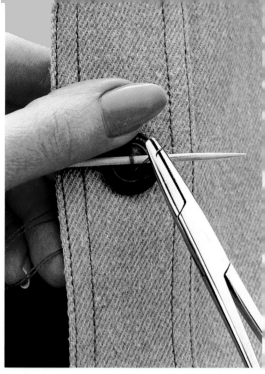

Needle gripper locks tight to hold the needle, allowing needle to be pulled through heavy fabric.

Glue substitutes for pinning or basting by holding fabric, leather, vinyl, felt, trims, patch pockets and zippers in place for permanent stitching. Use it for craft work as well as general sewing. Glue stick is water soluble, so it provides only a temporary bond. Liquid glue can be dotted in seam allowances to hold layers of fabric together.

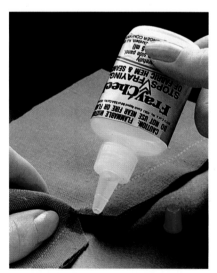

Liquid ravel preventer is a colorless plastic liquid which prevents fraying by stiffening fabric slightly. It is helpful when you have clipped too far into a seam allowance or want to reinforce a pocket or buttonhole. It darkens light colors slightly, so apply cautiously. The liquid becomes a permanent finish that will withstand laundering and dry cleaning.

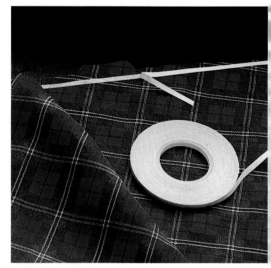

Basting tape is double-faced adhesive tape that eliminates pinning and thread basting. Use it on leather and vinyl as well as on fabric. The tape is especially helpful for matching stripes and plaids, applying zippers, and positioning pockets and trims. Do not machine-stitch through the tape, because the adhesive may foul your machine needle.

Loop turner is specially designed with a latch hook device at one end to grasp bias tubing or cording and turn it to the right side. It is quicker and easier than attaching a safety pin to one end and working the pin through. Because the wire is so fine, it can be used for very narrow tubing and button loops.

Bodkin threads ribbon, elastic or cord through a casing without twisting. Some bodkins have an eye through which ribbon or elastic is threaded; others have a tweezer or safety pin closure which grabs the elastic. The bodkin above has a ring which slides to tighten the prongs of the pincers.

Point turner pokes out the tailored points in collars, lapels and pockets without risking a tear. Made of wood or plastic, its point fits neatly into corners. Use the point to remove basting thread and the rounded end to hold seamlines open for pressing.

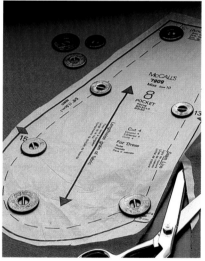

Folding cutting board protects a fine table's finish from pin or shears scratches. It also prevents fabric from slipping while cutting, and holds fabric more securely. Stick pins into it for faster pinning, square off fabric against marked lines, and use the 1" (2.5 cm) squares as an instant measure. The folding feature makes storage easy.

Weights hold a pattern in place for cutting. They eliminate time-consuming pinning and unpinning of the pattern and protect fabrics that would be permanently marked by pins. Weights are most easily used on smaller pattern pieces. Some sewers use items like cans of vegetables in place of retail weights.

Magnetic pin catcher and pin cushion keep all-steel pins in their place. The pin catcher attaches to the throat plate of the machine to catch pins as you pull them out while stitching. The magnetic, weighted pin cushion is more convenient than an ordinary one, and is especially handy for picking pins off the floor.

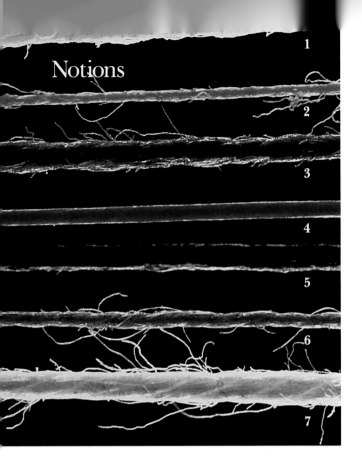

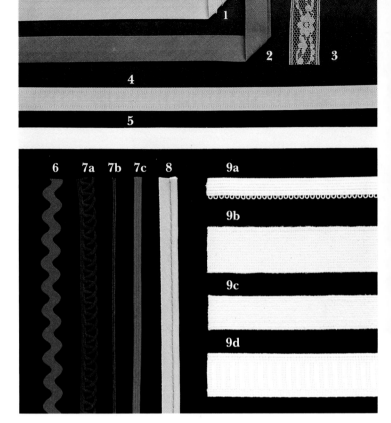

Thread

Select high-quality thread according to the fiber and weight of the fabric and the purpose of the stitching. As a general guideline, use a natural fiber thread for natural fiber fabrics and synthetic fiber thread for synthetic fabrics. Photo above has been enlarged 20 times to show detail.

1) Cotton-wrapped polyester thread is an all-purpose thread designed for hand and machine sewing on all fabrics: natural fibers and synthetics, wovens and knits.

2) Extra fine cotton-wrapped polyester thread reduces fabric puckering on lightweight fabrics, and does not build up or break during machine embroidery.

3) Topstitching and buttonhole twist is designed for topstitching, decorative programmed stitching, cording in machine-worked buttonholes and stitching hand-worked buttonholes.

4) Hand quilting thread is a strong cotton or polyester/cotton thread that does not tangle, knot or untwist while hand sewing through layers of fabric.

5) Button and carpet thread is suitable for hand sewing where extra strength is required.

6) Long-fiber polyester thread is smooth and even, and suitable for hand or machine stitching.

7) 100% mercerized cotton thread is used for natural fiber woven fabrics like cotton, linen and wool; it does not have enough stretch for knits.

Trims & Tapes

Choose trims and tapes that are compatible with your fabric and thread. Most trims and tapes can be machine stitched, but some must be applied by hand. Preshrink trims for washable garments.

1) Single-fold bias tape, ½" (1.3 cm) wide, and wide bias tape, ⅞" (2.2 cm) wide, available in prints and solid colors, are used for casings, trim and facings.

2) Double-fold bias tape binds a raw edge. It comes in ¼" (6 mm) and ½" (1.3 cm) folded widths.

3) Lace seam binding is a decorative lace hem finish.

4) Seam tape is 100% rayon or polyester, ⅜" (1 cm) wide, used to stay seams, finish hems and reinforce clipped corners.

5) Twill tape is used to stay seams or roll lines.

6) Rickrack comes in ¼" (6 mm), ½" (1.3 cm), and ⅝" (1.5 cm) widths for accent trim and edging.

7) Braid is available in loop (**7a**), soutache (**7b**), and middy (**7c**) styles. Use it for accent, scroll motifs, drawstrings, ties or button loops.

8) Corded piping is an accent trim inserted in seams to define and decorate edges.

9) Elastic is inserted in casings to shape waistbands, wrists and necklines. Knitted (**9a**) and woven (**9b**) elastics are softer than braided elastics (**9c**), curl less, and can be stitched directly onto the fabric. Non-roll (**9d**) waistband elastic has lateral ribs to keep it from twisting or rolling.

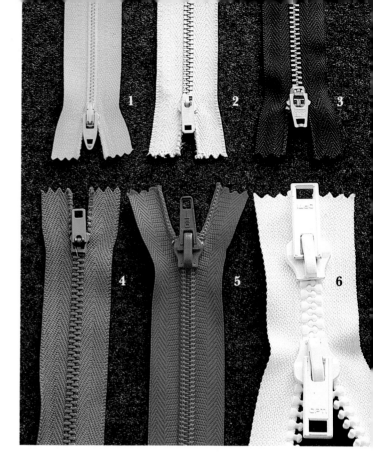

Buttons & Closures

Select these notions either to blend with the garment or stand out and make a fashion statement. Closures can be decorative as well as functional.

1) Sew-through, two-hole or four-hole buttons are commonly-used, all-purpose buttons.

2) Shank buttons have a "neck" or shank underneath the button.

3) Self-covered buttons can be covered with the same fabric as the garment for an exact color match.

4) Toggles are loop-and-bar fasteners with leather or leather-like trim, used on lapped areas.

5) Frogs are loop-and-ball fasteners that lend a dressy look to special outfits.

6) Snap and Velcro® tapes are used as closures on lapped areas of jackets, shirts or casual dresses.

7) Heavy-duty hooks and eyes are used to close waistbands on skirts or pants.

8) Hooks and eyes are inside closures available in sizes appropriate to various fabric weights.

9) Snaps are inside closures for areas that do not receive much stress, such as cuffs.

10) Jumbo snaps are hammered on or applied with a plier-like tool on the outside of a garment for a decorative effect.

Zippers

Zippers have metal or plastic teeth, or a synthetic coil of polyester or nylon attached to a woven tape. Both types come in all-purpose weights. Coil zippers are lightweight, more flexible, heat-resistant and rustproof. Metal zippers come in heavier weights for heavy fabrics and sportswear. Although zippers are usually designed to blend into the garment, some are big, colorful and made to be shown off.

1) Polyester all-purpose zippers are suitable for fabrics of all weights in skirts, pants, dresses and home decorating items.

2) Metal all-purpose zippers are strong, durable zippers for sportswear as well as pants, skirts, dresses and home decorating items.

3) Brass jean zippers are stamped metal zippers with a closed bottom, designed for jeans, work and casual wear in medium to heavyweight fabrics.

4) Metal separating zippers, available in medium and heavy weights, are used in jackets, sportswear and home decorating. Reversible separating zippers have pull tabs on the front and back of the zipper.

5) Plastic molded separating zippers are lightweight yet strong and durable, designed with extra fullness to give a smooth, straight finish to the application. Their decorative appearance makes them a natural for skiwear and outdoor wear.

6) Parka zippers are plastic molded separating zippers with two sliders, so they can be opened from the top and bottom.

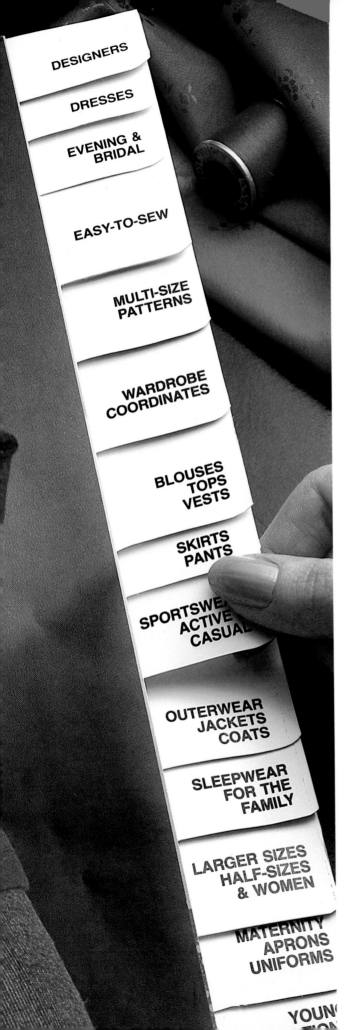

The Pattern

Shopping a pattern catalog is more creative than shopping a ready-to-wear catalog. In a pattern catalog, you aren't limited to the fabric, color, skirt length or buttons you see on the pages. You are the designer of your own fashion. You can choose the combination that flatters you and expresses your own personal style.

Pattern selection has never been better. Designer styles are available in the same season that they appear in ready-to-wear. There are easy patterns for the sewer with limited time. You will find patterns for accessories, home decoration, evening wear, men's and boys' fashions, and almost every kind of women's or children's garment.

The pattern catalog is divided into categories by size or fashion look, marked by index tabs. The newest fashions usually appear in the first few pages of each category. Pattern illustrations are accompanied by information on recommended fabrics and yardage requirements. An index at the back of the catalog lists patterns in numerical order along with their page numbers. The back of the catalog also includes a complete size chart for every figure type: male, female, children, and infants.

Match the pattern's level of sewing difficulty to your sewing experience. For success, select a pattern appropriate to your sewing skill. If your time or patience is limited, stay with simpler styles.

The number of pattern pieces listed on the back of the pattern is a clue to the complexity of the pattern. The fewer the pieces, the easier the pattern. Details like shirt cuffs, collar bands, pleats, and tucks also make a pattern more difficult to sew. Easy-to-sew patterns feature few of these details.

All pattern companies follow a uniform sizing based on standard body measurements. This is not exactly the same as ready-to-wear sizing. To select the right pattern size, first take your standard body measurements. Wear your usual undergarments and use a tape measure that doesn't stretch. For accuracy, have another person measure you. Record your measurements and compare them with the size chart on page 37.

How to Take Standard Body Measurements

1) Waistline. Tie a string or piece of elastic around your middle and allow it to roll to your natural waistline. Measure at this exact location with tape measure. Leave string in place as a reference for measuring hips and back waist length.

2) Hips. Measure around the fullest part. This is usually 7" to 9" (18 to 23 cm) below the waistline, depending on your height.

3) High bust. Place tape measure under arms, across widest part of back and above full bustline. Pattern size charts do not include a high bust measurement, but this measurement should be compared with the full bust to choose the right size pattern.

4) Full bust. Place tape measure under arms, across widest part of the back and fullest part of bustline. Note: If there is a difference of 2" (5 cm) or more between high and full bust, select pattern size by high bust measurement.

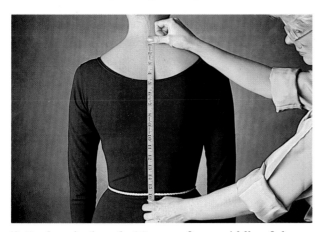

5) Back waist length. Measure from middle of the most prominent bone at the base of the neck down to waistline string.

6) Height. Measure without shoes. Stand with your back against a wall. Place a ruler on top of your head and mark the wall. Measure from the mark to the floor.

Female Figure Types

Young Junior Teen
About 5'1" to 5'3" (1.55 to 1.60 m) tall. Developing teen or preteen figure, with small, high bust. Waistline is larger in proportion to bust.

Junior Petite
About 5' to 5'1" (1.53 to 1.55 m) tall. Well-developed, shorter figure, with smaller body build and shorter back waist length than a Junior.

Junior
About 5'4" to 5'5" (1.63 to 1.65 m) tall. Well-developed figure, slightly shorter in height and back waist length than a Miss.

Miss Petite
About 5'2" to 5'4" (1.57 to 1.63 m) tall. Well-developed and well-proportioned shorter figure, with a shorter back waist length and slightly larger waist than a Miss.

Miss
About 5'5" to 5'6" (1.65 to 1.68 m) tall. Well-developed and well-proportioned in all areas. Considered the average figure.

Half-size
About 5'2" to 5'3" (1.57 to 1.60 m) tall. Fully-developed but shorter than the Miss. Shoulders are narrower than a Miss Petite. Waist is larger in proportion to bust than a Woman.

Woman
About 5'5" to 5'6" (1.65 to 1.68 m) tall. Same height as Miss, but larger and more fully mature, making all other measurements proportionately larger.

Maternity
Corresponds to Miss sizes. Measurements are for a figure five months pregnant, but patterns are designed to provide ease through the ninth month.

Female Figure Size Chart

To choose the right size pattern, take your measurements as directed on page 35. Then determine your figure type using the descriptions on the opposite page. Find your figure type on the chart below. Locate the column of numbers that most closely matches your measurements. Choose dress, blouse, and suit patterns by bust size; pants and skirt patterns by hip size.

Inches

Young Junior/Teen:

Size	5/6	7/8	9/10	11/12	13/14	15/16
Bust	28	29	30½	32	33½	35
Waist	22	23	24	25	26	27
Hip	31	32	33½	35	36½	38
Back Waist Length	13½	14	14½	15	15⅜	15¾

Junior Petite:

Size	3jp	5jp	7jp	9jp	11jp	13jp
Bust	30	31	32	33	34	35
Waist	22	23	24	25	26	27
Hip	31	32	33	34	35	36
Back Waist Length	14	14¼	14½	14¾	15	15¼

Junior:

Size	5	7	9	11	13	15
Bust	30	31	32	33½	35	37
Waist	22½	23½	24½	25½	27	29
Hip	32	33	34	35½	37	39
Back Waist Length	15	15¼	15½	15¾	16	16¼

Miss Petite:

Size	6mp	8mp	10mp	12mp	14mp	16mp
Bust	30½	31½	32½	34	36	38
Waist	23½	24½	25½	27	28½	30½
Hip	32½	33½	34½	36	38	40
Back Waist Length	14½	14¾	15	15¼	15½	15¾

Miss:

Size	6	8	10	12	14	16	18	20
Bust	30½	31½	32½	34	36	38	40	42
Waist	23	24	25	26½	28	30	32	34
Hip	32½	33½	34½	36	38	40	42	44
Back Waist Length	15½	15¾	16	16¼	16½	16¾	17	17¼

Half-size:

Size	10½	12½	14½	16½	18½	20½	22½	24½
Bust	33	35	37	39	41	43	45	47
Waist	27	29	31	33	35	37½	40	42½
Hip	35	37	39	41	43	45½	48	50½
Back Waist Length	15	15¼	15½	15¾	15⅞	16	16⅛	16¼

Woman:

Size	38	40	42	44	46	48	50	52
Bust	42	44	46	48	50	52	54	56
Waist	35	37	39	41½	44	46½	49	51½
Hip	44	46	48	50	52	54	56	58
Back Waist Length	17¼	17⅜	17½	17⅝	17¾	17⅞	18	18⅛

Maternity:

Size	6	8	10	12	14	16
Bust	34	35	36	37½	39½	41½
Waist	28½	29½	30½	32	33½	35½
Hip	35½	36½	37½	39	41	43
Back Waist Length	15½	15¾	16	16¼	16½	16¾

Centimeters

Young Junior/Teen:

Size	5/6	7/8	9/10	11/12	13/14	15/16
Bust	71	74	78	81	85	89
Waist	56	58	61	64	66	69
Hip	79	81	85	89	93	97
Back Waist Length	34.5	35.5	37	38	39	40

Junior Petite:

Size	3jp	5jp	7jp	9jp	11jp	13jp
Bust	76	79	81	84	87	89
Waist	56	58	61	64	66	69
Hip	79	81	84	87	89	92
Back Waist Length	35.5	36	37	37.5	38	39

Junior:

Size	5	7	9	11	13	15
Bust	76	79	81	85	89	94
Waist	57	60	62	65	69	74
Hip	81	84	87	90	94	99
Back Waist Length	38	39	39.5	40	40.5	41.5

Miss Petite:

Size	6mp	8mp	10mp	12mp	14mp	16mp
Bust	78	80	83	87	92	97
Waist	60	62	65	69	73	78
Hip	83	85	88	92	97	102
Back Waist Length	37	37.5	38	39	39.5	40

Miss:

Size	6	8	10	12	14	16	18	20
Bust	78	80	83	87	92	97	102	107
Waist	58	61	64	67	71	76	81	87
Hip	83	85	88	92	97	102	107	112
Back Waist Length	39.5	40	40.5	41.5	42	42.5	43	44

Half-size:

Size	10½	12½	14½	16½	18½	20½	22½	24½
Bust	84	89	94	99	104	109	114	119
Waist	69	74	79	84	89	96	102	108
Hip	89	94	99	104	109	116	122	128
Back Waist Length	38	39	39.5	40	40.5	40.5	41	41.5

Woman:

Size	38	40	42	44	46	48	50	52
Bust	107	112	117	122	127	132	137	142
Waist	89	94	99	105	112	118	124	131
Hip	112	117	122	127	132	137	142	147
Back Waist Length	44	44	44.5	45	45	45.5	46	46

Maternity:

Size	6	8	10	12	14	16
Bust	87	89	92	95	100	105
Waist	72	75	77.5	81	85	90
Hip	90	93	95	99	104	109
Back Waist Length	39.5	40	40.5	41.5	42	42.5

The Pattern Envelope

The pattern envelope contains a wealth of information, from a description of the garment to the amount of fabric needed. It gives ideas for fabric and color selection. The envelope helps you determine the degree of sewing difficulty with labels that indicate whether the style is a designer original, easy-to-sew or only suitable for certain fabrics. On the pattern envelope, you'll also find all the information needed to select fabric and notions.

The Envelope Front

Views are alternate designs of the pattern. They may show optional trims, lengths, fabric combinations or design details to appeal to a beginner, or challenge an experienced sewer.

Pattern company name and style number are prominently displayed on the pattern envelope.

Fashion photograph or illustration shows the main pattern design. It suggests suitable fabric types such as wool or cotton, and fabric designs such as print or plaid. If you are unsure of your fabric choice, use the pattern illustration as your guide. It is the designer's interpretation of the fashion.

Designer original patterns, indicated by the designer's name, often contain more difficult-to-sew details such as tucks, topstitching, linings or underlings. For sewers who have the time and skill, these patterns provide designer fashions that duplicate ready-to-wear.

Labels may identify a pattern that has easy construction methods, is designed for timesaving sewing, has special fitting or size-related information, or shows how to handle fabrics like plaids, knits or lace. Each pattern company has special categories and names for these designs.

Size and figure type are indicated at the top or side of the pattern. If the pattern is multi-sized, such as 8-10-12, you will find cutting lines for all three sizes on one pattern.

The Envelope Back

Body measurement and size chart is a reference to determine if you need to make alterations. For a multi-sized pattern, compare your measurements with those in the chart to decide which cutting line to use.

Garment descriptions include style, fit and construction information.

Style number is repeated on the back of the envelope.

Yardage block tells you how much fabric to buy for the size and garment view you have selected. Yardage for lining, interfacing and trims is also listed. To determine how much fabric you need, match the garment or view and the fabric width at the left with your size at the top of the chart. The number where the two columns meet is the number of yards to buy. The most common fabric widths are given. If the width of your fabric is not given, check the conversion chart at the back of the pattern catalog. Some patterns list the extra yardage required for napped fabrics or uneven plaids.

Metric equivalents of body measurements and yardage are included for countries that use the metric system.

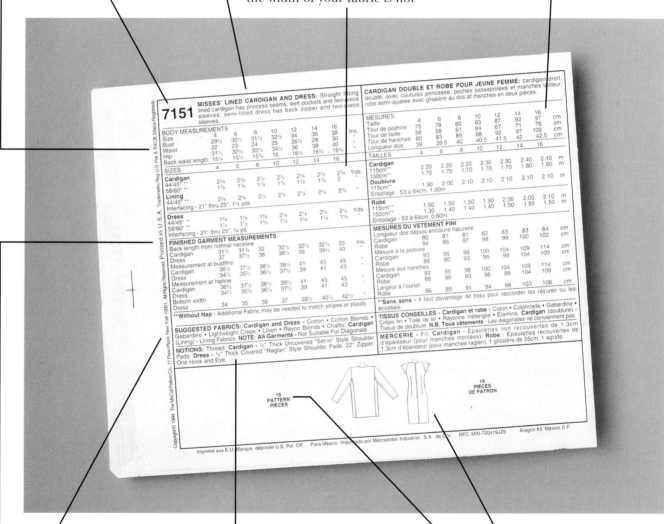

Fabric types suitable for the garments are suggested. Use them as a general guide to fabric selection. The special advice, such as "unsuitable for stripes or obvious diagonals," alerts you to fabrics that are not appropriate.

Finished garment measurements indicate finished length and width. You may need to make length adjustments. The "width at lower edge" is the measurement at the hemmed edge, indicating the fullness of the garment.

Notions, such as thread, zipper, buttons and seam binding, which are required for garment construction are listed. Purchase them at the same time as the fabric to ensure a good color match.

Back views show the details and style of the back of the garments.

Number of pattern pieces gives an idea of how easy or complicated the pattern is to sew.

Inside the Pattern

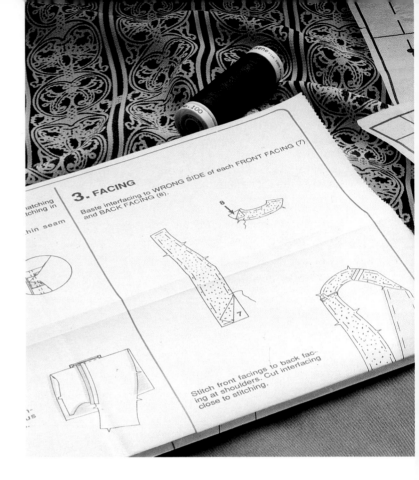

Open the pattern envelope to find the printed pattern pieces and the direction sheet which guides you, step-by-step, through the construction of the garment. Read through the direction sheet *before* cutting or sewing. Use it to plan and organize your sewing time, and alert you to the techniques you need to know as you progress.

Views of a single garment are labeled by number or letter. Patterns which include several different garments such as a skirt, jacket and pants (called *wardrobe patterns*) usually feature only one version of each. In this case, each garment is identified by name only. All pattern pieces are identified with a number and name, such as *skirt front*.

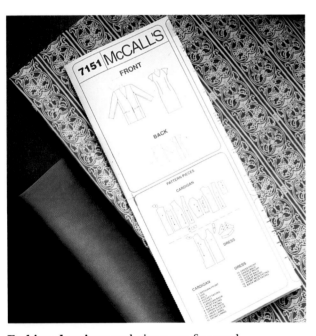

Fashion drawings and views are featured prominently on the direction sheet, sketched as they appear on the front of the envelope or as detailed line drawings. Some patterns illustrate each garment separately with the pattern pieces used in its construction. Most patterns illustrate all the pattern pieces together, with a key to identify the pieces used for each garment or view.

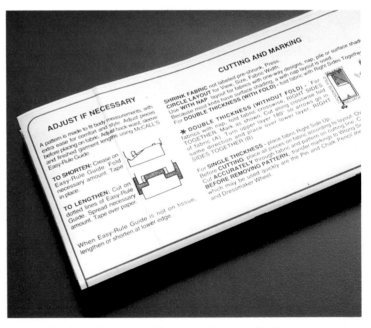

General instructions are given as a short refresher sewing course. These instructions may have a different name on each company's pattern, but they generally contain tips on how to use the pattern. Included is information on pattern and fabric preparation; explanation of pattern markings; cutting, layout and marking tips; and a short glossary of sewing terms. The easy-to-sew and beginner patterns often incorporate these tips into the step-by-step instructions.

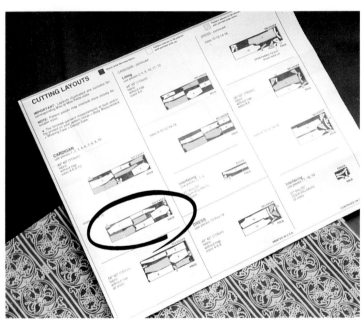

Cutting layouts are shown for each garment view. They differ according to the width of the fabric, pattern size and whether the fabric is with or without nap. Layouts for interfacing and lining are also included. When the fabric is to be cut in a single thickness or on the crosswise grain, the pattern layout indicates this with a symbol, explained in the general instructions. A pattern piece, right side up, is illustrated without shading; wrong side up, it is shaded or scored. Circle the layout for the correct pattern size, fabric width and view.

Sewing directions are a step-by-step guide to constructing the garment, arranged by views. Beside each instruction is a sketch illustrating the sewing technique. The right side of the fabric usually appears shaded; the wrong side, plain. Interfacing is indicated with dots. Together, the sketch and the directions give you a clear picture of exactly what to do. Remember that these are only general directions. An alternative technique may be more effective for the fabric you are using.

Fabric Essentials

All fabrics are based on two kinds of fibers: *natural* or *man-made*. Natural fibers are those derived from plants or animals: cotton, wool, silk and linen. Man-made fibers are produced by chemical processes. They include polyester, nylon, acetate, spandex and many others.

Combining natural and man-made fibers produces *blends* which give you the best qualities of several fibers. For example, the strength of nylon may be added to the warmth of wool, the easy care of polyester to the comfort of cotton.

There is an almost endless variety of blends available, and each one behaves differently. Check the fiber content on the bolt end for the kinds and quantities of fibers used. Care instructions are also listed. Examine the *hand* of the fabric — how it feels, how it drapes, whether it crushes easily or ravels, whether it stretches. Drape the fabric over your hand or arm to determine if it is as soft or crisp, heavy or light, as you need for a particular project.

Fabrics are also classified by *fabrication*, meaning how they are made. All fabrics are either *woven, knit* or *nonwoven*. The most common woven is the plain weave construction. This is found in fabrics like muslins, poplin and taffeta. Denim and gabardine are diagonal weaves. Cotton sateen is a satin weave. Knits also have several classifications. Jersey is an example of a plain knit. Sweater knits can be made by the purl, patterned or raschel knit processes. Felt is an example of a nonwoven fabric.

Selecting the right fabric for your sewing project takes a little practice. Refer to the back of the pattern envelope for suggestions, and learn to feel the hand of fabric. Quality fabric doesn't have to be expensive. Choose well-made fabric that will wear well and stay looking good.

Easy-to-Sew Fabrics

Poplin   **Cotton broadcloth**   **Shirtings**   **Linen-likes**   **Firm knits**   **Firm wool**   **Denim**

There are many fabrics that are easy and quick to sew. These fabrics are generally plain weave or firm knit, of medium weight. Most do not require complicated seam finishes or special handling, since they ravel little or not at all.

Small prints, overall prints and narrow stripes are easy to sew because they do not require matching at the seams. Prints, especially if they are dark, can hide stitching imperfections.

Plain weave fabrics like poplin or cotton broadcloth are always good choices. Stable or moderate-stretch knits do not need seam finishing, and their stretchability makes fitting easier. Natural fiber fabrics, such as cottons and lightweight wools, are easy to sew because stitching easily blends into these fabrics.

For more examples of easy-to-sew fabrics, consult the suggested fabrics that are listed on the backs of easy-to-sew patterns.

Handling Special Fabrics

Certain fabrics, because of their design or fabrication, need special attention during layout and construction. Some easy-to-sew fabrics fall into this category. The special handling required is usually not difficult. Often you need only add one more step, such as a seam finish, or exercise a little more care.

1) Napped and pile fabrics like velvet, velveteen, velour, flannel and corduroy require special care in cutting out. These fabrics appear light and shiny when brushed in one lengthwise direction, and dark when brushed in the other direction. To prevent your garment from having a two-toned look, you must follow the "with nap" layouts on the pattern instruction sheet. Decide which way you want the nap to lie, and cut all pattern pieces with the top edges facing the same direction.

Although satin and moiré taffeta are not napped fabrics, their shiny surfaces reflect light differently in each lengthwise direction. Decide which effect you prefer, and use a one-way layout.

2) Sheer fabrics look best with special seams and seam finishes. Unfinished seam allowances detract from the fragile, see-through look of voile, batiste, eyelet or chiffon. French seams are a classic choice, but other seam finishes can also be used.

3) Twill weave fabrics like denim and gabardine have diagonal ridges. If these ridges are very noticeable, use a "with nap" layout for cutting, and avoid patterns that are not suitable for obvious diagonals. Denim ravels easily and requires enclosed seams.

4) Plaids and stripes require special care in layout and cutting (pages 72 to 74). To match plaids and large stripes at seams, you need to buy extra fabric. Buy ¼ to ½ yard (0.25 to 0.5 m) more than the pattern calls for, depending on the size of the design.

5) Knits must be handled gently during construction to keep them from stretching out of shape. Special stitches and seam finishes (page 102) are needed to maintain the right amount of stretch.

6) One-way design fabrics, such as some flower and paisley prints, require a "with nap" cutting layout so the design does not go up one side of the garment and down the other. Border prints are cut on the crosswise rather than lengthwise grain of the fabric. They usually require more yardage. Select patterns which show a border print view and specify the correct yardage.

Guide to Fabrics and Sewing Techniques

Type	Fabric	Special Seams	Machine Needle Size	Thread
Sheers	Crisp: organdy, organza, voile Soft: batiste, lawn, chiffon, China silk, georgette, gauze	French, mock French, self-bound, double-stitched	8 (60), 9 (65), or 11 (75)	Extra-fine: mercerized cotton, cotton-covered polyester or long-fiber polyester
Lightweight	Silk shirtings, broadcloth, calico, oxford cloth, chambray, lightweight linens, challis, seersucker, eyelet, charmeuse	French, mock French, self-bound, stitched-and-pinked or multi-zigzag, double-stitched	8 (60), 9 (65), or 11 (75)	Extra-fine: mercerized cotton, cotton-covered polyester or long-fiber polyester
Light to mediumweight knits	Tricot, interlocks, jerseys, light sweater knits, stretch terry, stretch velour	Double-stitched, straight and zigzag, narrow zigzag	11 (75), 14 (90), ballpoint	All-purpose: cotton/polyester, long-fiber polyester
Mediumweight	Wool flannel, linen types, crepe, gabardine, chino, poplin, chintz, corduroy, velvet, velveteen, velour, taffeta, double knits, sweatshirt knits, denim, quilted fabric	Welt, lapped, flat-fell, mock flat-fell, as well as plain seam with appropriate edge finish	11 (75), 14 (90), ballpoint for knits	All-purpose: cotton/polyester, long-fiber polyester
Medium to heavyweight	Heavy wool flannel, fleece, fake fur, canvas, heavy denim, heavy cotton duck, coating	Welt, lapped, flat-fell, mock flat-fell, stitched-and-pinked	16/100 18/100	Heavy-duty: cotton/polyester, long-fiber polyester, topstitching and buttonhole twist
No grain (nonwoven)	Leather, suede (natural and man-made), buckskin, calfskin, reptile, plastic, felt	Welt, lapped, mock flat-fell, topstitched, plain seam	11/75 14/90 16/100	All-purpose: cotton-wrapped polyester, long-fiber polyester Leather: avoid cotton-wrapped polyester

Classic Fabric Textures & Designs

Whether or not you have had much sewing experience, this group of fabrics probably looks familiar because it includes fabrics that are always in fashion. Some require out-of-the-ordinary sewing techniques, and some need special handling because they have unique surface textures. Others rate extra attention because they have woven, knitted, or printed designs that affect pattern layout.

1) Loose weaves have coarse or uneven textures and tend to fray. The primary sewing challenge with loosely woven fabrics is to control raveling.

2) Plaids require careful pattern layout. Study the fabric before pattern layout to decide which bars are dominant, where to position them on the pattern pieces, and whether the design has a one-way direction. Arrange the pattern pieces so the fabric design matches at the most noticeable seams. Careful pinning or basting ensures against mismatches.

3) Stripes require handling similar to that of plaids. Careful layout and basting is necessary to match stripes attractively.

4) Large prints are among the most dramatic types of fabric designs. Print repeats can be as large as 24" (61 cm). With prints this size, position the print motifs for pleasing balance.

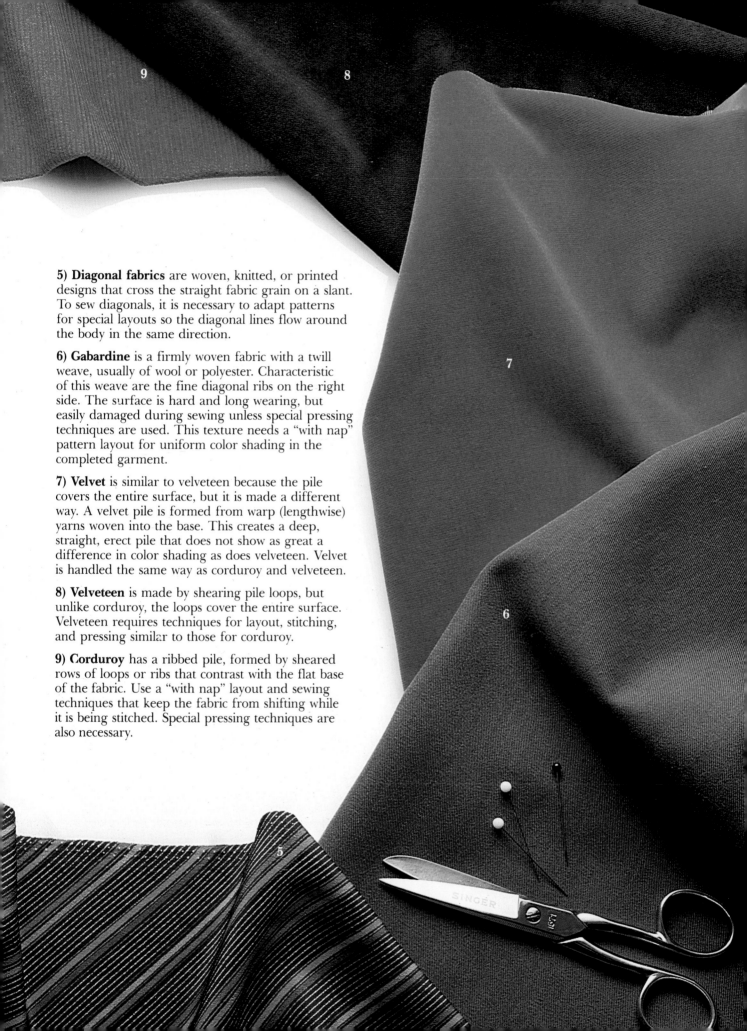

5) Diagonal fabrics are woven, knitted, or printed designs that cross the straight fabric grain on a slant. To sew diagonals, it is necessary to adapt patterns for special layouts so the diagonal lines flow around the body in the same direction.

6) Gabardine is a firmly woven fabric with a twill weave, usually of wool or polyester. Characteristic of this weave are the fine diagonal ribs on the right side. The surface is hard and long wearing, but easily damaged during sewing unless special pressing techniques are used. This texture needs a "with nap" pattern layout for uniform color shading in the completed garment.

7) Velvet is similar to velveteen because the pile covers the entire surface, but it is made a different way. A velvet pile is formed from warp (lengthwise) yarns woven into the base. This creates a deep, straight, erect pile that does not show as great a difference in color shading as does velveteen. Velvet is handled the same way as corduroy and velveteen.

8) Velveteen is made by shearing pile loops, but unlike corduroy, the loops cover the entire surface. Velveteen requires techniques for layout, stitching, and pressing similar to those for corduroy.

9) Corduroy has a ribbed pile, formed by sheared rows of loops or ribs that contrast with the flat base of the fabric. Use a "with nap" layout and sewing techniques that keep the fabric from shifting while it is being stitched. Special pressing techniques are also necessary.

Loose Weaves

Loosely woven fabrics are frequently made from unusual yarns, which are thick and lightly spun to preserve natural irregularities and create a hand-loomed look. Two sewing considerations are to control the raveling and to maintain the soft, loose hand of the fabric.

The loosely woven basketweave **(1)** has two or more yarns woven together in a basket effect. Heavy raw silk **(2)** is ravel-prone because of the thick and thin crosswise yarns. Gauze fabrics **(3)**, lightweight and crinkly, should be handled with sewing techniques for sheer fabrics. The homespun look **(4)** is achieved with lightly spun yarns that ravel easily. A pulled thread look **(5)** creates a novelty windowpane effect.

Pattern Selection

Choose a pattern that has the potential for omitting linings, facings, and interfacings, as well as closures such as buttons and zippers. Many jacket, blouse, and skirt patterns, especially pullover or wrap styles, can be adapted this way. The less stable the fabric, the more loosely fitted the pattern selected should be, but in most cases simple styles are the best. The stability of loosely woven fabrics varies. Test the stability by draping the fabric over your hand and letting a length hang freely. See how much it stretches and whether it drapes softly. Gently tug on the true bias grain to get a feeling for the amount the fabric gives in this direction.

Fabric Preparation

Preshrink all loose weaves, using the care method planned for the finished garment. To prevent excessive raveling, zigzag crosswise cut ends or bind them with sheer bias tricot binding before washing. To wash, treat loose weaves like delicate fabrics. Air dry to prevent shrinkage from the heat of a dryer. Roll the fabric in towels to remove excess moisture. Spread on a flat surface, and straighten the grain.

Layout, Cutting & Marking

Because the individual yarns of the fabric stand out, it is important to arrange the fabric straight and on-grain for pattern layout. Any wavy grainlines will show clearly on the finished garment. When the fabric texture comes from nubby, irregular yarns, use a "with nap" layout so the texture in all the garment sections looks the same. Space pins closely to anchor the pattern pieces securely to the fabric.

If you are working with a fabric that frays readily, cut out the pattern with 1" (2.5 cm) seam allowances. Wider seam allowances are easier to handle for special seam and edge finishes, and they provide ample fabric for clean cuts on raw edges that must be trimmed. Transfer pattern markings with marking pen or thread basting.

Special Seam Techniques

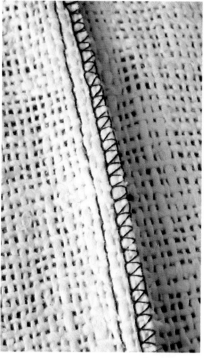

Plain seam with raw edges enclosed in sheer tricot bias binding is quick, neat treatment. Use zigzag, 3-step zigzag, or long straight stitches, 10 to 12 per inch (2.5 cm).

Flat-fell seam, formed on right side of garment, makes reversible seam which is ideal for roll-up sleeves or other areas showing both faces of seams.

Overlocked seam, sewn on 4-thread overlock machine or 3-thread machine with a row of straight stitches, covers raw edges with thread.

Special Hem Techniques

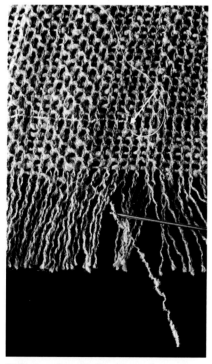

Topstitch to stabilize hem edges. This method is fast and attractive. Finish raw edge before hemming; use a zigzag stitch or a 2-thread or 3-thread overlock stitch.

Bind edge with sheer tricot bias binding. Hand hem with blind catchstitch or blind hem, worked loosely between garment and hem.

Fringe edge. Pull a thread at desired depth of fringe. Stitch on thread-pulled line (arrow); then one by one remove fabric yarns below stitching.

Knits

A knit is a fabric made from interlocking looped stitches. Because of this construction, knits shed wrinkles well, are comfortable to wear, and are easy to sew because they do not ravel. There are many kinds of knits, and most of those available for sewing can be grouped into five general categories.

Firm, stable knits do not stretch significantly and are handled similarly to woven fabrics. In this group are double knits (**1**), which have fine lengthwise ribs on both sides. It is difficult to tell the right and wrong side of a double knit unless the right side has a decorative design. Raschel knit (**2**) is a lacy or open knit texture that does not stretch because lengthwise threads are locked into some of the knitted loops. Some raschel knits are made from bulky yarns and look like bouclé wovens or hand knits. Others are made from finer yarns and look crocheted.

Lightweight single knits have fine ribs running lengthwise on the right side and loops running crosswise on the wrong side. Pull the crosswise edge of a single knit and it will roll to the right side. Single knits such as jersey (**3**), tricot (**4**), and interlock (**5**) do not stretch lengthwise, but they do have crosswise give.

Textured knits may be single or double knits. This category is distinguished by a surface texture, usually on the right side. Knitted terry (**6**) and velour (**7**) are pile knits that look like their woven namesakes; however, they usually have a great deal of crosswise stretch. Also in the category of textured knits are sweater knits (**8**). Patterned sweater knits have floats on the wrong side where colored yarns are carried from one motif to another. This limits their crosswise stretch. Comfortable sweatshirt fleece (**9**) looks like a single knit on the right side; the wrong side has a soft, brushed surface. It is usually fairly stable with little stretch in either direction.

Two-way stretch knits have a great degree of stretch crosswise and lengthwise and a high percentage of resilient spandex fibers. Absorbent cotton/spandex and cotton/polyester/spandex knits (**10**) are favored for active sportswear such as leotards, body suits, and aerobic exercise outfits. Strong nylon/spandex knits (**11**) are resilient, even when wet, and are usually selected for swimwear.

Ribbing is a very stretchy knit that can be used for tops and for finishing knit garments at wrists, ankles, neck, and waist. One type is tubular ribbing (**12**), which is sold by the inch (2.5 cm) and must be cut open along one lengthwise rib for sewing. Another type is rib trim (**13**), which is color coordinated with sweater knits; one edge is prefinished, and the other is sewn to the garment.

Techniques for Knits

Patterns for knits depend on the stretch characteristics and weight of the knit. The list of suggested fabrics on the back of a pattern envelope usually includes a combination of knit and woven fabrics. If a knit is soft and lightweight, such as jersey, it is suitable for patterns that have gathers, draping, and similar features. If it is firm, such as double knit, a pattern with tailoring or a shaped, fitted silhouette is suitable. If it is bulky or textured, such as a sweater knit, a pattern with few seams and details works best to show off the knit texture.

Certain patterns, however, require knits that stretch. These are closely fitted pattern styles, such as swimsuits and leotards, which would be too small to wear if made from a fabric without elasticity, or tops and pants that use the knit for a comfortable close-to-the-body fit. Most patterns designed for knits have a stretch gauge printed on the back of the envelope. Test the knit that you have selected against the ruler gauge. When the pattern specifies

"two-way stretch knit," test the crosswise and lengthwise stretchability of the knit.

Patterns designed for knits often have ¼" (6 mm) seam allowances. If the pattern you have selected has ⅝" (1.5 cm) seam allowances, trim them to ¼" (6 mm) when using knit sewing techniques.

Fabric Preparation

For best results, preshrink knits. Wash and dry them if they will be washed as part of their routine care. Use a bulk drycleaner if the finished garment will be drycleaned. It is not necessary to preshrink ribbing unless using a dark-colored ribbing on a light-colored garment.

If, after preshrinking, a knit still has a crease where it was folded on the bolt, steam the crease. If the crease cannot be removed by steaming, it is permanent. Refold the knit for pattern layout to prevent the crease from showing on the garment.

To straighten the ends of knits, draw a chalk line across the cut crosswise edges at right angles to the ribs. Cut the fabric on the chalk line.

How to Use a Stretch Knit Gauge

Correct knit for pattern stretches easily to right-hand side of the gauge printed on pattern envelope. To test, fold crosswise edge of knit over 3" to 4" (7.5 to 10 cm), and test fold against gauge. Knit that stretches even more than gauge requirements may still be used for pattern.

Wrong knit for pattern is forced beyond reasonable limits to satisfy gauge printed on pattern envelope. Ribs of knit are distorted, and stretched edge folds over on itself because of too much stress on fabric. Knit does not have enough natural elasticity for this pattern style.

Pressing

Press knits on the lengthwise ribs by lifting and lowering the iron. Use a low iron temperature setting, and raise the temperature as needed. Do not press across the ribs or handle the fabric until it is completely cooled. Either action can stretch knits out of shape.

Block sweater knits instead of pressing. To block, pat the fabric or the garment into shape on a flat surface. Steam with a hand steamer, or hold a steam iron above the knit surface. Allow the fabric to dry and cool completely before further handling.

Pattern Layout

Always use a "with nap" pattern layout on knits. Because of knit construction, they have a directional quality that shows up as a difference in color shading in the completed garment.

Stretch both crosswise edges of a knit before pattern layout to see if the knit runs. If so, the runs will occur more readily along one edge than the other. Position the run-prone edge at the garment hemline during pattern layout. The hem is subject to less stress, so the knit will be less likely to run after the garment is sewn.

When laying out and cutting a knit fabric, do not allow it to hang off the work surface. The weight of the fabric can distort the portion on the work surface, pulling it off-grain.

On bulky or textured knits, it is easier to lay out the pattern on a single layer of fabric. Position the textured side down; pin and mark on the smoother, wrong side of the knit. Use weights instead of pins on knits with open or lacy textures.

Interfacings

Interface knits to stabilize details, such as buttonholes, plackets, and patch pockets, and to support shaped areas such as collars. Select a supple interfacing that does not change the character of the knit. Two types of interfacings especially suitable for knits are fusible tricot and stretch nonwoven.

Tips for Interfacing Knits

Fusible tricot interfacing adds support and body to fashion knits without adding stiffness. It also allows for some crosswise stretch. Use tricot to stabilize detail areas such as cuffs, pockets, and plackets.

Stretch nonwoven interfacing stabilizes knit lengthwise but allows knit to stretch crosswise. Use this interfacing for flexible shaping in collars, necklines, facings, tabs, and zipper openings.

Sheer & Silky Fabrics

Sheer fabrics can have a soft or crisp hand; crisp sheers are easier to cut and sew. Soft sheers are batiste (**1**), chiffon (**2**), China silk (**3**), and georgette (**4**). Crisp sheers include fabrics such as organza (**5**), voile (**6**), and organdy (**7**).

The major consideration with sheer fabrics is their transparent quality. The stitches on the inside of a sheer garment show from the outside. Whether revealed clearly or as mere shadows, details such as seams, facings, and hems must be neat and narrow to look well made.

Silky fabrics are made from natural silk fibers or synthetic fibers that look like silk, such as polyester, nylon, rayon, and acetate. The polyester types are popular because they are less costly than silk fabrics. Most synthetic silk-like fabrics do not shrink or fade,

and can be washed and dried by machine. This group of fabrics includes charmeuse (**8**), crepe de chine (**9**), lightweight jacquard weaves (**10**), lightweight satin-backed crepe (**11**), and tissue faille (**12**).

Even when silk and synthetic silk-like fabrics do not have the see-through character of sheers, they do have similar fine weaves and light weights. Inner construction can show as ridges on the outside of silky garments. That is why many of the same sewing supplies and techniques are suggested for both kinds of fabrics. An additional consideration with silk-like fabrics is their smooth, slick texture, which makes them slippery to handle. You will need to take special steps when laying out and cutting the pattern pieces to control these fabrics.

Guide to Sewing Sheer and Silky Fabrics

Equipment & Techniques	Soft Sheers Batiste, chiffon, China silk, georgette **Crisp Sheers** Organdy, organza, voile	Lightweight Silkies Charmeuse, crepe de chine, jacquard weaves, satin-backed crepe, tissue faille
Machine Needles	Size 8 (60), 9 (65), or 11 (75)	Size 8 (60), 9 (65), or 11 (75)
Stitch Length	12 to 16 per inch (2.5 cm)	12 to 16 per inch (2.5 cm)
Millimeter Stitch Setting	2.5 to 2	2.5 to 2
Thread	Extra-fine long staple polyester; silk or mercerized cotton. These threads are often sold as notions for lingerie, machine embroidery, or quilting. Use finest thread possible.	
Hand Needles	Betweens, sizes 8 to 12	Betweens, sizes 8 to 12
Interfacings	Sheer nonwoven fusible or sew-in, self-fabric, organza	Fusible tricot, sheer nonwoven fusible or sew-in, batiste, self-fabric, lining fabric, organza, organdy
Special Seams	French, hairline, overlocked, double-stitched	French, overlocked, double-stitched
Special Hems	Overlocked, rolled overlocked, hand-rolled, tricot-bound, hairline, narrow topstitched	

Techniques for Sheer & Silky Fabrics

Keep in mind the delicate nature of sheer and silky fabrics when choosing patterns. The most suitable pattern designs are those that fit loosely and have graceful, flowing lines. Look for soft details such as gathers, ruffles, shirring, or draping. Crisp sheers, however, can be sewn from patterns with tailored, shirt-style details. Bias-cut pattern sections can be difficult to handle on silk and synthetic silk fabrics, which stretch a great deal as well as slip and slide.

For sheers, the fewer seams, darts, facings, and other details to sew, the less inside construction will show through to the right side. Also, the less time you will spend with special finishing techniques. Avoid patterns that require zippers, and omit in-seam pockets because zippers and pockets are bulky and can create an unattractive show-through on the outside of the garment.

Fabric Preparation

For best results, wash and dry sheer and silky fabrics before you begin working with them if they will be washed as part of their routine care. This preshrinks the fabric and removes resins, which can cause skipped stitches and make stitching difficult on synthetic fabrics. Follow the care instructions provided by the fabric manufacturer. Typical care instructions are to machine wash in a gentle cycle and tumble dry at a low temperature setting. Before

washing, stitch along cut edges of the fabric to prevent excessive fraying.

Pure silk and silk/synthetic blend fabrics require special consideration. Silk fabrics can be drycleaned, but hand washing may be preferred. Warm water releases a natural substance from within the silk fibers, which renews the fabric and gives it a refreshed look. Prewashing also frees you from worry about water spotting. However, silk fabrics cannot be made colorfast, and dyes will run. Hand washing is not recommended for strong colors, prints, and iridescents but can be used for light solid colors. Use a sample of your fabric as a test to see how it reacts to hand washing; then prepare the entire length of fabric accordingly.

Also preshrink other fabrics, such as interfacings and linings. Even a tiny amount of shrinkage on these inner fabrics will show up as puckers or bubbles on thin, lightweight outer fabrics.

If you decide to dryclean your silk garment, prepare the fabric for sewing by steam pressing on the wrong side. Use a press cloth to protect the fabric. Set the iron at the lowest end of the steam setting.

Pressing

The best approach to pressing sheer and silky fabrics is to work with fabric scraps first. Determine

How to Hand Wash Silks

1) Swish fabric gently in lukewarm water. Use mild detergent, mild soap, or natural shampoo such as castile. Rinse in cool water.

2) Roll fabric in towel to remove excess moisture. Do not wring or twist; this causes wrinkles, which are difficult to remove.

3) Press on wrong side of fabric while it is wet. Use dry iron at cool temperature, such as synthetic setting, keeping grainlines true.

the optimum temperature setting on your iron, beginning with a low setting and raising it as needed. Fabrics made from rayon or polyester fibers scorch easily and require a cool iron temperature. Use a press cloth to protect fragile fabrics and fibers, or use a soleplate cover on your iron. Avoid a metal-coated ironing board cover because it reflects too much heat into the fabric.

Most pure silk fabrics can be pressed at a low steam setting, but test to see if steaming leaves spots. This is a hazard especially on pure silk fabrics that have not been prewashed before pattern layout and on lustrous fabrics such as charmeuse.

Avoid overpressing. Thin, lightweight fabrics are quickly penetrated by heat and need less pressing effort than heavier fabrics. A light touch is all that is necessary. Use a hand steamer on finished garments.

Layout & Cutting

In general, fine, lightweight fabrics are easier to handle during pattern layout if you cover the cutting surface with a sheet, other matte-surfaced fabric, or flannel-backed vinyl tablecloth with the flannel side up. Cardboard cutting boards and cork-covered or padded work surfaces also help to make slippery fabrics more controllable.

To pin patterns in position, use superfine pins (.5 mm diameter). They penetrate the fabric weave without marring it. Prepare new pins by wiping off the manufacturer's oil coating to prevent leaving spots, or use the pins first on dark fabric. In spite of their name, silk pins are too coarse for these fabrics and should be reserved for use with heavier fabrics such as raw silk.

The fastest way to cut out fine fabrics is with a rotary cutter. The blade cuts fabric edges neatly and does not shift the fabric as you work. Another good cutting tool is a bent-handled dressmaker's shears. The shape of the handle allows you to rest one cutting blade on the work surface for accurate strokes that barely disturb the fabric layers. Serrated-edge shears can also be helpful. The special blades firmly grip thin and slippery fabrics, a benefit not only for initial cutting but also for trimming raw edges. Whichever tool you use, be sure it is sharp; blades of shears should be in good alignment. Also, synthetic fabrics cause a fuzz buildup, which dulls the cutting blades; wipe this off with a soft cloth.

Use a "with nap" layout for all fabrics that have luster or shine. This one-way pattern layout guarantees uniform color shading in the finished garment. Some fabrics look lighter or brighter in one direction than the other; study the fabric before pattern layout and decide which shading you prefer.

Layout Techniques for Slippery Fabrics

 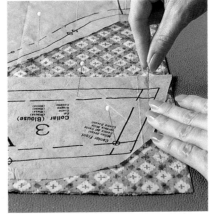 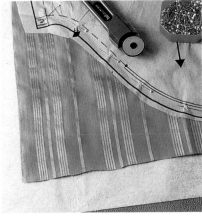

Fold fabric right side out, so less-slick wrong sides face each other. Pick up fabric along folded edge, and let fabric fall naturally to ensure accuracy of crosswise grain.

Push pins straight down through pattern seam allowance, fabric, and padded or cork-covered work surface to secure slippery layers. If using cardboard cutting board, avoid using superfine pins because cardboard dulls them quickly.

Sandwich extremely slippery or thin fabrics between two layers of tissue paper for better control. Place tissue paper on cutting board; place fabric and pattern on tissue; pin through all layers. Pin only in seam allowances.

Lustrous Fabrics

The lustrous surface of special occasion fabrics can come from the weave of the fabric, as is true for satin, or from fibers with sheen, such as silk and acetate. Special finishes also create surface luster, or metallic yarns or sequins can be added to give an ordinary fabric glamorous sparkle.

1) Satin is a weave that produces a shiny surface texture from floating yarns. The combination of fibers such as silk, rayon, or polyester with the distinctive weave makes the fabric likely to water-spot; protect the fabric with a press cloth, and use a dry iron when pressing. Use superfine pins to avoid snagging surface yarns.

2) Crepe-backed satin is also called satin-backed crepe because the fabric is reversible; one face has the matte, pebbly texture of crepe, and the other face has the smooth, shiny texture of satin. One side may be used as a binding or trim for the other.

3) Satin peau is a satin with a firm twill weave on the right side. Some peaus are double faced, with fine crosswise ribs on both sides. Because pins and ripped-out stitches can leave marks, pin only in seam allowance; test-fit to avoid ripping stitches.

4) Taffeta has a crisp hand and drapes stiffly. Test sewing techniques on scraps, because pins and ripped-out stitches can leave marks. When the fiber content includes acetate, steam can leave spots.

5) Moiré taffeta is passed between heated rollers to give it a watermarked surface texture.

6) Brocade comes in all weights, from light to heavy, and has raised tapestry-style motifs. The motifs should be balanced on major garment sections and matched at prominent seams. Most brocades are woven, but some are knit. Careful pressing on a padded surface preserves the surface texture. When brocades have shiny metallic threads, set the iron at a low temperature for pressing. To make metallic brocades more comfortable, underline with batiste.

7) Metallic fabrics have metallic yarns woven or knit into them. Most metallics are sensitive to heat and discolor when steam is used. Finger press seams with a thimble or blunt end of a point turner; or use a cool, dry iron.

8) Lamé is a smooth, shiny metallic fabric, either knit or woven. Knit metallics drape and ease better than the wovens. Besides traditional gold, silver, and copper tones, lamé is available in iridescent colors.

9) Sequined fabrics have a knit or sheer woven base. A simple pattern style is especially important for these fabrics. Or use sequined fabric for only a part of the garment, such as the bodice.

Techniques for Lustrous Fabrics

Many fabrics fit into the lustrous category, and some have unique sewing requirements. However, all of these fabrics are alike in two ways: A "with nap" pattern layout is used for uniform color shading in the finished garment, and the less handling, the better. Keep handling to a minimum by choosing patterns in simple styles with few seams and darts. Avoid buttoned closings and details such as shaped collars and welt pockets. Use a simple pinked finish on plain seams, or treat raw edges with liquid fray preventer instead of using elaborate dressmaker techniques. Take special care when pressing, using a light touch and covering the pressing surface with a scrap of self-fabric so nap faces nap. To prevent ridges when pressing seams, press over a seam roll or place strips of heavy brown paper between seam allowance and garment.

Guide to Sewing Lustrous Fabrics

Equipment & Techniques	Mediumweight Crepe-backed satin, lamé, satin, satin peau, silk, taffeta, moiré	Heavily Textured Brocade, sequined fabrics
Machine Needles	Size 11 (75)	Size 14 (90) or 16 (100)
Stitch Length	8 to 12 per inch (2.5 cm)	8 to 12 per inch (2.5 cm)
Millimeter Stitch Setting	3.5 to 2.5	3.5 to 2.5
Thread	All-purpose cotton or cotton/polyester, silk for silk fabrics	All-purpose cotton or cotton/polyester
Hand Needles	Betweens, size 7 or 8	Betweens, size 7 or 8
Interfacings	Sew-in nonwoven or woven	Sew-in nonwoven or woven
Special Seams	Plain seam: pinked, overedge, three-step zigzag, or liquid fray preventer finish	Plain seam or lined to edge
Special Hems	Catchstitched, topstitched, horsehair braid, faced	Faced

Tips for Handling Lustrous Fabrics

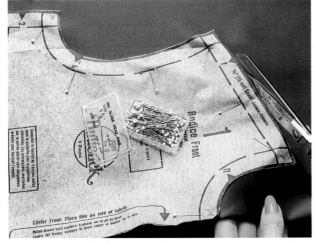

Layout. Pin only in seam allowances to prevent pin marks. Use extra-fine silk pins for finely woven fabrics such as satin and taffeta. Shears must be sharp or strokes will chew raw edges of fabric. Cut directionally for smoothest edges. Always use "with nap" layout for fabrics with luster.

Seams. Use plain seams with a simple edge finish. Raw edges can be pinked, overlocked, or finished with three-step zigzag. If fabric frays easily, apply thin coat of liquid fray preventer to raw edges. Slip envelopes between seam allowances and garment to protect garment from stray drops.

Lace & Embroidered Fabrics

Laces look fragile and delicate but are actually easy to sew. True laces have a net or mesh background, which has no grainline and does not ravel. You can cut into the fabric freely for creative pattern layouts, seams need no time-consuming edge finishes, and hemming requires little more than trimming close to the edges of prominent motifs.

The openwork designs of lace fabrics have rich histories. Some laces still bear the names of the European localities where they were once made by hand from silk, cotton, or linen fibers. Today, many laces are made by machine from easy-care cotton blends, polyester, acrylic, or nylon.

1) Alençon lace has filled-in motifs outlined by soft satin cord on a sheer net background. One or both lengthwise edges usually have a finished border.

2) Chantilly lace has delicate floral motifs worked on a fine net background and outlined with silky threads. A popular bridal fabric, Chantilly lace usually has an allover pattern.

3) Eyelet is a finely woven cotton or polyester/cotton fabric embroidered with a satin-stitched openwork design. Even though eyelet embroideries are not true laces, they require pattern layout and pressing techniques similar to those for laces.

4) Peau d'ange is a form of Chantilly lace made with a flossy yarn to give it a soft texture.

5) Venice lace is made from heavy yarns and unique stitches that give it a three-dimensional texture. Picot bridges join the motifs. Venice lace does not have the net background that is typical of most laces.

6) Point d'esprit has an open net or fine tulle background with a pattern of embroidered dots.

7) Cluny lace is made from heavy cotton-like yarns and looks hand-crocheted. It usually has paddle or wheel motifs and may have raised knots as part of the design.

8) Schiffli is an embroidered sheer or semi-sheer fabric decorated on a Schiffli machine, which imitates hand embroidery stitches.

Guide to Sewing Laces

Equipment & Techniques	Delicate Chantilly, peau d'ange, point d'esprit	Embroidered Eyelet, Schiffli	Textured Alençon, Cluny, Venice
Machine Needles	Size 8 (60) or 9 (65)	Size 9 (65) or 11 (75)	Size 11 (75)
Stitch Length	12 to 16 per inch (2.5 cm)	10 to 12 per inch (2.5 cm)	10 to 12 per inch (2.5 cm)
Millimeter Stitch Setting	2.5 to 2	3 to 2.5	3 to 2.5
Thread	Extra-fine	All-purpose	All-purpose
Hand Needles	Betweens, size 7 or 8	Betweens, size 7 or 8	Betweens, size 7 or 8
Interfacings	Omit	Omit	Omit
Special Seams	Lapped, overlocked, double-stitched	Overlocked, double-stitched	Lapped, double-stitched
Special Hems	Self-hem, appliquéd	Self-hem	Self-hem, appliquéd, horsehair braid

Techniques for Sewing Lace & Embroidered Fabrics

Select a pattern that suits the texture and weight of the lace fabric. Use heavy laces such as Alençon and Cluny for simple, fitted pattern silhouettes. Select lightweight laces, such as Chantilly, for patterns with full skirts and sleeves, and details such as ruffles.

Patterns for bridal and evening gowns that are illustrated in lace fabrics may require specific forms of lace, such as edgings of specific widths or a wide allover lace. Check the back of the pattern envelope to see if the lace fits the pattern requirements.

When considering a pattern that is not illustrated in laces, select a pattern with sections sized to fit the fabric width. If planning to use a bordered lace on sleeves, you may have to use a short-sleeved pattern if the lace is not wide enough for long sleeves, or place the lace at the lower edge of an organza sleeve. Facings, hems, and pockets are usually eliminated so you may need less fabric. Because lace has no grainline, it is possible to turn the pattern pieces to use an edge or border as a finished edge.

Fabric Preparation

Lace rarely requires any preparation for sewing. Most laces must be drycleaned. Although shrinkage is rare, if the care label on a lace fabric indicates it is washable, and you are combining it with other fabrics and trims to make a washable garment, then you should preshrink the lace. Add it to the other components of the garment as you preshrink them.

Facings, Interfacings & Underlinings

Facings and interfacings are not used on lace garments. Finish outer edges with lace trim, lace borders, or sheer tricot bias or French binding. Cut collars and cuffs as single layers, and finish the outer edges with lace trim or appliqué. Use a narrow seam to join them to the garment.

If you need to add body or support to lace, underline the lace with tulle netting. For example, you may choose to underline a fitted lace bodice or sleeves. The tulle netting adds strength without showing through or changing the character of the lace. A lining fabric in a contrasting color can also be used as an underlining. Although this makes the lace opaque, it shows off the lace design and hides seams, darts, and other details of inner construction.

Layout & Cutting

Pattern layout is an important preliminary step for lace fabrics. Begin by studying the details of the lace design. Unfold the fabric fully on the work surface, laying contrasting fabric underneath if necessary to make the design easier to read.

Note the placement of prominent motifs, the spacing of the repeats, and the depth of any borders. These affect pattern layout because the most noticeable motifs should be matched at the seams and centered or otherwise balanced on major garment sections, just like large fabric prints. If the design has one-way motifs, use a "with nap" pattern layout.

Plan at this point how to use the motifs creatively. Some laces have large primary motifs and smaller secondary motifs or borders that can be cut out and used as appliqués. To use borders as prefinished hems, determine the finished skirt and sleeve lengths before pattern layout. If you plan to trim the border from the fabric and sew it to the garment as a decorative edging, you do not need to determine lengths in advance so precisely.

Before cutting, decide which seam treatment you will be using. Allover laces can be sewn like sheer fabrics, with narrow seams. However, if you are working with a re-embroidered lace or a special heirloom lace with a large motif, lapped seams may be better. They will not interrupt the flow of the lace design around the garment because the seam is nearly invisible. With this method, pattern sections must be pinned in place and cut out one by one in sequence. You may use a combination of seams in one garment, with lapped seams at shoulder and side seams and narrow zigzag or double-stitched seams for set-in sleeves.

Once lace is cut, there is little margin for fitting changes. Fit the pattern before layout to avoid ripping out stitches later. Cut the pattern from lining or underlining fabric to use for fitting, as well as for the inside of the finished garment. Another method is to make a muslin trial garment. A third method is to make a full pattern from pattern tracing fabric and baste the sections together for a fitting. You can then use this pattern to cut out the lace.

Pressing

Avoid overhandling lace with pressing. If a light touch-up is needed, press with right side down on a well-padded surface to avoid flattening the lace texture. Use a press cloth to prevent the tip of the iron from catching or tearing the net background. If you are working with lace made from synthetic fibers, such as polyester or nylon, use a low temperature setting on the iron. Finger press seams, darts, and other construction details. Wear a thimble and press firmly. If further pressing is necessary, steam lightly, then finger press.

Lace Appliqués

Lace appliqués, either purchased as single medallions or cut from lace fabric, make elegant trims on special-occasion garments. These trims are often used as accents on bridal and evening gown bodices when the skirt is cut from lace fabric. They can also be used as feminine details on silky lingerie and blouses.

Three different methods can be used to apply individual lace motifs to a garment. To stitch appliqués in place, use either the hand or machine method. Another quick technique is securing appliqués with fusible web. This method is suitable for laces and background fabrics that are not sensitive to heat and steam.

Attaching Lace Appliqués

Use lace fabric. Clip around lace motif. Leave one or two rows of net around edges to give motif definition and to keep re-embroidered lace cordings from raveling. Or purchase lace appliqué.

Hand-stitch. Use short running stitches ¼" (6 mm) from appliqué edges. Keep stitches loose so background fabric stays smooth and appliqué is not flattened. (Contrasting thread is used to show detail.)

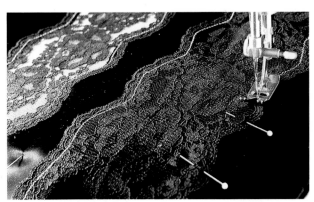

Machine-stitch. Use a narrow zigzag or short straight stitch ¼" (6 mm) inside edges. Under the motif, trim fabric close to zigzag stitching for sheer effect. (Contrasting thread is used to show detail.)

Fuse. Position garment, right side up, on covered pressing surface. Place appliqué on garment. Slip circles of fusible web under appliqué. Cover with paper towels or absorbent press cloth. Fuse, following manufacturer's directions.

Interfacing

Interfacing plays a supporting role in almost every garment. It is the inner layer of fabric used to shape and support details like collars, cuffs, waistbands, pockets, lapels and buttonholes. Even simple styles often need interfacing to add stability to necklines, facings or hems. Interfacing adds body to garments and helps keep them crisp through repeated washings and wearings.

Interfacings come in many different fibers and weights. The pattern may require more than one kind. Choose interfacing according to the weight of the fashion fabric, the kind of shaping required and the way the garment will be cleaned. Generally, interfacing should be the same weight or lighter than the fashion fabric. Drape two layers of the fabric and the interfacing together to see if they hang well. Areas like collars and cuffs usually need stiffer interfacing. For sheer fabrics, another piece of the fashion fabric may be the best interfacing.

Interfacings are available in *woven* or *nonwoven* fabrics. Woven interfacing has a lengthwise and crosswise grain. It must be cut with the same grain as the part of the garment to be interfaced. Nonwoven interfacing is made by bonding fibers together; it has no grain. Stable nonwovens can be cut in any direction and will not ravel. Stretch nonwovens have crosswise stretch, most effective for knits.

Both woven and nonwoven interfacings are available in *sew-in* and *fusible* versions. Sew-in interfacing must be pinned or basted, and is ultimately held in place by machine stitching. Fusibles have a coating on one side which, when steam-pressed, melts and fuses the interfacing to the wrong side of the fabric. Fusibles come in plastic wrappers which have directions for applying. Follow them precisely, since each fusible is different. When applying fusibles, use a damp press cloth to protect the iron and provide extra steam.

Choosing between fusible and sew-in interfacing is usually a matter of personal preference. Sew-ins require more hand work. Fusibles are quick and easy, and give more rigidity to the garment. However, some delicate fabrics cannot take the heat that fusing requires. Textured fabrics such as seersucker cannot be fused because the texture would be lost.

Interfacings are made in weights from sheer to heavy and usually come in white, gray, beige or black. There are special timesaving interfacings for waistbands, cuffs and plackets. These have pre-marked stitching lines to keep edges even.

Another interfacing aid is *fusible web,* available in strips of various widths. It bonds two layers of fabric together, making it possible to bond a sew-in interfacing to the fashion fabric. Fusible web can also be used to put up hems, hold appliqués in place and secure patches before stitching.

Guide to Interfacings

Fusible woven interfacings are available in different weights and crispness, from medium to heavyweight. Cut them on the same grain as the garment piece, or on the bias for softer shaping.

Fusible nonwoven interfacings come in all weights, from sheer to heavyweight. Stable nonwovens have little give in any direction and can be cut on any grain.

Fusible knit interfacings are made of nylon tricot, which is stable in the lengthwise direction and stretches on the crosswise grain to be compatible with lightweight knit and woven fabrics.

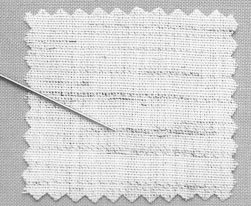

Sew-in woven interfacings preserve the shape and qualities of the fabric, and should be used for natural shaping with woven fabrics. Weights range from sheer organza and batiste to heavyweight hair canvas.

Sew-in nonwovens provide a choice of weight, color, stretch, stable or all-bias combinations. They are appropriate for knits and stretch fabrics as well as for wovens. Preshrink all nonwoven interfacings.

Fusible web is a bonding agent used to join two layers of fabric without stitching. Although it is not an interfacing, it adds some stiffness to the fabric but does not prevent stretching.

Nonwoven fusible waistbanding is precut in widths or strips to be used for extra firm, crisp edges such as waistbands, cuffs, plackets and straight facings. It has premarked stitching or fold lines.

Nonwoven sew-in waistbanding is a heavyweight, very firm finished strip for stiff, stable waistbands or belts. It is available in several widths. It can be sewn to the back or facing of a waistband, but is too stiff to sew into a waistband seam.

How to Apply Fusible Interfacing

1) **Position** interfacing on warm fabric, resin side down; smooth into place. Lightly mist interfacing with water, or steam shrink. Position press cloth and dampen with liberal misting, even when using steam iron.

2) **Start** at center of large or long pieces of interfacing, and work toward each end to fuse. Do not slide iron from one position to the next. To ensure complete coverage, overlap fused areas with iron.

3) **Use** two-handed pressure, and lean on iron; fuse for recommended time, 10 to 15 seconds for most fusible interfacings. Otherwise, bond will not be permanent and will eventually separate from fabric.

4) **Press** the fused area from right side of fabric for better bonding. Use a press cloth or iron soleplate guard to protect fabric surface. Cool and dry fused fabrics before moving them; interfacing is easily reshaped or distorted while warm.

Layout, Cutting & Marking

Once you have chosen the pattern and fabric and assembled the proper equipment, you're ready to start creating your garment. Before you cut, make sure the fabric is properly prepared and the pattern correctly laid out.

Much of fabric preparation and layout has to do with the fabric grain. *Grain* is the direction in which the fabric threads run.

Woven fabrics consist of lengthwise threads intersecting crosswise threads. When these threads cross one another at perfect right angles, the fabric is *on-grain*. If the intersection of lengthwise and crosswise threads does not form right angles, the fabric is *off-grain*. It is essential that your fabric be on-grain before cutting. If fabric is cut off-grain, the garment will never hang or fit correctly.

The direction of the lengthwise threads is called the *lengthwise grain*. This grainline runs parallel to the *selvage*, a narrow, tightly-woven border which runs along both lengthwise sides of the fabric. Because lengthwise threads are stronger and more stable than crosswise threads, most garments are cut so the lengthwise grain runs vertically. The crosswise threads form the *crosswise grain*, which runs at right angles to the selvage. In most fabrics, it has a slight amount of give. Fabrics with border prints are often cut on the crosswise grain so the border will run horizontally across the garment.

Any diagonal line intersecting the lengthwise and crosswise grains is called a *bias*. Fabric cut on the bias has more stretch than fabric cut on the grainline. A *true bias* is formed when the diagonal line is at a 45-degree angle to any straight edge. This angle provides the most stretch. Strips cut on the true bias are often used to finish curved edges such as necklines and armholes. Plaids and stripes can be cut on the bias for an interesting effect. Garments cut on the true bias usually drape softly.

Knit fabrics are formed by interlocking loops of yarn called *ribs*. The ribs run parallel to the lengthwise sides of the fabric. Their direction can be compared to the lengthwise grain of woven fabrics. The rows of loops at right angles to the ribs are called *courses* and are comparable to the woven crosswise grain. Knits have no bias and no selvage. Some flat knits have perforated lengthwise edges that look something like a selvage, but these cannot be relied on to establish true lengthwise grain. Knits have the most stretch in the crosswise direction, and are cut with the crosswise grain running horizontally around the body for maximum comfort.

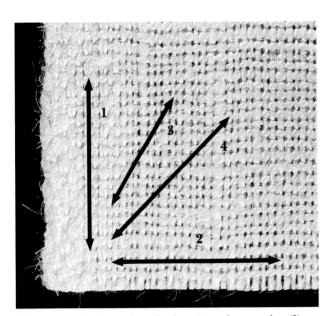

Woven fabrics have lengthwise (1) and crosswise (2) threads. The lengthwise threads are stronger, since they must withstand greater tension during weaving. Bias (3) is any diagonal direction. True bias (4) is a 45-degree angle. It has the most stretch.

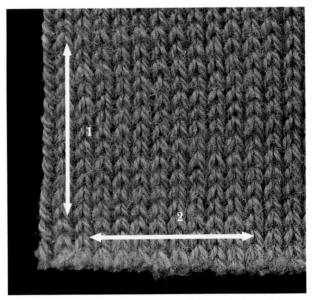

Knit fabrics have lengthwise (1) ribs parallel to the length of the fabric. Crosswise courses (2) run at right angles to the ribs. Some knits are flat. Others are made in a tubular shape; these can be cut open along a lengthwise rib if a single thickness is needed for layout.

Preparing the Fabric

Before laying out the pattern, take the necessary steps to prepare the fabric for cutting. The label on the bolt tells whether the fabric is washable or dry-cleanable and how much, if any, the fabric will shrink. If the fabric has not been preshrunk by the manufacturer, or if the label says it will shrink more than one per cent, you must preshrink the fabric before cutting. It is often advisable to preshrink knits, since this removes the sizing that sometimes causes skipped stitches. Zippers and trims may also need preshrinking. Dry-cleanable fabrics can be preshrunk by steam pressing or by a professional dry cleaner. This is especially important if you plan to use fusible interfacing, which requires more steam

than normal pressing and may cause shrinkage. To make sure the fabric is on-grain, begin by straightening the crosswise ends of your fabric. This may be done by pulling a crosswise thread, or cutting along a woven design or crosswise rib of a knit. Next, fold the fabric lengthwise, matching selvages and crosswise ends. If the fabric bubbles, it is off-grain. Fabric that is slightly off-grain can be straightened by steam pressing. Pin along selvages and both ends, matching edges. Press from the selvages to the fold. Fabric that is very much off-grain must be straightened by pulling fabric in the opposite direction from the way the ends slant. Permanent-finish fabrics cannot be straightened.

How to Preshrink Fabric

Preshrink washable fabric by laundering and drying it in the same manner you will use for the finished garment. You may also immerse it in hot water. After 30 minutes to one hour, gently squeeze water out and dry fabric as you would the finished garment.

Steam press to preshrink dry-cleanable fabrics. Steam evenly, moving iron horizontally or vertically (not diagonally) across the grain. After steaming, let fabric dry on smooth, flat surface for four to six hours, or until thoroughly dry.

How to Straighten Crosswise Ends of Fabric

Pull threads to straighten woven fabric. Clip one selvage and gently pull one or two crosswise threads. Push fabric along threads with your other hand until you reach opposite selvage. Cut fabric along pulled thread.

Cut on a line to straighten a stripe, plaid, check or other *woven* design. Simply cut along a prominent crosswise line. Do not use this method for *printed* designs, because they may be printed off-grain.

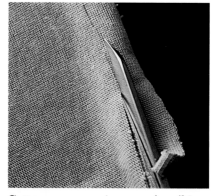

Cut on a course (a crosswise rib) to straighten ends of a knit. It may be easier to follow along the course if you first baste-mark it with contrasting thread, or mark with marking pencil or chalk.

Laying Out the Pattern

Get ready to lay out the pattern by preparing a large work area such as a table topped with a cutting board, or other large flat surface. Assemble all the pattern pieces for the view you are making and press them with a warm, dry iron to remove wrinkles.

Locate the correct layout diagram on the pattern direction sheet. Pattern layouts are reliable guides for laying out the pattern quickly and efficiently. Find the layout for the view, fabric width, and pattern size you are using. When working with a napped or other directional fabric (page 75), choose a "with nap" layout. Circle the layout with a colored pen to make sure you refer to the correct layout each time.

Fold the fabric as indicated on the layout. Most fabrics are cut with the right side folded in. This makes it easier to mark and faster to stitch, since some pieces will be in position to sew. Cottons and linens are usually folded right side out on the bolt; wools, wrong side out. The right side of the fabric may appear shinier or flatter, or have a more pronounced weave. Selvages look more finished on the right side. If you cannot tell which is the right side, simply pick the side you like best and consistently use that as the right side. A slight difference in shading that is not apparent as you cut may be noticeable in the finished garment if two different sides are used.

The layout diagram indicates the placement of the selvages and fold. Most garments are cut with the fabric folded along the lengthwise grain. If the fabric is to be cut folded on the crosswise grain, the fold is labeled "crosswise fold" on the layout. The crosswise fold should not be used on napped or other directional fabrics.

Place the pattern pieces on the fabric as indicated in the layout. The symbols and markings used in layout diagrams are standardized for all major pattern companies. A white pattern piece indicates that this piece is to be cut with the printing facing up. A shaded piece should be cut with the printing facing down. A dotted line indicates that a pattern piece should be cut a second time.

When a pattern piece is shown half white and half shaded, it should be cut from folded fabric. Cut the other pieces first and refold the fabric to cut this piece. A pattern piece shown extending beyond the fold is cut from a single layer rather than the usual double layer of fabric. After cutting the other pieces, open the fabric right side up and position this piece by aligning the grainline arrow with the straight grain of the fabric.

After all pattern pieces are in place, pin them to the fabric according to the directions below. Do not begin cutting until all pattern pieces are in place.

How to Pin Pattern Pieces in Place

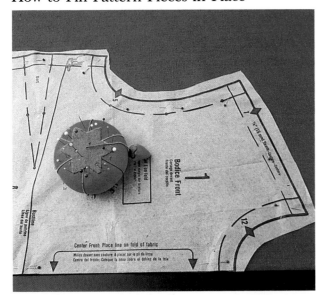

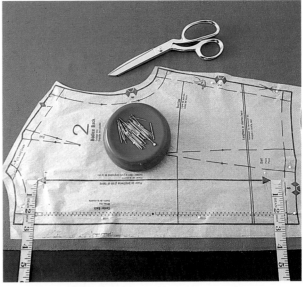

1) Position pattern pieces to be cut on the fold first. Place each directly on folded edge of fabric. Pin corners of pattern diagonally. Continue pinning in the seam allowance, placing pins parallel to the cutting line. Space pins about 3" (7.5 cm) apart, closer together on curves or on slippery fabrics.

2) Place straight-grain pattern pieces on fabric with grainline arrow parallel to the selvage of woven fabrics, parallel to a rib for knits. Measure from each end of the arrow to the selvage or rib, shifting the pattern until the distances are equal. Pin both ends of the grainline so pattern will not shift. Continue pinning as directed in step 1.

Laying Out
Plaids & Stripes

Select simple styles for plaids and stripes. Complicated fashions can detract from or distort the fabric design. Avoid diagonal bustline darts, long horizontal darts and patterns designated "not suitable for plaids and stripes."

Always buy extra yardage to allow for matching the design at the seams. The extra amount needed depends on the size of the *repeat* (the four-sided area in which the pattern and color of the design are complete) and the number and lengths of major pattern pieces. Usually an extra ¼ to ½ yard (0.25 to 0.5 m) is sufficient.

It is easier to work with even plaids and balanced stripes than uneven plaids and unbalanced stripes. *Even plaids* have the same arrangement of colors and stripes in both lengthwise and crosswise directions. The area of repeat is perfectly square. In *uneven plaids*, the color and stripes form a different arrangement in the lengthwise or crosswise direction, or both. *Balanced stripes* repeat in the same order in both directions; *unbalanced stripes* do not. To avoid having to match two layers of yardage it is recommended that each pattern piece be layed out in a single layer.

Placement Tips

Before cutting and layout, decide the placement of plaid design lines within the garment and where they will fall on the body. Avoid placing a dominant horizontal line or block of lines at the bustline and waistline if possible. Experiment with the fabric draped from shoulder to hem. Some plaid garments look more balanced when the hemline falls at the bottom of a dominant crosswise line. If you wish to draw the eye away from the hemline, place the hemline between two dominant lines. When laying out plaids and stripes, match *stitching* lines, not cutting lines.

To match at the seams, lay out each piece in a single layer beginning with garment front. Place dominant vertical lines at the center front and center back, or position the pattern so the center front is halfway between two dominant vertical lines. Position the sleeve in the same way, using the shoulder dot as the guide for centering the sleeve on or between the dominant vertical lines.

Although it is not always possible to match the design at every seam, try to match: crosswise bars at vertical seams such as center front and back, and side seams; set-in sleeves to the bodice front at armhole notches; lengthwise stripes where possible; and pockets, flaps and other details to the area of the garment they will cover. The plaid may not match at the shoulder seams or the back notch in the armhole of a set-in sleeve.

Identifying even and uneven plaids. An even plaid has lengthwise and crosswise color bars that match when the repeat is folded diagonally through the center (1). An uneven plaid may have differing color bars in one or more directions (2). Or an uneven plaid may have matching color bars but not form a mirror image when folded diagonally because the repeat is not square (3). This type of uneven plaid is the most difficult to identify.

Tips for Laying Out Plaid Fabrics

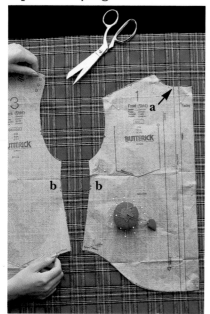

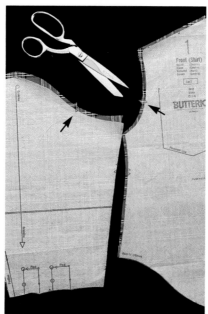

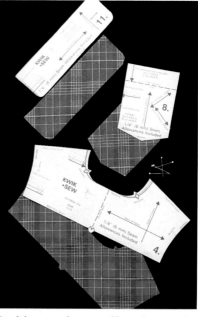

Lay out each piece in a single layer, beginning with front pattern piece. Use dominant part of design **(a)** for center front and center back. Match notches at side seams **(b)** of front and back.

Center sleeve at same dominant part of design as center front. The design should match at the notches (arrows) of the sleeve front and armhole of garment front; notches at back may not match.

Position pockets, cuffs, yokes, and separate front bands on the true bias to avoid time-consuming matching. Center a dominant design block in each pattern piece.

How to Lay Out Uneven Plaids

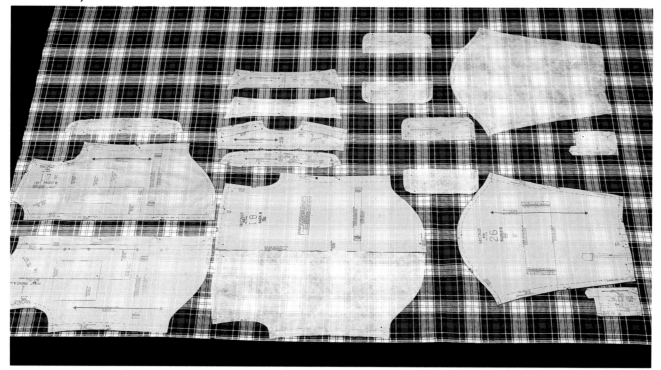

Lay out pattern on single layer of fabric, flipping pattern pieces over to cut right and left halves. Place most dominant color bar at center front and center back or position the pattern so the center front is halfway between two dominant vertical lines. Place pattern pieces in one direction only, using "with nap" layout. Plaid will repeat around the garment instead of forming a mirror image on each side of the center front and center back seams.

Laying Out Directional Fabrics

Directional fabrics include *napped* fabrics such as corduroy, velveteen and flannel; *plush* fabrics such as fake fur; *shiny* fabrics such as taffeta and satin; and *print* fabrics which have one-way designs. Other fabrics which can be directional include some *twill weave* fabrics such as denim and gabardine, and *knits* such as jersey, single or double knits which appear lighter or darker depending on the direction of the grain.

To prevent the garment from having a two-toned look or having its design running in two different directions, all pattern pieces must be laid out with their tops facing the same direction. Napped fabrics can be cut with the nap running either up or down. Nap running up gives a darker, richer look. Nap running down looks lighter and usually wears better. Plush fabrics look best with the nap running down. Shiny fabrics can be cut in whichever direction you prefer. One-way designs should be cut so that the design will be right side up when the garment is completed.

How to Lay Out Directional Fabrics

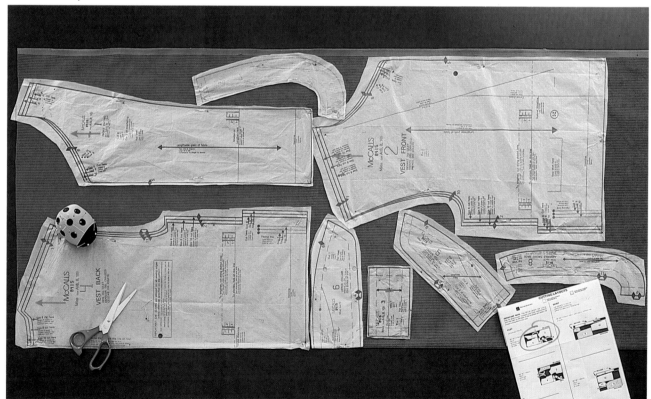

Choose the direction your fabric will run, then lay out the pattern pieces according to the "with nap" layout on the pattern direction sheet. To ensure proper placement, mark each pattern piece with an arrow pointing to the top of the piece. Sometimes the pattern calls for a crosswise fold. In this case, fold the fabric as the layout indicates, then cut along the foldline. Turn the top layer of fabric around so the nap runs in the same direction as the nap of the lower layer of fabric, and cut both layers at the same time.

Cutting Tips

Arrange your cutting table so you can move around it to get at the pattern from all angles. If your cutting surface is not this accessible, cut groups of pattern pieces apart from the rest of the fabric so you can turn these smaller pieces around.

Accuracy is important, since a mistake in cutting cannot always be corrected. Before cutting, double check placement of pattern pieces and alterations. Before cutting plaids, one-way designs, or directional fabrics, make sure the fabric is folded and laid out correctly. Basting tape (page 30) may be helpful to keep fabric from shifting. Heavy or bulky fabric can be cut more accurately one layer at a time. Slippery fabric is easier to cut if you cover the table with a sheet, blanket, or other non-slip material.

Choose sharp, plain, or serrated blade, bent-handled shears, 7" or 8" (18 or 20.5 cm) in length. Take long, firm strokes, cutting directly on the dark cutting line. Use shorter strokes for curved areas. Keep one hand on the pattern near the cutting line to prevent the pattern from shifting and to provide better control.

The rotary cutter (page 28) is especially useful for cutting leather, slippery fabrics, or several layers of fabric. The rotary cutter can be used by either right or left-handed sewers. Use a cutting mat to protect the cutting surface.

Notches can be cut outward from the notch markings, or with *short* snips into the seam allowance (page 79). Be careful not to snip beyond the seamline. Use snips to mark the foldlines and stitching lines of darts and pleats, and the center front and center back lines at the top and bottom. Mark the top of the sleeve cap above the large dot on the pattern with a snip. On bulky or loosely woven fabric where snips cannot be easily seen, cut pattern notches out into the margin. Cut double or triple notches as one unit, not separately.

After you finish cutting, save scraps to test stitching or pressing techniques, make trial buttonholes, or cover buttons. For accurate marking and easy identification, leave each pattern piece pinned in place until you are ready to sew that piece.

Your pattern may call for *bias strips* of fabric to enclose raw edges such as necklines or armholes. Ideally, these are cut from a piece of fabric long enough to fit the area to be enclosed. Bias strips may also be pieced together to form a strip of the correct length.

How to Cut & Join Bias Strips

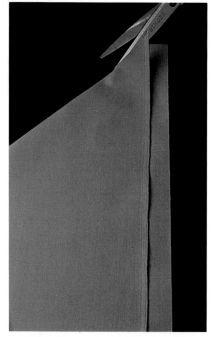 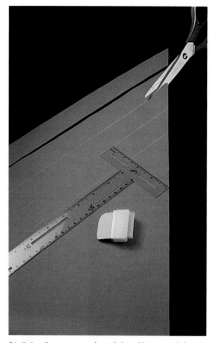 

1) Fold fabric diagonally so that a straight edge on the crosswise grain is parallel to the selvage or lengthwise grain. The foldline is the true bias. Cut fabric along the foldline to mark the first bias line.

2) Mark successive bias lines with a marking pencil or chalk, and yardstick or see-through ruler. Cut along marked lines. When a bound finish is called for in a pattern, the pattern will specify the length and width of bias strips needed.

3) Join bias strips if piecing is necessary. With right sides together, pin strips together with shorter edges aligned. Strips will form a "V." Stitch a ¼" (6 mm) seam. Press seam open. Trim points of seams even with edge of bias strip.

Marking Tips

In marking, key pattern symbols are transferred to the wrong side of the fabric after cutting and before the pattern is removed. These markings become continuous reference points to help you through all stages of garment construction. Pattern symbols that should be marked include construction symbols and position marks for placement of details.

Marking is usually done on the *wrong* side of the fabric. Some pattern symbols, such as pocket placement and buttonholes, should be *transferred* from the wrong side to the right side of the fabric (not *marked* on the right side). To do this, hand or machine-baste through the marking on the wrong side. The thread becomes the marking on the right side. Foldlines can be marked by pressing.

There are several ways to transfer markings, each suitable for different fabrics. Choose whichever gives you the fastest, most accurate marking.

Pins are a quick way to transfer markings. They should not be used on fine fabrics or those on which pin marks would be permanent, such as silk or synthetic leathers. Use pin marking only when you plan to sew immediately, since pins may fall out of loose weaves or knits.

Tailor's chalk or dressmaker's pencil, used with pins, is suitable for most fabrics.

Tracing wheel and tracing paper provide a quick, accurate method. It works best on plain, flat-surfaced fabrics. The wheel may damage some fabrics, so always test on a scrap first. Before marking, place a piece of cardboard under the fabric to protect the table. On most fabrics, both layers can be marked at one time.

Liquid markers are felt-tip pens designed especially for fabric. The marker transfers through the pattern tissue onto the fabric. The ink rinses out with water or disappears on its own, so liquid markers can be used on the right side of most fabrics.

Machine basting transfers markings from the wrong side of the fabric to the right side. It can also be used to mark intricate matching points or pivot points. After marking on the wrong side, machine-stitch through the marking. Use a long stitch length or speed-basting stitch, with contrasting color thread in the bobbin. The bobbin thread marks the right side. To mark a pivot point, stitch on the seamline with regular-length stitching and matching thread. Leave the stitching in place as a reinforcement.

Snips or clips can be used on most fabrics except very loosely woven tweeds and some bulky wools. With the point of scissors, snip about ⅛" to ¼" (3 to 6 mm) into the seam allowance.

Pressing can be used to mark foldlines, tucks, or pleats. It is a suitable method for any fabric that holds a crease.

How to Mark with Chalk, Pencil or Liquid Marker

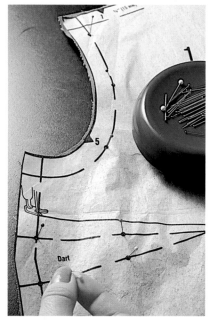

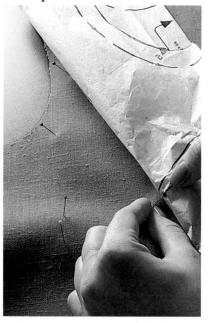

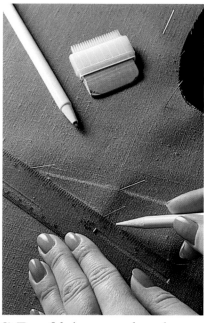

1) Insert pins straight down through pattern and both layers of fabric at marking symbols.

2) Remove pattern carefully by pulling over pin heads. Mark top layer with chalk, pencil or marker at pinpoints on wrong side.

3) Turn fabric over and mark other layer at pinpoints. Remove pins and separate layers.

How to Mark with Basting or Pressing

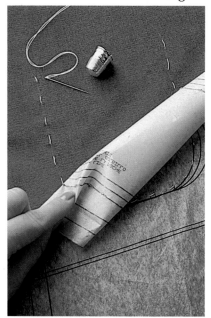

Hand-baste with long and short stitches to mark one layer of fabric. Stitch through pattern and fabric along a solid line, using short stitches on the tissue side and long stitches through fabric. Carefully pull pattern tissue away.

Machine-baste to transfer pencil, chalk or tracing paper markings from the wrong side to the right side. Use contrasting thread in the bobbin, longest stitch on machine. Do not use machine basting on fabrics which mar. Do not press over machine basting.

Press to mark foldlines, tucks and pleats. Pin pattern to a single layer of fabric. Fold pattern and fabric along marking line. Press along the fold with a dry iron.

How to Mark with Tracing Wheel and Tracing Paper

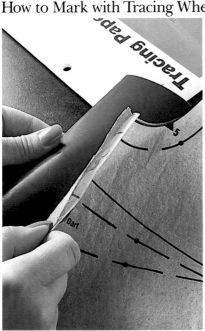

1) **Place** tracing paper under pattern, with carbon sides facing the wrong side of each fabric layer.

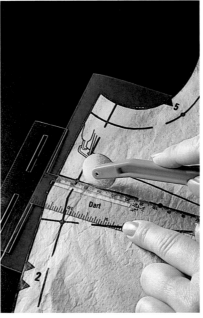

2) **Roll** tracing wheel over lines to be marked, including center foldlines of darts, using a ruler to help draw straight lines.

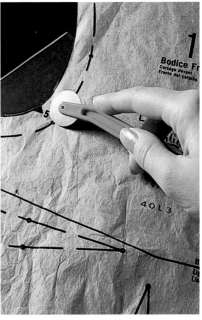

3) **Mark** dots and other large symbols with short lines perpendicular to the stitching line, or an "X." Use short lines to mark the ends of darts or pleats.

Timesaving Marking Techniques

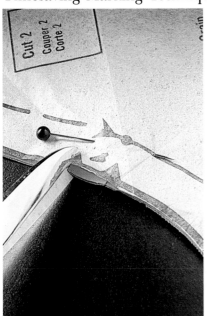

Snips can be used to mark notches, ends of darts, foldlines, or center front and back locations. Make tiny snips, ⅛" (3 mm) deep, into seam allowance. Snip through pattern and both fabric layers with point of scissors.

Pins can mark darts, dots or foldlines without the help of marking pencil. Insert pins through pattern and fabric. Pull pattern carefully over heads. Mark bottom layer with second set of pins. Secure first set of pins to mark top layer.

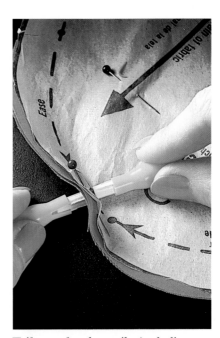

Tailor tacker has tailor's chalk inserted in two holders. One side has a pin which is inserted through pattern marking to meet chalk on the other side. Twist both sides of tacker so chalk marks two fabric layers in one timesaving step.

Sewing Techniques

General Guidelines for Pattern Adjustments

Pattern adjustments change the measurement and shape of standard pattern pieces to fit your figure. To streamline the entire fitting process, make as many fitting changes as you can before you cut. Step-by-step instructions for specific adjustments are given on the following pages. The basic guidelines below apply to most changes you are likely to make.

Press pattern pieces with a warm, dry iron before you start. It is not accurate to work with wrinkled tissue pieces.

Pin-fit the pattern to preview how well the fashion style fits your figure. Adjust the pattern on your body, or decide how extensively you need pattern adjustments. If you need many adjustments, reconsider your choice of pattern style. Another style may fit your figure with fewer adjustments. Also, pin-fit after making pattern adjustments as a fast check of their accuracy.

Work in a logical order, completing lengthening or shortening pattern adjustments first. Then work from the top of the pattern down to make additional adjustments to fit body width and contours.

Watch for chain reactions. Adjustments on one pattern piece usually require matching adjustments on adjoining pattern sections. If you change the neckline seam, for example, you must change the neck facing to match. Sometimes a compensating rather than a matching adjustment is necessary. For example, if you lower the shoulder seams to fit sloping shoulders, you must also lower the underarm seam to retain the armhole size.

Maintain the original grainline as printed on the pattern pieces, so the finished garment hangs properly. Extend the grainline from one edge of the pattern piece to the other before cutting. This helps preserve grainline as you make adjustments.

Blend the adjusted stitching and cutting lines back into the original lines. When adjustments are blended correctly, the original shape of the pattern piece will not be distorted.

To blend a seam, draw a continuous line where one has become broken during pattern adjustment. To blend a straight line, use a ruler or straight edge, connecting the beginning and end of the new line. To blend a curved line, use a curved ruler to reconstruct the original curve of the pattern, blending to each end from a point halfway between the broken seamline.

Blend the seamline first, then the cutting line. On multiple-sized patterns where no seamlines are marked, blend the cutting line only, and stitch the specified seam allowance, usually ⅝" (1.5 cm).

When there is a dart in the seamline, fold the dart out before blending the line. Be sure to mark all notches and darts on the new blended seamline.

Choosing an Adjustment Method

Wherever possible, two methods are given for the most common pattern adjustments: the minor, or in-seam, method and the major, or cut-and-slide, method. Choose one method or the other, depending on how much of an adjustment you need to make.

Minor in-seam pattern adjustments are quick and easy, because you can mark them directly on the printed pattern within the seam allowance or on the pattern tissue margin. In-seam methods have narrow limitations. Usually you can add or subtract no more than ⅜" to ½" (1 to 1.3 cm).

In the photos, to clarify where an addition would normally be marked on the margin of the tissue pattern, the margin has been trimmed and a contrasting tissue placed under the pattern. This procedure is not necessary on patterns that have not been used previously, because they have generous tissue margins around them.

Major cut-and-slide pattern adjustments allow you to add or subtract greater amounts than in-seam methods and to make adjustments exactly where they are needed to fit your figure. Cut-and-slide methods also have limits, usually to a maximum of 2" (5 cm). The specific amount is stated with the step-by-step instructions. Do not attempt to adjust beyond the stated maximums or you will distort the shape of the pattern pieces and cause the finished garment to hang off-grain. It will also be more difficult to make matching or compensating adjustments on adjoining pattern sections.

If you need a greater adjustment than cut-and-slide methods allow, consider working with another pattern size. Or distribute the adjustment over additional pattern seams and details instead of concentrating the adjustment in one area.

Basic Length Adjustments

Before making any other pattern adjustments, adjust the length of pattern pieces to fit your personal length proportions. If your figure is close to average, basic length adjustments may be the only changes needed on most patterns.

Basic length adjustments are made in two areas: above and below the waist. Use your back waist length measurement to determine the correct pattern length above the waist. To determine the correct pattern length below the waist, measure from the waist in back to the proposed hemline. Make these length adjustments using the adjustment lines printed on the pattern pieces.

Adjustments for Special Figures

Most people can make basic length adjustments by using the printed lengthening and shortening lines on the pattern. If your bust point does not match the placement on the pattern it may be necessary to adjust

the length above the bust or to adjust the darts so that they point to the fullest part of the bust. If you have a full bust, adjust the front pattern length above the waist, as on pages 86 and 87.

For Half-sizes or Miss Petite figure types, reduce the pattern length proportionately, by dividing the total adjustment into smaller amounts. Shorten the pattern at the chest and sleeve cap and at the hip adjustment line, in addition to using the printed adjustment lines above the bust and waist. Length may also be adjusted at the hemline.

Standard pattern shortening adjustments for Miss Petite remove ¼" (6 mm) at chest, ¾" (2 cm) above waist, 1" (2.5 cm) at hip adjustment line, and 1" (2.5 cm) at hem to shorten pattern by 3" (7.5 cm). Standard adjustments for Half-sizes are similar, but the chest adjustment is omitted because armhole size does not need to be reduced. Customize standard length adjustments to suit your personal proportions.

How to Determine Length Adjustments

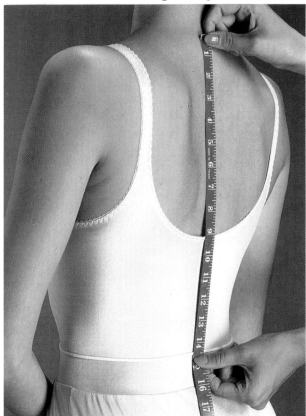

Above the waist. Measure back waist length from prominent bone at back of neck to natural waistline. Compare with back waist length measurement for your pattern size given on pattern envelope to determine how much to adjust bodice front and back patterns.

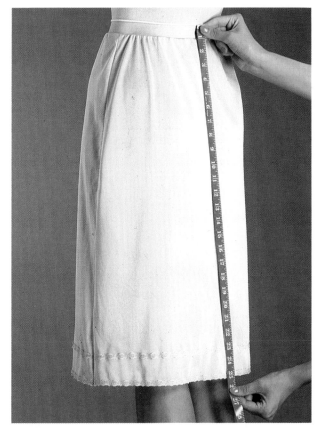

Below the waist. Measure at center back from waist to proposed garment hemline, or use a garment of correct length to determine this measurement. Compare with finished garment length given on back of pattern envelope to determine how much to adjust skirt front and back patterns.

How to Shorten Patterns

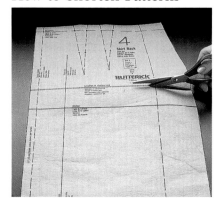

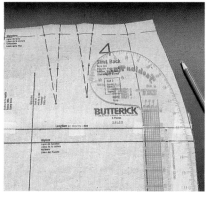

1) Cut pattern on the printed adjustment lines. If skirt pattern provides no adjustment lines, cut off excess length at bottom edge.

2) Lap cut sections. Overlap equals total amount pattern must be shortened. Tape sections together, keeping grainline straight.

3) Blend stitching and cutting lines. Make matching adjustments on back and front pattern pieces.

How to Lengthen Patterns

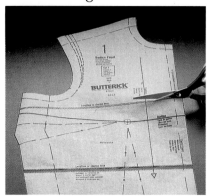

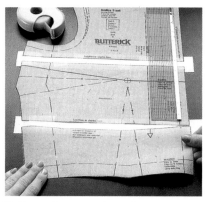

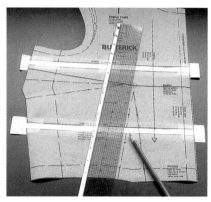

1) Cut pattern on the printed adjustment lines.

2) Spread cut sections the amount needed. Place paper underneath to bridge gap. Tape sections in place, keeping grainline straight.

3) Blend stitching and cutting lines. Make matching adjustments on back and front patterns.

How to Shorten Patterns for Half-sizes and Petites

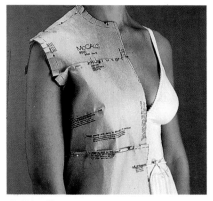

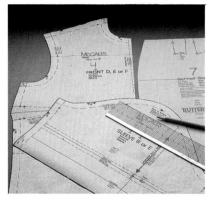

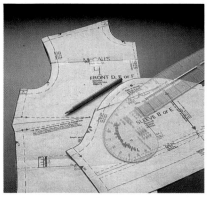

1) Pin-fit or measure pattern to determine how much length to remove across chest above armhole notches, at adjustment line above waist, at hipline, and at adjustment line below waist.

2)Draw adjustment lines on front and back, midway between armhole and shoulder seam notches. Draw similar line across sleeve cap. Draw hip adjustment line 5" (12.5 cm) below waist on skirt front and back.

3) Cut pattern pieces on each adjustment line; lap to shorten. Shorten back and front patterns equally. Shorten sleeve cap by same amount removed from bodice at chest.

Fitting the Bust

When fitted correctly, the bodice of a garment drapes smoothly over the bust without pulling, and the waistline of the garment lies at natural waistline and is parallel to the floor. Adjust bodice back length according to back waist length measurement. Make similar adjustments on bodice front. In addition, front bodice seams or darts may need to be adjusted to fit your bust size and shape.

If your bust is fuller than standard, you may need to add additional length and width to the bodice front pattern. Keep in mind that bodice front and back side seam lengths must match. If you have selected a pattern featuring loose or oversized fit, you can use some of the design ease in the pattern to fit a full bust and make a lesser adjustment.

For an average or small bust, pin-fitting, as in step 3 below, will determine whether it is necessary to raise or lower darts. Repositioning the darts may be all that is needed to improve pattern fit.

If you make bust adjustments on the pattern beyond simply raising or lowering darts, you may want to test your adjustments by making a bodice fitting shell from the adjusted pattern. Many fitting solutions are easier to visualize in fabric, and this extra step can save time in the long run.

Ease, or extra room, is necessary for comfort at the bustline. Add the minimum amount of ease to your bust measurement, as shown on the chart below, before comparing with the pattern to judge whether pattern adjustments are needed.

The ease amounts given on the chart are general guidelines. At times you may want to fit with more or less ease. For example, thick fabrics require more ease than lightweight ones. Knits require less ease than wovens, and very stretchy knits require no ease at all or even negative ease for formfitting garments.

Minimum Ease

Garment	Minimum Bust Ease
Blouse, dress, jumpsuit	2½" to 3" (6.5 to 7.5 cm)
Unlined jacket	3" to 4" (7.5 to 10 cm)
Lined jacket	3½" to 4½" (9 to 11.5 cm)
Coat	4" to 5" (10 to 12.5 cm)

How to Determine Pattern Adjustments

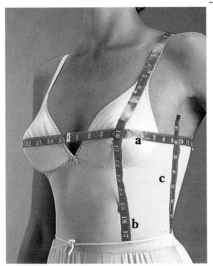

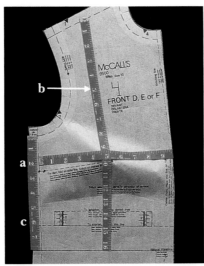

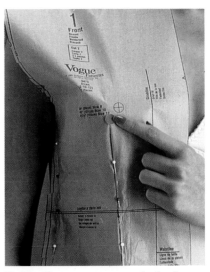

1) Measure bust **(a)** at fullest part, keeping tape measure parallel to floor. Add minimum ease to bust measurement. Measure the front waist length **(b)** from midpoint of shoulder, over bust point, straight down to waist. Measure the side length **(c)** from 1" (2.5 cm) below underarm to waist. Use two fingers under arm to determine distance.

2) Measure pattern front and back at bustline **(a)**. Measure bodice front pattern from midpoint of shoulder, over bust point, to waist **(b)**. Note any differences to decide if pattern length must be adjusted above waist or bust (opposite). Measure side seam of bodice front pattern from underarm to waist **(c)**. Note any differences to decide if pattern length must be adjusted.

3) Pin-fit pattern to mark the bust point. Note if bust shaping or darts on the pattern should be raised or lowered for good fit. Compare pattern measurement with body measurement plus minimum ease to determine how much width to add for full bust or how much to remove for small bust.

High Bust

Poor fit, when the bust is higher than average, shows in pulls across the fullest part of the bust and in wrinkles under the bust. Dart does not point to fullest part of curve. Underarm dart must be raised; dart from the waistline (if any) needs to be lengthened.

Low Bust

Poor fit, when the bust is lower than average, shows in pulls across the fullest part of the bust and in wrinkles above the bust. Darts are too high and need to be lowered and shortened.

How to Raise or Lower Darts

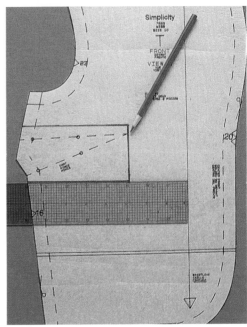

1) Draw horizontal lines on pattern ½" (1.3 cm) above and below the underarm dart, at right angle to grainline. Connect the lines with a vertical line through dart point. Cut out dart on marked lines.

How to Fit a Full Bust without Darts

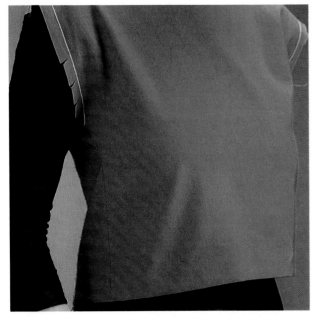

Accommodate full bust on less closely fitted pattern styles by making an adjustment that does not create a dart. This method can be used to increase the pattern a limited amount. Exceeding the maximum adjustment distorts the fabric grain at the lower edge of the garment. This adjustment is not appropriate on plaids, checks, or stripes.

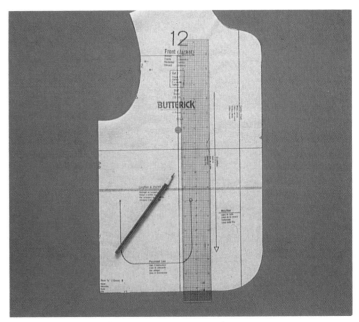

1) Draw line across bodice front midway between armhole notch and shoulder seam, at right angle to grainline. Draw second line 2" to 4" (5 to 10 cm) below armhole, at right angle to grainline. Draw third line through bust point, parallel to grainline to connect first two lines; extend line to lower edge.

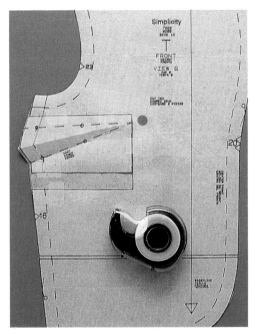

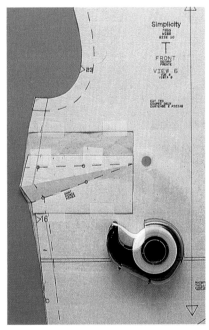

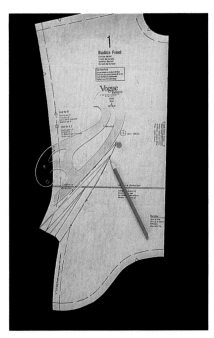

2) Raise dart the amount needed for a high bust. Position dart so that it points to the bust point (dot) or fullest part of figure. Place paper under pattern. Tape cut edges in place, keeping edges even. Redraw side seam.

2a) Lower dart the amount needed for a low bust. Position dart so that it points to the bust point (dot) or fullest part of figure. Place paper under pattern. Tape cut edges in place, keeping edges even. Redraw side seam.

Diagonal dart requires change in direction so that it points to bust point. Mark new dart point on pattern. Redraw dart, connecting side seam ends of the dart and new dart point.

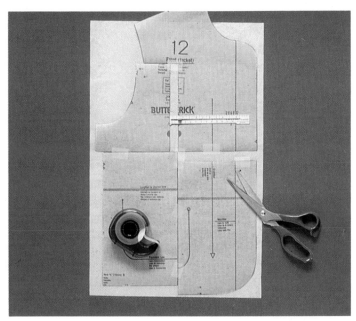

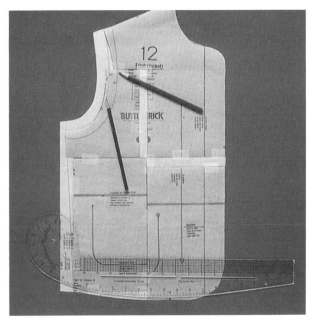

2) Cut pattern on adjustment lines. Slide armhole portion *out* a maximum of ¾" (2 cm) to add total of 1½" (3.8 cm) to bodice width. Slide center front waist section *down* no more than 2" (5 cm) to add bodice length. Tape to paper.

3) Blend stitching and cutting lines at armhole and side seams. Use curved ruler to blend lower cutting line from the center front, tapering back to the original side seam.

Fitting the Waist & Abdomen

Although a waistband or waistline should fit snugly, it must be slightly larger than your waist for good fit. For wearing comfort, a finished waistband should be from ½" to 1" (1.3 to 2.5 cm) larger than your actual measurement. In addition, allow ½" (1.3 cm) of ease from pattern waist measurement to waistband. Apply the same fitting guidelines to garments with faced waistlines. If garment has a waistline seam and no band, allow the total amount, 1" to 1½" (2.5 cm to 3.8 cm), for basic ease.

One indication of good waist fit is the way the side seams hang. They should hang straight, visually bisecting the body, without being pulled to the front or the back. Figure and posture variations may cause distortion of the side seams and require separate adjustment of skirt front and back. For example, a body with a full abdomen will need additional width and length in front, while a person with swaybacked posture may need to shorten the skirt pattern at center back. Adjustments for full abdomen and swayback should be determined and made at the same time that the waist width adjustment is made.

How to Determine Pattern Adjustments

1) Measure your waist. Compare with the waist measurement for your pattern size. Minimum wearing ease is included in the pattern, so adjust the pattern accordingly, enlarging or reducing as needed.

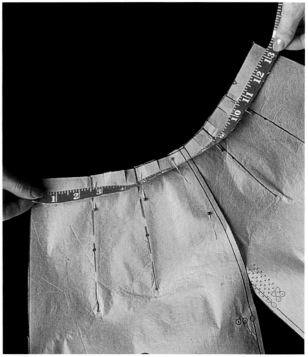

2) Pin out waistline darts, tucks, or pleats to measure pattern to compare with body measurements plus ease. Measure at the waistline seam; on a garment without a waistline seam, measure at the waistline mark at the narrowest part of the waistline area. Double the pattern measurement to compare with your waist measurement.

Small Waist

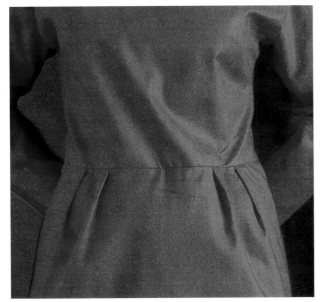

Poor fit has waistline or waistband that is too large, although garment fits at hips and bust. A dress with a waistline seam is baggy, with loose vertical folds at the waist. On a skirt or pants, waistband stands away from waist and tends to slide down.

Minor Adjustment

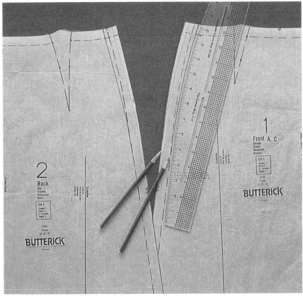

Remove one-fourth the amount needed at each seam. Maximum of ⅜" (1 cm) per seam allowance may be removed from pattern sizes smaller than 16. From size 16 and larger, remove maximum of ⅝" (1.5 cm). Blend stitching and cutting lines, using curved ruler. On dart-fitted skirts or pants, do not make darts deeper to reduce waistline unless additional garment contouring is needed to fit broad curvy hips or full round seat. Adjust width on adjoining pattern pieces.

Major Adjustment

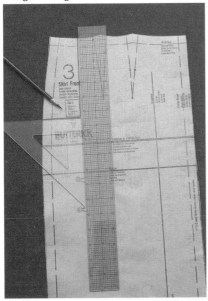

1) Draw a line 5" (12.5 cm) long, parallel to lengthwise grainline, between side seam and dart. Draw a second line from bottom of first line to side seam, at right angle to grainline.

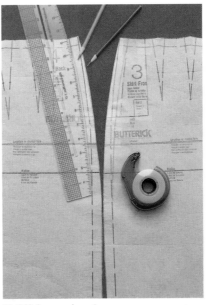

2) Slide section *in* to remove up to 1" (2.5 cm) from waist seam. Tape paper underneath. Blend stitching and cutting lines. Make matching adjustment on back, removing up to 2" (5 cm) from each seam for a total reduction of 4" (10 cm).

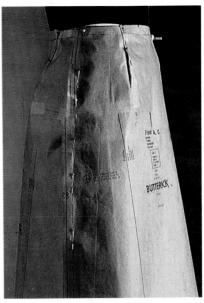

3) Pin-fit pattern to check position of waistline darts. It may be necessary to reshape or move the darts closer to center front and back for good fit. Make a corresponding width adjustment to adjoining waistband, facing, or bodice pattern.

Large Waist

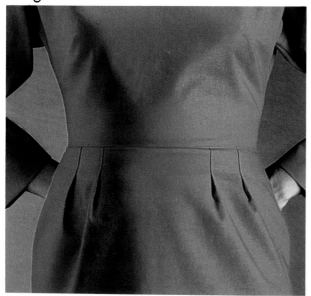

Poor fit is indicated by horizontal wrinkles near the waist, which cause the waistline of a dress to rise. A waistband on skirt or on pants creases from strain. Wrinkles fan out from waist or form horizontal folds below waistband.

Minor Adjustment

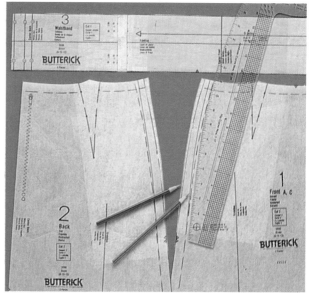

Add one-fourth the amount needed at each seam, adding up to ⅜" (1 cm) per seam allowance for total of ¾" (2 cm) per seam. On dart-fitted skirts, each dart can be reduced up to ¼" (6 mm) to enlarge waistline. Blend stitching and cutting lines, using curved ruler. Make corresponding width adjustment to adjoining waistband, facing, or bodice patterns.

Major Adjustment

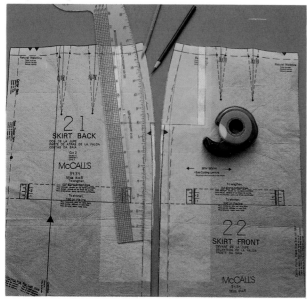

1) Draw adjustment lines and cut pattern as in step 1 for small waist (page 89). Slide section *out* up to 1" (2.5 cm). Tape paper underneath. Blend stitching and cutting lines to waist, using curved ruler, and to hem, using straightedge. Make matching adjustment on back pattern, adding up to 2" (5 cm) per seam for total of 4" (10 cm).

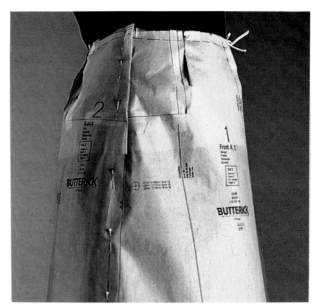

2) Pin-fit pattern to check position of waistline darts. It may be necessary to reshape darts or move them closer to the side seams for a better fit. Make a corresponding width adjustment to adjoining waistband, facing, or bodice sections.

Prominent Abdomen

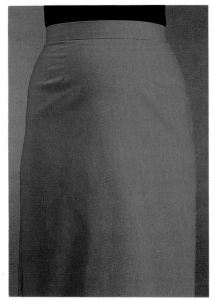

Poor fit is indicated by horizontal wrinkles across the front below the waistline. Diagonal wrinkles from abdomen to sides pull side seams forward. Waistline and hemline may ride up. Extra length and width are needed at center front.

Minor Adjustment

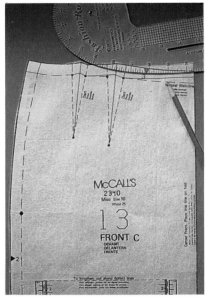

1) Raise waist stitching line on front skirt or pants pattern up to ⅜" (1 cm) at center front to add more length. Fold out darts, and blend stitching and cutting lines, using curved ruler.

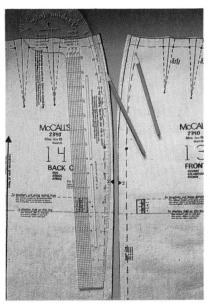

2) Add up to ½" (1.3 cm) at side seam of the front pattern piece. Remove same amount from back pattern piece to maintain the waist circumference. To further improve fit, convert front darts to gathers or unpressed pleats.

Major Adjustment

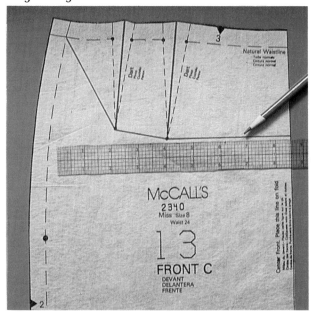

1) Draw diagonal adjustment lines on pattern from intersection of side seam and waistline seam through dart points, extending at right angle to center front. Cut on line. Cut on dart foldline to, but not through, dart point.

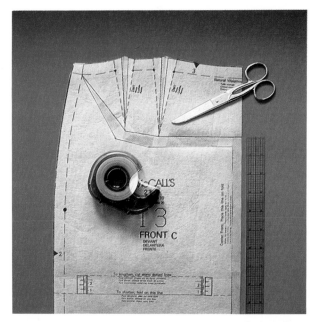

2) Slide center section *up* the amount needed and *out* half the amount needed, opening darts and diagonal slash. Extend center front line from new position to hemline. Darts can also be converted to gathers or unpressed pleats. Blend stitching and cutting lines at waistline.

Flat Abdomen

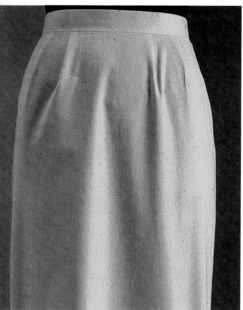

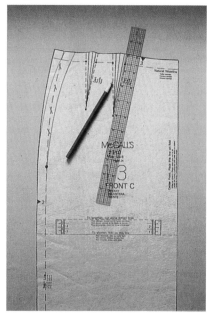

Adjustments for Flat Abdomen

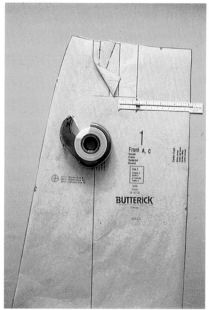

Poor fit is indicated by vertical wrinkles and excess fabric at center front. Hipbones may protrude. Darts are poorly located and too deep for flat abdomen contour.

Redraw shallower darts by removing an equal amount on each side of dart foldline. To restore the original waistline measurement, remove the same amount from side seam, blending from a point on waistline seam to hipline with curved ruler.

Move darts closer to side seam for prominent hipbones. Cut out dart as for raising or lowering bust dart (pages 86 and 87), and slide it to correct position after pin-fitting pattern. Fold out dart, and blend waistline stitching and cutting lines, using curved ruler.

Swayback

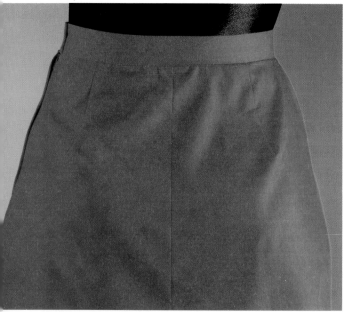

Adjustment for Swayback

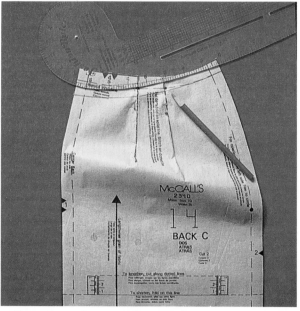

Poor fit is caused by posture variation; area directly beneath waist in back does not fit smoothly, or skirt bags in seat area, indicating that garment is too long at center back. Diagonal wrinkles form, indicating that dart width or length is wrong for body shape. Pin out excess to determine amount to shorten at center back.

Adjust darts, if necessary, to accommodate protrusion of seat. If dart width is changed, make corresponding width adjustment at side seam to maintain waist size. Lower the waist stitching line on the back skirt pattern the amount needed. Fold darts toward center and blend stitching and cutting lines, using curved ruler.

Fitting Hips

When garments fit well at the hipline, they feel comfortable whether you are standing or sitting. They also look smooth, without strained wrinkles or excess fabric folds.

Before adjusting for width, make any basic lengthening or shortening adjustments below the waistline. Length adjustments may eliminate the need for adjusting pattern hip circumference. If you have one hip higher than the other, it may be necessary to make a copy of the pattern and adjust a separate pattern piece for each side of the body. If your hips are fuller or slimmer than the average, adjust the pattern to include the right amount of ease. For wearing comfort, there must be a minimum of 2" (5 cm) ease, or extra room, at the hipline of the garment for sizes smaller than 16. For size 16 or larger, there must be at least 2½" (6.5 cm) of ease. You may need more than minimum ease for good fit if you have full hips or are using a thick fabric. You may need less if you are working with a knit.

How to Determine Pattern Adjustments

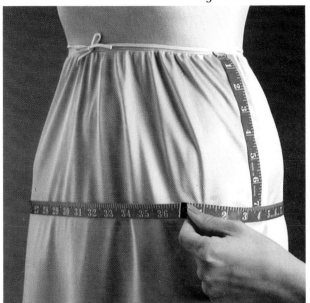

1) **Measure** hips, as viewed from the side, where seat protrudes most, keeping tape measure parallel to floor. Determine where hipline falls by measuring at side seam from waist to fullest part of hips. Add 2" to 2½" (5 to 6.5 cm) minimum ease to measurement.

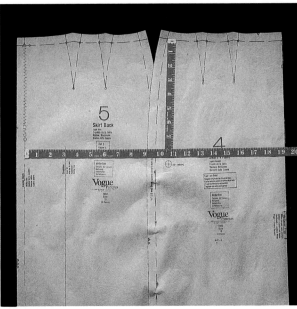

2) **Mark** pattern side seam at point where fullest part of hipline falls. Lap the back and front pattern pieces at mark. Measure hipline from center front to center back at this position. Double this measurement to arrive at total finished circumference. Compare with hip measurement plus ease to determine if adjustment is needed.

Full Hips

Poor fit causes horizontal wrinkles across hips. Skirt cups under seat in back. Skirt tends to ride up, because there is not enough width at hip level to fit full hips. Pattern needs enlarging at hipline.

Minor Adjustment

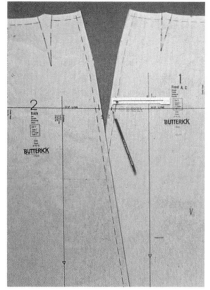

1) Mark hipline at side seam of back and front patterns. Add one-fourth the amount needed at each side seam, next to mark. Add maximum of ⅜" (1 cm) per seam allowance for total of ¾" (2 cm) per seam.

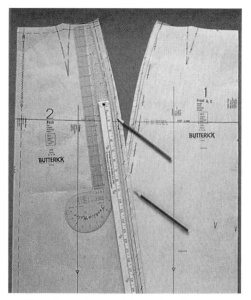

2) Blend stitching and cutting lines from hip to waist with curved ruler. Mark new stitching and cutting lines from hip to hem with straightedge.

Small Hips

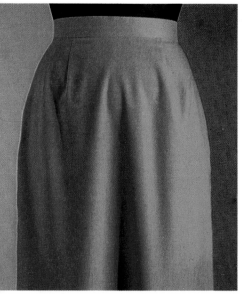

Poor fit causes excess fabric to drape in folds and look baggy. Skirt hipline is too broad for figure with slender hips. Pattern width needs reduction at hipline, and darts may have to be reduced. If darts are reduced, side waist seam must be decreased equal amount, as on page 89.

Minor Adjustment

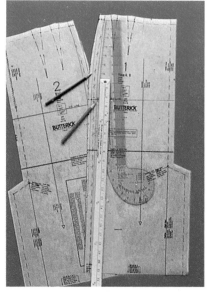

Mark hipline at side seam on back and front patterns. Remove one-fourth the amount needed at each side seam, next to mark. Remove up to ⅜" (1 cm) per seam allowance for total of ¾" (2 cm) per seam. Mark new stitching and cutting lines as in step 2, above.

Major Adjustment

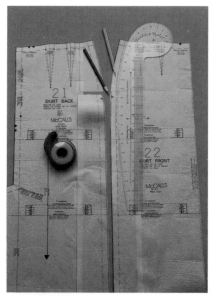

Reduce dart size as needed. Make side waist adjustment (page 89). Draw adjustment line and cut as for major adjustment for full hips, step 1, opposite. Slide section in to remove one-fourth of the extra width at the hipline. Blend stitching and cutting lines from waist to hip area with curved ruler. Mark hip area to hem with straightedge.

Major Adjustment

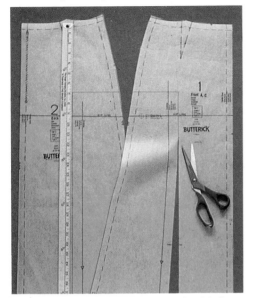

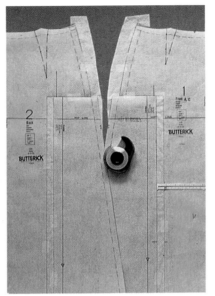

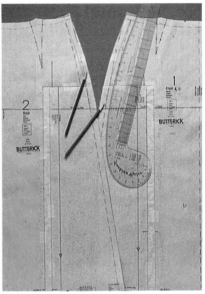

1) Draw a line parallel to the hipline approximately 5" (12.5 cm) below the waistline. Draw a second line parallel to lengthwise grainline from end of first line to hem. Cut on lines.

2) Slide section *out* to add one-fourth the amount needed. Add maximum of 1" (2.5 cm) to sizes under 16 for total of 2" (5 cm) per seam, and 1½" (3.8 cm) to sizes 16 and above for total of 3" (7.5 cm) per seam.

3) Blend stitching and cutting lines from hip to waist with curved ruler. Mark the hip area to the hem with a straightedge.

Uneven Hips

How to Adjust Pattern for One High Hip

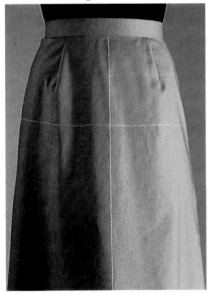

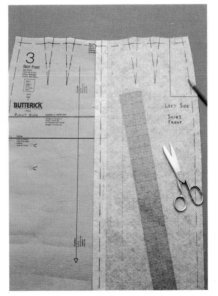

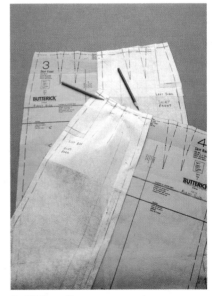

Poor fit causes diagonal wrinkles on one side. Fabric is off grain in hip area. One hip may be fuller, slimmer, or higher than other hip. Make necessary width adjustments in darts and side seam.

1) Trace front and back skirt pattern pieces. Label right and left sides. Draw adjustment line on poor fit side 5" (12.5 cm) long, parallel to lengthwise grainline, beginning midway between side seam and dart. Draw a second line at right angle from bottom of first line to side seam. Cut on adjustment lines.

2) Slide adjustment section up to add necessary length for fitting high hip. Tape paper underneath. Adjust skirt back and front to match. Fold darts or tucks as they will be pressed. Blend stitching and cutting lines at waist and side seams.

Fitting As You Sew

You must make any basic changes in length on the pattern pieces before cutting out fabric sections; however, many improvements in fit can be made during construction. Try on your garment after sewing the major front, back, side, and shoulder seams. Pin any shoulder pads in place. Check the fit while wearing the undergarments and accessories, such as belt and shoes, you plan to wear with the finished garment. Taking in or letting out seams at this point in the sewing is easy.

While sewing progresses, try on the garment for fit as many times as needed. For example, it's a good idea to test the fit after sewing in one sleeve. Make sure ease at the sleeve cap is distributed to fit your figure, and check sleeve length. Then you can sew the other sleeve with confidence that it will fit.

Tips for Fitting As You Sew

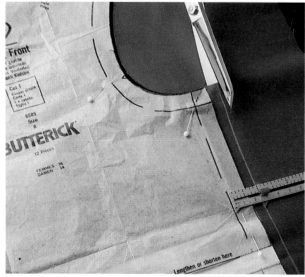

Allow 1" (2.5 cm) seams at sides of garment if you think changes in fit will be necessary. Seams can be let out to add as much as 2" (5 cm) around garment if needed. If extra allowance is not needed, trim seam to standard width after fitting.

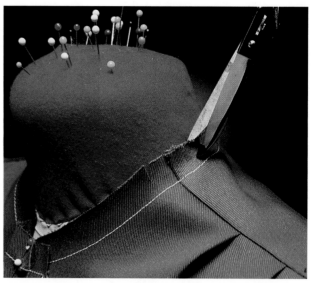

Staystitch neck and armhole edges on seamlines. Try on garment, right side out. Clip up to ¼" (6 mm) from staystitching until neck seamlines fall in proper position on figure.

Mark alterations on outside of garment with pins, or use thread to baste-mark delicate fabrics.

Use chalk or marking pen to transfer changes to inside of garment by tracing pinned or basted folds. Traced lines are new stitching lines for seams.

Seams

A seam is the basic element in all garment construction. It is created by stitching two pieces of fabric together, usually ⅝" (1.5 cm) from the cut edge. Perfect seams are the most obvious sign of a well-made garment. Puckered, crooked, or uneven seams spoil the fit as well as the look.

In addition to holding a garment together, seams can be used as a design element. Seams placed in unusual locations or topstitched with contrasting thread add interest to a garment.

Most plain seams require a *seam finish* to prevent raveling. A seam finish is a way of treating or enclosing the raw edges of seam allowances so they are more durable and do not ravel.

Variations of the plain seam include *bound, encased, topstitched,* and *eased* seams. Some, such as the flat-fell seam, add strength or shape. Others, such as French or bound seams, improve the appearance of the garment or make it longer wearing.

Techniques for Machine Stitching Seams

Position the bulk of the fabric to the left of the machine needle, with cut edges to the right. Support and guide fabric gently with both hands as you stitch.

Use guidelines etched on the throat plate of the machine to help you sew straight seams. For extra help, use a seam guide or strip of masking tape placed the desired distance from the needle.

Use the thread cutter located at the back of the presser bar assembly to cut threads after stitching. Or use a thread clipper to cut threads.

How to Sew a Plain Seam

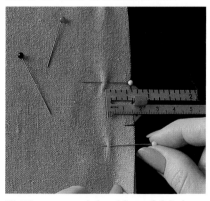

1) Pin seam, right sides of fabric together, at regular intervals, matching notches and other markings precisely. Place pins at right angles to seamline, usually ⅝" (1.5 cm) from edge, with points just beyond seamline and heads toward cut edge for easy removal.

2) Secure the stitching with backstitching. Then stitch forward on the seamline, removing the pins as you come to them. Backstitch ½" (1.3 cm) at end to secure the stitching. Trim threads.

3) Press over stitching line on wrong side to press seam flat. This blends stitches into fabric. Then press seam open. Use your fingers or the blunt end of a point turner to open seams as you press. If seam is curved, such as hip area of skirt or pants, press over curved area of a tailor's ham.

How to Sew Curved Seams

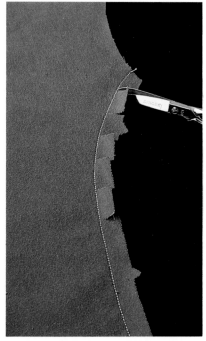

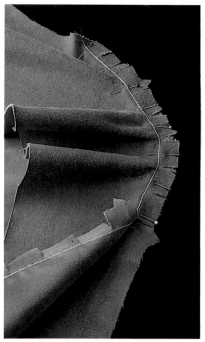

1) Stitch a line of reinforcement stitching just inside seamline of inner curve of center panel. Clip into seam allowance all the way to the stitching line at intervals along the curve.

2) Pin inner and outer curves, right sides together with clipped edge on top, spreading clipped inner curve to match all markings and fit outer curve.

3) Stitch on seamline with clipped seam on top, using shorter stitch than usual for the fabric and being careful to keep the lower layer of fabric smooth.

4) Cut out wedge-shaped notches in the seam allowance of outer curve by making small folds in seam allowance and cutting at slight angle. Be careful not to cut into stitching line.

5) Press seam flat to embed and smooth the stitches. Turn over and press on the other side.

6) Press seam open over curve of tailor's ham, using tip of iron only. Do not press into body of garment. If not pressed to contour, seam lines become distorted and look pulled out of shape.

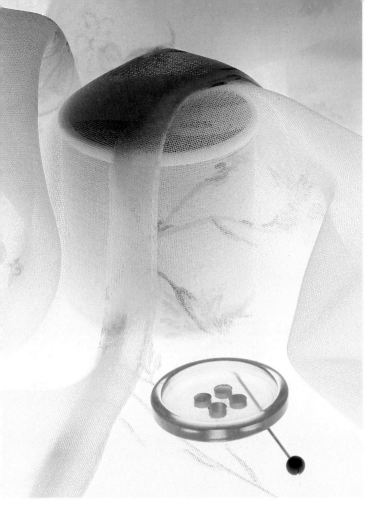

Encased Seams

Encased seams differ from bound seams in that no additional fabric or binding is used. The cut edges of seam allowances are enclosed within the seam itself. Encased seams are best suited to lightweight fabrics, since the additional bulk created is not a problem. These seams are especially appropriate for sheer fabrics, because no raw or contrasting edges show through. Use a straight-stitch foot and needle plate (page 14) to keep sheer fabric from being pulled into the feed.

Use encased seams for blouses, unlined jackets, lingerie or sheer curtains. They are also an excellent choice for children's clothes, because they stand up to rugged wear and repeated laundering.

Self-bound seam begins with a plain seam. One seam allowance is then folded over the other and stitched again.

French seam looks like a plain seam on the right side and a narrow tuck on the wrong side. It begins by stitching the wrong sides of the fabric together. This seam is difficult to sew in curved areas, so is best used on straight seams.

Mock French seam begins with a plain seam. Seam allowances are trimmed, folded to the inside and stitched along the folds. The self-bound and mock French seam can be used in curved or straight areas.

How to Sew a Self-bound Seam

1) Stitch a plain seam. Do not press open. Trim one seam allowance to ⅛" (3 mm).

2) Turn under the untrimmed seam allowance ⅛" (3 mm). Then turn again, enclosing the narrow trimmed edge and bringing the folded edge to the seamline.

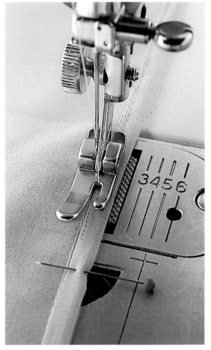

3) Stitch on the folded edge, as close as possible to first line of stitching. Press seam to one side.

How to Sew a French Seam

1) Pin *wrong* sides of fabric together. Stitch ⅜" (1 cm) from edges on right side of fabric.

2) Trim seam allowance to ⅛" (3 mm). Fold *right* sides together, with stitching line exactly on fold. Press flat.

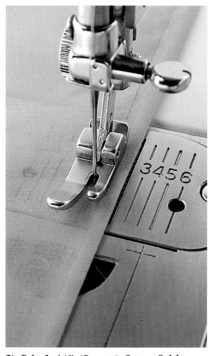

3) Stitch ¼" (6 mm) from fold. This step encases cut edges. Check right side to be sure no raveled threads are showing. Press seam to one side.

How to Sew a Mock French Seam

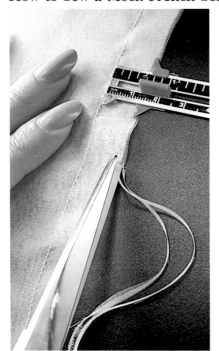

1) Stitch a plain seam. Trim both seam allowances to ½" (1.3 cm). Press open.

2) Press ¼" (6 mm) on each seam allowance toward inside of seam, so cut edges meet at stitching line.

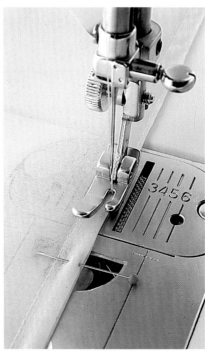

3) Stitch edges together, stitching as close to folds as possible. Press seam to one side.

How to Sew a Flat-fell Seam

1) Pin fabric, *wrong* sides together, at seamline with pin heads toward raw edges. Stitch, taking the usual ⅝" (1.5 cm) seam allowance.

2) Press seam allowances to one side. Trim the lower seam allowance to ⅛" (3 mm).

3) Turn under ¼" (6 mm) on the upper seam allowance and press.

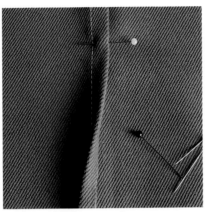

4) Pin folded seam allowance to garment, concealing trimmed lower edge.

5) Edgestitch on fold, removing pins as you come to them.

6) Finished seam is a reversible flat seam with two visible rows of stitching on each side.

How to Sew a Mock Flat-fell Seam

1) Stitch a plain seam. Press seam allowances to one side. Trim lower seam allowance to ¼" (6 mm).

2) Topstitch on right side of garment, ¼" to ½" (6 mm to 1.3 cm) from the seamline. Edgestitch close to the seamline.

3) Finished seam looks like the flat-fell seam on the right side, but has one exposed seam allowance on wrong side.

Stretch Seams

Stretch fabrics for casual or action wear include jersey, stretch terry, stretch velour and other knits. Stretch woven fabrics include stretch denim, stretch poplin and stretch corduroy. For swimwear and leotards, Lycra® knits are available. Seams in these fabrics must stretch or "give" with the fabric. Some sewing machines have special knit stitches that incorporate stretch.

Test the seam or knit stitch on a scrap of fabric to determine its appropriateness to the weight and stretchiness of the fabric. Some of the special knit stitches are more difficult to rip than straight stitching, so be sure the garment fits before stitching. Because knits do not ravel, they usually do not require seam finishing.

Double-stitched seam gives an insurance row of stitching to a seam. Use this method if your machine does not zigzag.

Straight and zigzag seam combines a straight seam with the stretchiness of zigzag. This is a suitable finish for knits that tend to curl along the raw edges.

Narrow zigzag seam is used for knits that do not curl along edges. It is a fast, easy stretch seam.

Straight stretch stitch is formed by a forward/backward motion of reverse-action machines. It makes a strong, stretchy seam appropriate for stressed areas such as armholes.

Straight with overedge stitch has a special pattern which combines a straight stretch stitch with diagonal stitching. It joins and finishes the seam in one step.

Elastic stretch stitch is an excellent choice for swimwear and leotards. The stitch combines a narrow and wide zigzag pattern.

Taped seams are used in areas where you do not want stretch, such as shoulder seams.

How to Sew a Taped Seam

1) Pin fabric, right sides together, so that twill tape or seam binding is pinned over seamline. Position seam binding so it laps ⅜" (1 cm) into the seam allowance.

2) Stitch, using double-stitched, straight and zigzag, overedge or narrow zigzag seam. Press seam open or to one side, depending on selected seam.

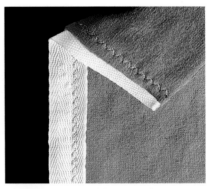

3) Trim seam allowance close to stitching, taking care not to cut into seam binding.

Seam Finishes

A seam finish lends a couture touch and improved appearance to any garment. Finish seams to prevent woven fabrics from raveling and knit seams from curling. Seam finishes also strengthen seams and help them stand up to repeated washings and wearing, making the garment look new longer.

Seams should be finished as they are stitched, before being crossed by another seam. A finish should not add bulk or show an obvious imprint on the right side of the garment after it is pressed. If you are not sure which seam finish to use, try several on a fabric scrap to see which works best.

The seam finishes shown here all begin with a plain seam. They can also be used as edge finishes for facings and hems.

Selvage finish requires no extra stitching. Appropriate for straight seams of woven fabrics, it requires adjusting the pattern layout so that the seam is cut on the selvage.

Stitched and pinked seam finish is suitable for firmly-woven fabrics. It is a quick and easy finish that prevents raveling and curling.

Turned and stitched finish (also called *clean-finished*) is suitable for light to mediumweight woven fabrics.

Zigzag seam finishes prevent raveling and are good for knits, because they have more give than straight-stitched finishes. These finishes use the built-in stitches on automatic zigzag machines.

Basic Seam Finishes

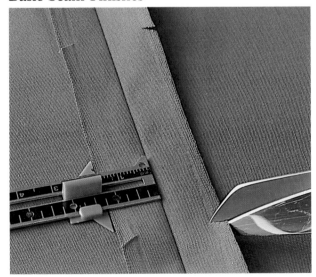

Selvage finish. Adjust pattern layout so that edges of seam are cut on selvage. To prevent shrinking and puckering, clip diagonally into both selvages at 3" to 4" (7.5 to 10 cm) intervals after seam is stitched.

Stitched and pinked finish. Stitch ¼" (6 mm) from edge of each seam allowance. Press seam open. Trim close to stitching with pinking or scalloping shears.

How to Sew a Turned and Stitched Finish

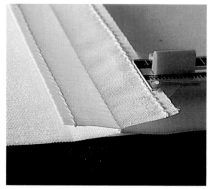

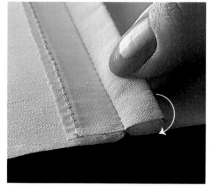

1) Stitch ⅛" to ¼" (3 to 6 mm) from edge of each seam allowance. On straight edges, this stitching may not be necessary.

2) Turn under seam allowance on stitching line. The stitching helps the edge turn under, especially on curves.

3) Stitch close to edge of fold, through seam allowance only. Press seam open.

How to Sew a Zigzag Finish

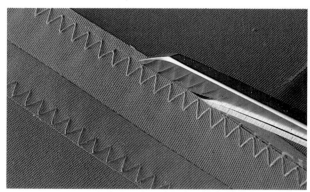

1) Set zigzag stitch for maximum width. Stitch near, but not over, edge of each seam allowance.

2) Trim close to stitching, being careful not to cut into stitching.

Other Zigzag Finishes

Overedge zigzag finish. Trim seam edges evenly, if necessary. Adjust zigzag stitch length and width to suit fabric. Stitch close to edge of each seam allowance so that stitches go over the edge. If fabric puckers, loosen tension by turning to a lower number.

3-step zigzag finish. Use stitch that puts three short stitches in space of one zigzag width. Set machine for pattern stitch and adjust length and width to suit fabric. Stitch close to edge of seam allowance, being careful not to stretch fabric. On some machines, a *serpentine* stitch gives same results. Trim close to stitching line.

Bound Seam Finishes

These finishes totally enclose the cut edge of seam allowances and prevent raveling. They also enhance the appearance of the inside of the garment. Bound seam finishes are a good choice for unlined jackets, especially those made of heavy fabrics or those which ravel easily.

The most commonly used bound finishes are the bias bound, tricot bound and Hong Kong finishes. Mediumweight fabrics such as chino, denim, linen, gabardine and flannel, and heavyweight fabrics such as wools, velvet, velveteen and corduroy can utilize any of the three. Begin each of these finishes by sewing a plain seam. Bound finishes can also be used on hem or facing edges.

Bias bound is the easiest bound finish. Use purchased double-fold bias tape, available in cotton, rayon or polyester, to match the fashion fabric.

Tricot bound is an inconspicuous finish for delicate, sheer fabrics or bulky, napped fabrics. Purchase sheer bias tricot strips or cut ⅝" (1.5 cm) wide strips of nylon net or lightweight tricot. The nylon net must be cut on the bias; the tricot, on the crosswise grain for maximum stretch.

Bias Bound

Fold bias tape around cut edge of seam, with wider side of tape underneath. Stitch close to edge of inner fold, catching the wider fold edge underneath.

Tricot Bound

Fold sheer tricot strip in half lengthwise and encase cut edge of seam. Stretch strip slightly as you sew, and it will naturally fold over cut edge. Stitch with straight stitch or medium-width zigzag.

Serger Seams & Seam Finishes

Serged seams can be used on many garments. Your instruction manual may include suggestions for where stitches are used. Garment style, fabric selection, and personal preference will help you decide which seams to use. The serged seam alone is not always suitable for garment construction. Many seams are sewn using both the serger and the conventional machine. For example, pants, jackets, or garments requiring adjustable fit, or seams that will be subjected to a great amount of stress, should be sewn with a pressed-open conventional seam and overedged seam allowances.

Types of Seams & Seam Finishes

Overlock seams (pages 18 and 19) are appropriate for wovens and knits. Choose the 3-thread overlock for loosely fitted or nonstressed seams. The more secure 4-thread and 5-thread safety stitches are used primarily for wovens because the chainstitch may pop when stretched. The 3-thread and 4-thread mock safety stitches, designed for durable stretch seams, may also be used on wovens.

Overedge seam finish (page 108) for conventional seams is used when it is desirable to keep the entire 5/8" (1.5 cm) seam allowance. It is the best choice for tailored garments sewn from wools, linens, and silk suitings. It is also recommended whenever fit is uncertain to allow for letting out seams.

Reinforced seam (page 108) is recommended for seams that will be stressed.

French seam (page 108) is used for sheers and loosely woven fabrics. The seam will add bulk, so it is best used on full, gathered items like skirts and curtains.

Rolled seam (page 108) may be used instead of French seams for sheers that are firmly woven and for laces.

Mock flat-fell seam (page 108) is used for denim and other heavyweight woven fabrics.

Reversible lapped seam (page 109) is used for reversible garments or for thick, loosely woven fabrics to provide added strength.

Gathered seam (page 109) is finished in one easy step using differential feed and a shirring foot. An alternate method uses the conventional machine with the serger.

Mock flatlock seam (page 110) is used for a decorative effect, with decorative thread used in the upper looper.

Flatlock on a fold (page 110) is used for the decorative effect of a flatlock seam on fabric that has been folded and stitched.

Types of Stabilized Seams

There are several methods for stabilizing seams in serger garment construction. The type of fabric you are sewing and the desired effect will determine which method you choose.

Fusible stabilized seam (page 111) uses fusible interfacing strips to stabilize seams. Interfacing can also be used as a stable base for decorative edge finishes on stretchy knit or bias-cut fabrics.

Elastic stabilized seam (page 111) uses transparent elastic to allow full stretch and recovery in a serged seam, but prevents fabric from stretching out of shape.

Nonstretch stabilized seam (page 111) uses twill tape, seam tape, or ribbon to prevent stretching of the fabric at the seamline.

Slight-stretch stabilized seam (page 111) uses tricot bias binding to reinforce and stabilize a seam where slight stretch is desired. Use this method for stabilizing seams in sweater knits and T-shirt knits, which need support without completely restricting the stretch of the fabric.

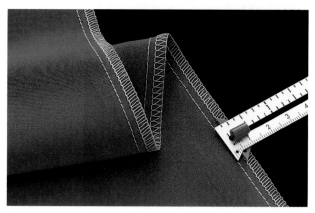

Overedge seam finish for conventional seam. Stitch ⅝" (1.5 cm) seam, right sides together, using conventional machine. Stitch seam allowances, slightly trimming raw edge, using overedge or overlock stitch.

Reinforced seam. Stitch ⅝" (1.5 cm) seam, right sides together, using conventional machine; use narrow zigzag on moderate-stretch knits. Serge seam allowances together ⅛" (3 mm) from seamline.

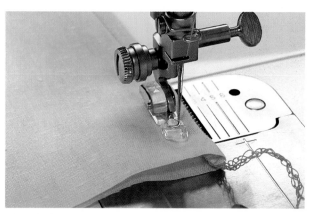

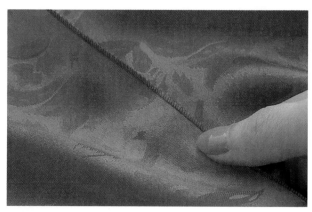

French seam. Overedge seam, wrong sides together, with left needle positioned ¼" (6 mm) inside seam allowance. Fold fabric, right sides together, enclosing overedged fabric; press. Straight-stitch close to enclosed stitches, using zipper foot on the conventional machine.

Rolled seam. Place fabric right sides together. Stitch seam, using a rolled hem stitch, with needle positioned on seamline; trim excess seam allowance. Press. Use tricot bias binding to stabilize lace edge, as shown on page 111, if desired.

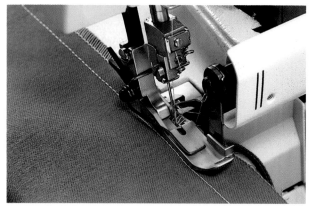

Mock flat-fell seam. 1) Place fabric right sides together. Stitch, using a conventional machine. Serge seam allowances together, trimming slightly.

2) Press seam allowance toward one side; topstitch from right side next to seamline, using a conventional machine. Topstitch again, ¼" (6 mm) away, through all layers.

How to Sew a Reversible Lapped Seam

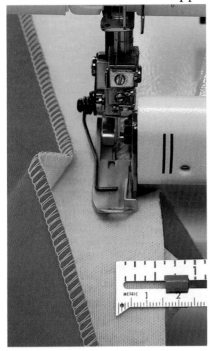

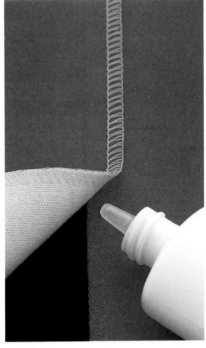

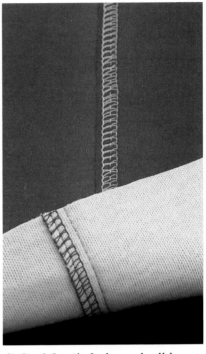

1) Stitch each single-layer seam allowance, using overedge or overlock stitch and aligning needle to seamline.

2) Lap garment sections so seamlines meet; glue-baste.

3) Straight-stitch through all layers ⅛" (3 mm) from serged stitches, from both sides of garment, using conventional machine.

How to Sew a Gathered Seam

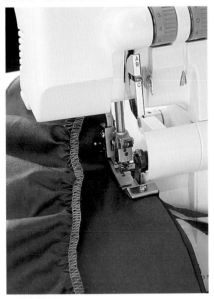

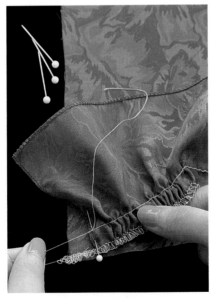

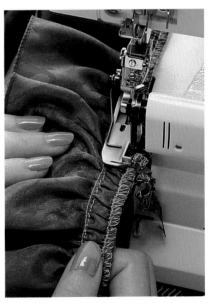

1) Replace regular presser foot with shirring foot; set differential feed to a larger number. Align edges of two fabric layers together; position layers so fabric to be gathered is on the bottom. Overlock the seam with needle positioned on the seamline.

Alternate method. 1) Baste in seam allowance near seamline, using conventional machine. Overedge seam allowance, slightly trimming raw edge. Align overedged fabric to corresponding section, right sides together, matching as necessary; pin. Pull bobbin thread and serger needle thread, gathering fabric to fit.

2) Stitch seam, using conventional machine. Overedge seam allowances, using serger. Or, overlock seam, with left needle positioned on seamline, trimming away excess seam allowance; remove pins as they approach knives.

How to Sew a Mock Flatlock Seam

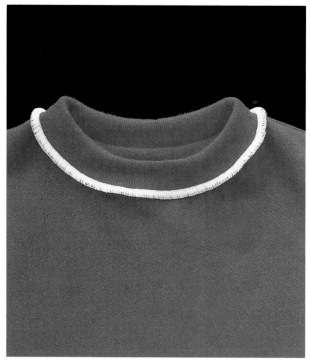

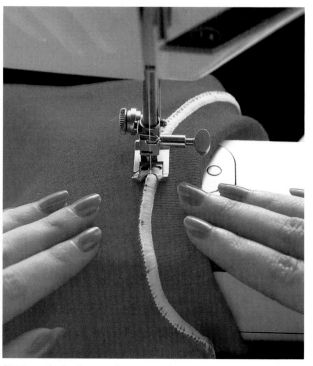

1) Use decorative thread (page 16) in upper looper. Serge fabric, wrong sides together; press seam to one side with decorative thread on top.

2) Topstitch decorative serged seam through all layers, using conventional machine.

How to Flatlock on a Fold of Fabric

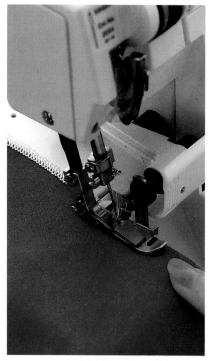

1) Mark stitch placement line on right side of fabric. Fold, *wrong* sides together, on marked line. Adjust serger for flatlock stitch. Place fabric slightly to the left of knives.

2) Serge seam without trimming fold of fabric. Position stitches half on and half off fabric.

3) Open the fabric, and pull the stitches flat.

Stabilized Seams

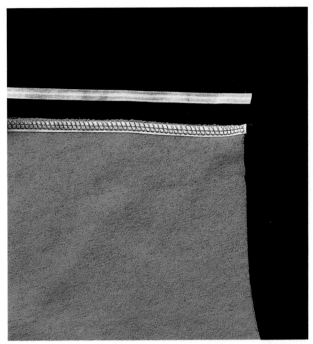

Fusible stablilized seam. Cut ¾" (2 cm) strip of fusible knit interfacing the length of the seam. Fuse to wrong side of garment. Stitch seam.

Elastic stabilized seam. Use elastic tape foot, if available; adjust foot tension to drag slightly against elastic. Serge seam, stitching through elastic; elastic should not gather seam. If using regular presser foot, place elastic over seamline and serge without trimming elastic; increase differential feed to ease fabric, if desired.

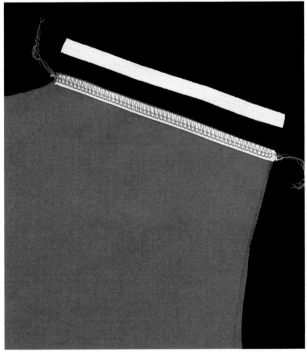

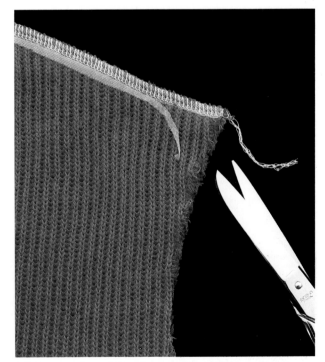

Nonstretch stabilized seam. Serge as in elastic stabilized seam, above; use twill tape, seam tape, or ribbon, and adjust foot tension so it does not drag on stabilizer. Decrease differential feed slightly, if desired, to prevent puckering of seam.

Slight-stretch stabilized seam. Cut ¾" (2 cm) strip of tricot bias binding the length of the seam. Serge through relaxed strip; trim excess binding close to stitches. Increase differential feed slightly, if desired, to ease fabric and prevent overstretching seam.

Darts

A dart is used to shape a flat piece of fabric to fit bust, waist, hip or elbow curves. There are two types of darts. A *single-pointed dart* is wide at one end and pointed at the other. A *shaped dart* has points at both ends. It is usually used at the waistline, with the points extending to the bust and hips. Besides providing a closer fit, darts are also used to create special designer touches and unique styles.

Perfect darts are straight and smooth, not puckered at the ends. The darts on the right and left sides of the garment should have the same placement and length.

How to Sew a Dart

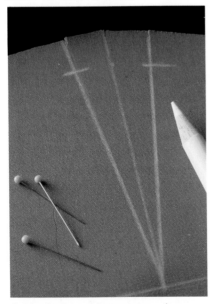

1) Mark dart using appropriate marking method for fabric. Mark point of dart with horizontal line.

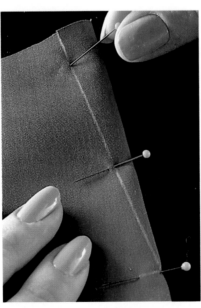

2) Fold dart on center line, matching stitching lines and markings at the wide end, the point and in between. Pin in place, with heads of pins toward folded edge for easy removal as you stitch.

3) Stitch from wide end to point of dart. Backstitch at beginning of stitching line, then continue stitching toward point, removing pins as you come to them.

Dart Techniques

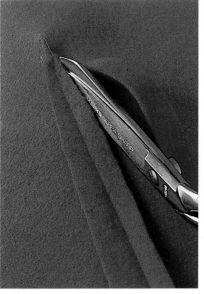

Shaped darts are stitched in two steps, beginning at the waistline and stitching toward each point. Overlap stitching at waist about 1" (2.5 cm). Clip dart fold at waistline and midway along points, to within ⅛" to ¼" (3 to 6 mm) of stitching to relieve strain and allow dart to curve smoothly.

Wide darts and darts in bulky fabrics should be slashed open on the fold line and trimmed to ⅝" (1.5 cm) or less. Slash to within ½" (1.3 cm) of point. Press dart open and press point flat.

Press darts over the curve of a tailor's ham to maintain the built-in curve. Vertical darts are usually pressed toward the center front or center back. Horizontal darts are usually pressed downward.

4) Taper to point of dart. When ½" (1.3 cm) remains, shorten stitch length to 12 to 16 stitches per inch (2.5 cm). Take last two to three stitches directly on fold. Do not backstitch at the point, because this may cause puckering. Continue stitching off edge of fabric.

5) Raise presser foot and pull dart toward front. About 1" (2.5 cm) back from point of dart, lower presser foot and secure thread by stitching several times in fold of the dart with stitch length set at 0. Clip threads close to knot.

6) Press folded edge of dart flat, being careful not to crease fabric beyond the point. Then place dart over curve of tailor's ham and press in proper direction (above). For a neat, flat finish, press darts before they are stitched into a seam.

Gathers

A soft, feminine garment line is often shaped with gathers. They may be found at waistlines, cuffs, yokes, necklines or sleeve caps. Soft and sheer fabrics produce a draped look when gathered; crisp fabrics create a billowy effect.

Gathers start with two stitching lines on a long piece of fabric. The stitching lines are then pulled at each end to draw up the fabric. Finally, the gathered piece is sewn to a shorter length of fabric.

The stitch length for gathering is longer than for ordinary sewing. Use a stitch length of 6 to 8 stitches per inch (2.5 cm) for mediumweight fabrics. For soft or sheer fabrics, use 8 to 10 stitches per inch. Experiment with the fabric to see which stitch length gathers best. A longer stitch makes it easier to draw up the fabric, but a shorter stitch gives more control when adjusting gathers.

Before you stitch, loosen the upper thread tension. The bobbin stitching is pulled to draw up the gathers, and a looser tension makes this easier.

If the fabric is heavy or stiff, use heavy-duty thread in the bobbin. A contrasting color in the bobbin also helps distinguish it from the upper thread.

How to Sew Basic Gathers

1) Stitch a scant ⅝" (1.5 cm) from raw edge on right side of fabric, starting and ending at seamline. Loosen upper tension and lengthen stitches appropriate to fabric. Stitch a second row in seam allowance, ¼" (6 mm) away from first row. This double row of stitching gives better control in gathering than a single row.

2) Pin stitched edge to corresponding garment section, right sides together. Match seams, notches, center lines and other markings. Fabric will droop between the pinned areas. If there are no markings to guide you, fold straight edge and gathered edge into quarters. Mark fold lines with pins. Pin edges together, matching marking pins.

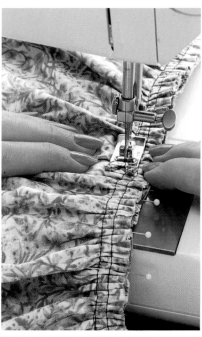

3) Pull both bobbin threads from one end, sliding fabric along thread to gather. When half the gathered section fits the straight edge, secure bobbin threads by twisting in a figure-8 around pin. Pull bobbin threads from other end to gather remaining half.

4) Pin gathers in place at frequent intervals. Distribute gathers evenly between pins. Reset stitch length and tension for regular sewing.

5) Stitch, gathered side up, just outside gathering lines. Adjust gathers between pins as you stitch. Hold gathers taut with fingers on both sides of needle. Keep gathers even, so folds of fabric do not form as you stitch.

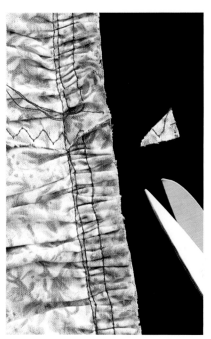

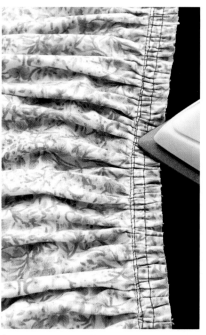

6) Trim seam allowances of any seams that have been sewn into the stitching line, trimming off corners at a diagonal.

7) Press seam allowance on wrong side, using tip of iron. Then open out garment and press seam in the direction it will lie in the finished garment. Press seam toward gathers for puffy look, toward garment for smoother look.

8) Press into gathers with point of iron on right side of garment, lifting iron as you reach seam. Do not press across gathers; this will flatten them.

Gathering with Elastic

Gathers formed with elastic offer comfortable and easy fit in knits and active sportswear. This technique ensures uniform gathers and creates shape that is relaxed and not as close to the body as other shapebuilders.

Elastic can be stitched directly to the garment or inserted in a casing. A casing is a tunnel for elastic, created with a turned-under edge or with bias tape stitched to the fabric. Choose an elastic that is suitable to the sewing technique and area of the garment where it is used (page 32).

Elastic in a casing can be any width. Use a firm, braided or non-roll elastic. Braided elastic has lengthwise ribs, and narrows when stretched.

Stitched elastic calls for woven or knitted elastics which are soft, strong and comfortable to wear next to the skin. On short areas such as sleeve or leg edges, it is easiest to apply the elastic while the garment section is flat, before side seams are stitched. When using stitched elastic at a waistline, overlap the ends of the elastic and stitch to form a circle before pinning to the garment.

Cut elastic the length recommended by the pattern. This length includes a seam allowance. To add elastic when the pattern does not call for it, cut the elastic slightly shorter than the body measurement plus seam allowance. Allow 1" (2.5 cm) extra for a stitched elastic seam, ½" (1.3 cm) extra for overlapping elastic in a casing.

How to Sew Elastic in Casing (waistline seam)

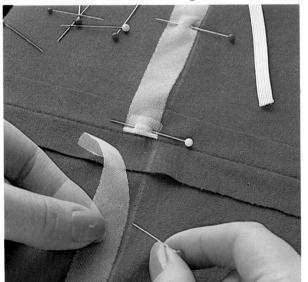

1) Pin sheer bias tricot strip or bias tape that is ¼" (6 mm) wider than the elastic to inside of garment along marked casing lines, beginning and ending at one side seam. Turn under ¼" (6 mm) at each end of bias tape and pin to seamline. For easy application, work on ironing board with garment wrong side out.

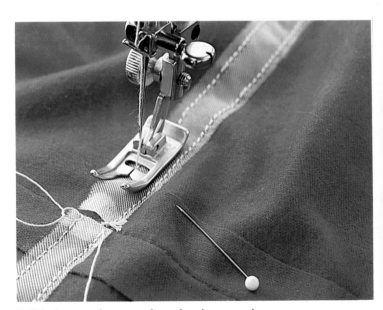

2) Stitch tape close to edges, leaving opening at seam to insert elastic. Do not backstitch at ends of stitching, because this stitching shows on the right side of the garment. Instead, pull all four ends to inside and knot.

How to Sew Stitched Elastic

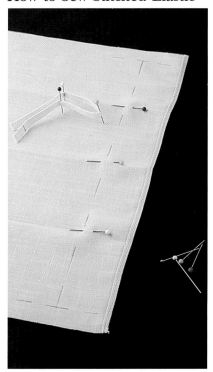

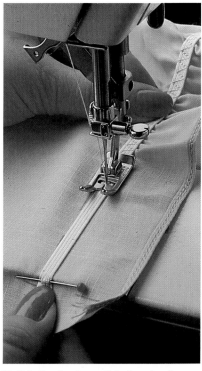

1) Fold elastic and fabric into fourths. Mark fold lines of elastic and garment with pins.

2) Pin elastic to wrong side of garment, matching marking pins. Leave ½" (1.3 cm) seam allowance at each end of elastic.

3) Stitch elastic to fabric, elastic side up, stretching elastic between pins, with one hand behind needle and other hand at next pin. Apply with a zigzag, multi-stitch zigzag or two rows of straight stitching, one along each edge of elastic.

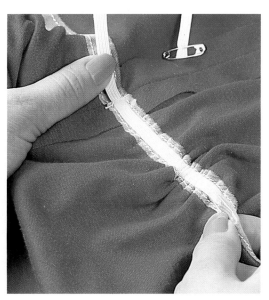

3) Insert elastic through casing using a bodkin or safety pin, taking care not to twist elastic. Place a large safety pin across free end of elastic to prevent it from pulling through.

4) Lap ends of elastic ½" (1.3 cm) and sew together with straight or zigzag stitches, stitching forward, backstitching, and forward again. Clip thread ends. Ease elastic back into casing.

5) Slipstitch ends of casing together. Distribute gathers evenly along the elastic.

Sleeves

When two garment pieces to be joined are uneven in length, the longer one must be *eased* to fit the shorter one. Eased seams most often occur at shoulder seams, yokes, elbows, waistbands, or sleeves. These seams add freedom of movement without adding the bulk of gathers. The mark of perfection in an eased seam is the absence of small tucks or gathers in the seamline. The most common use of an eased seam is a set-in sleeve. It is a basic technique that, with practice, can be performed expertly.

How to Set in a Sleeve

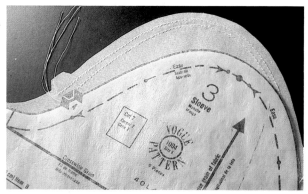

1) Easestitch cap of sleeve (the area between front and back notches) on right side, slightly inside seamline. Easestitch sleeve cap again, ⅜" (1 cm) from edge.

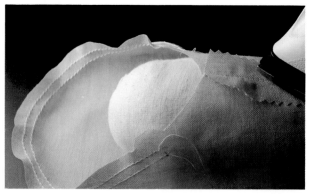

2) Stitch underarm sleeve seam, right sides together. Press seam flat, then press seam open. Use sleeve board or seam roll to prevent impression of seam on top of sleeve.

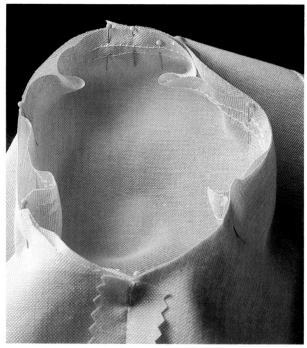

3) Turn sleeve right side out. Turn garment inside out. Insert sleeve into armhole, right sides together, matching notches, small dot markings, underarm seam, and shoulder line. Insert pins on seamline for best control of ease.

4) Draw up bobbin threads of easestitching lines until cap fits armhole. Distribute fullness evenly, leaving 1" (2.5 cm) flat (uneased) at shoulder seam at top of sleeve cap.

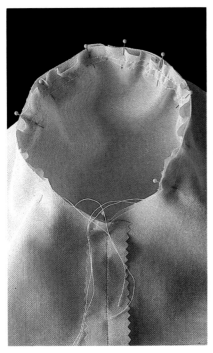

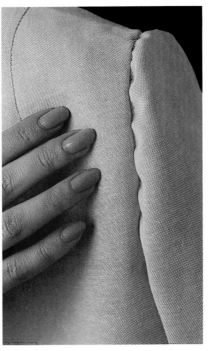

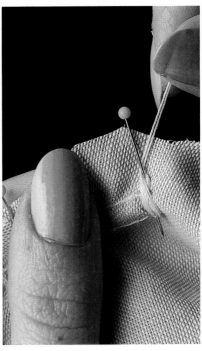

5) Pin sleeve to armhole at close intervals, using more pins in front and back where the bulk of the ease is located.

6) Check sleeve from right side for smooth fit and correct drape. Adjust if necessary. There can be tiny pleats or puckers in seam allowance, but not in seamline.

7) Secure ends of easestitching thread by making a figure-8 over each pin at front and back notches.

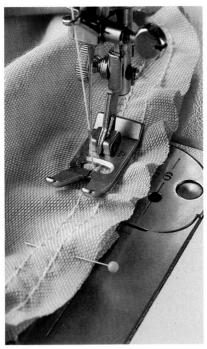

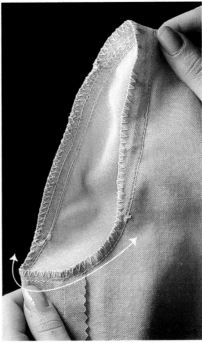

8) Stitch just outside easestitching line, sleeve side up, starting at one notch. Stitch around sleeve, past starting point, to other notch, reinforcing underarm with two rows of stitching. Remove pins as you come to them.

9) Trim seam allowance to ¼" (6 mm) between notches at underarm only. Do not trim seam allowance of sleeve cap. Zigzag seam allowances together.

10) Press seam allowance of sleeve cap only, using press mitt or end of sleeve board. Do not press into the sleeve.

Collars

Collars are important details worthy of careful sewing. A well-made collar circles your neck without rippling or pulling and keeps its neat appearance through repeated cleanings. Pointed tips should match. Edges should be smooth and flat.

Interfacing, usually cut from the collar pattern piece, adds shape, support, and stability. Most collar styles benefit from the slightly firm finish provided by fusible interfacings. Select the special crisp type of fusible interfacing suitable for men's shirts if you are working with classic shirting fabrics such as oxford cloth or broadcloth. If your fabric is soft or delicate, like challis or crepe de chine, choose a lightweight fusible that bonds at low iron temperatures.

Convertible collar looks similar to the notched collar and lapels on a tailored blazer. The front facings fold back to form the lapels. This collar can be worn open or closed. The top button is usually omitted on casual wear.

Shirt collar with a stand comes from menswear traditions. There are two separate sections: the collar, and the *stand* between collar and neckline. In some patterns the stand is an extension of the collar section. This eliminates one seam and is faster to sew, but the sewing methods for both versions are similar. For a professional look, topstitch collar edges and stand seams close to the edge.

Standing collar may be shaped or cut double depth and folded along its length to form a self-facing.

Tips for Sewing Collars

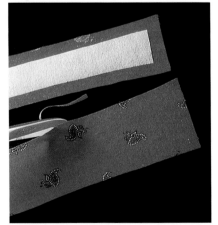

Trim outer edges of undercollar a scant ⅛" (3 mm) so the seam rolls toward the underside of the collar when stitched and turned. Pin right sides of collar and undercollar together with outer edges even.

Press collar seam open on a point presser; turn collar right side out. Gently push collar points out with a point turner. Press collar flat, allowing the seam to roll slightly toward the undercollar.

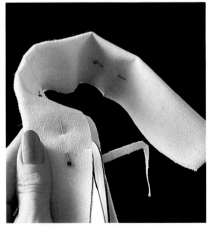

Roll collar into its finished position and pin. If necessary, trim raw edge of undercollar so it is even with upper collar edge. This makes the collar roll properly when it is sewn in place.

How to Sew a Pointed Collar (nonfusible interfacing)

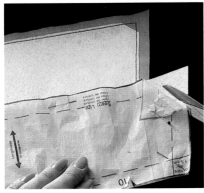

1) Trim corners of interfacing diagonally just inside seamline. Machine-baste interfacing to wrong side of upper collar, ½" (1.3 cm) from edge. Trim interfacing close to stitching.

2) Trim a scant ⅛" (3 mm) from outer edges of undercollar. This keeps undercollar from rolling to right side after collar is stitched to the neckline. Pin right sides of collar and undercollar together with outer edges even.

3) Stitch on seamline, taking one or two short stitches diagonally across each corner instead of making a sharp pivot. This makes a neater point when the collar is turned.

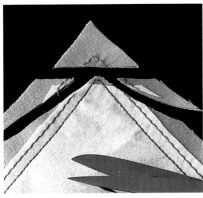

4) Trim corners, first across the point, close to stitching, then at an angle to the seam on each side of the point.

5) Grade seam allowances by trimming undercollar seam allowance to ⅛" (3 mm) and collar to ¼" (6 mm).

6) Press seam open on a point presser. Turn collar right side out.

7) Push points out gently with a point turner.

8) Press collar flat, rolling seam slightly to the underside so it will not show on finished collar.

How to Sew a Round Collar (using fusible interfacing)

1) Trim seam allowances from fusible interfacing and fuse to wrong side of upper collar, following manufacturer's instructions on package.

2) Trim scant ⅛" (3 mm) from outside edge of undercollar, as for pointed collar (page 121). Stitch right sides of collar and facing together, using shorter stitches on curves.

3) Trim seam allowances close to stitching line, using pinking shears **(1)**. Or, grade and clip seam allowances **(2)**. Press seam open, even though seam is enclosed. This flattens stitching line and makes collar easier to turn.

How to Line a Facing with Interfacing

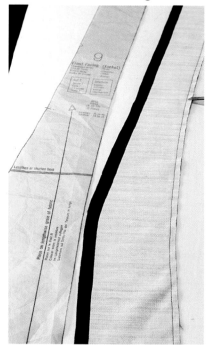

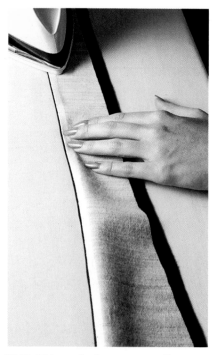

1) Stitch fusible interfacing to facing, right sides together, using ¼" (6 mm) seam allowance; nonadhesive side of interfacing is right side. Clip curves.

2) Press seam away from facing. To prevent interfacing from fusing to ironing board, be careful that the edge of the iron does not go beyond the seam allowance.

3) Fold interfacing on seamline. Finger-press fold, and position interfacing on wrong side of facing. Fuse interfacing to facing. Attach facing to garment.

How to Attach a Convertible Collar

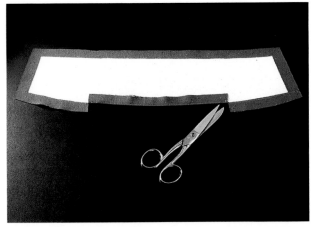

1) Staystitch upper collar neck seam before stitching to undercollar. Clip collar seam allowance to staystitching at shoulder marks. Press seam allowance to wrong side between clips.

2) Interface front facings up to foldline, finishing facing edges with a finish appropriate to the fabric. Turn under facing seam allowances at shoulder seams; press.

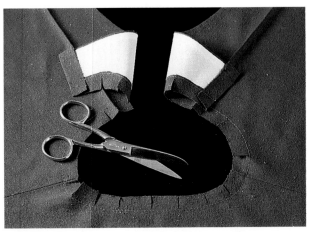

3) Stitch shoulder seams. Staystitch garment neck edge on seamline. Clip seam allowance at frequent intervals, stopping short of staystitching. Stitch upper and undercollars. Turn right side out, and press.

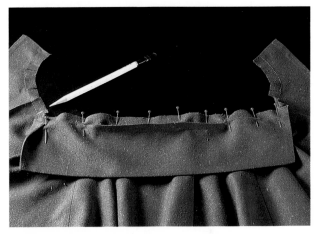

4) Pin undercollar only to garment between shoulder seams. Keep collar neck edge free. Pin upper collar and undercollar to front neck edge, matching markings.

5) Fold front facings over collar. Pin through all layers. Stitch neckline seam, right side of garment up; do not catch folded edge of collar in stitching. Trim across corners, and grade seam; turn facings right side out.

6) Bring folded edge of upper collar over neck seam, and edgestitch or slipstitch in place. Slipstitch facings to shoulder seam allowances.

Waistbands & Cuffs

Because a waistband supports the entire garment, it must be a strong and sturdy outer edge finish. A basic waistband for skirts and pants is cut on the lengthwise grain of the fabric where there is the least amount of stretch. The waistband is stabilized with interfacing, doubled and sewn to the waistline edge, enclosing the seam allowance.

Most waistbands call for a turned-under edge as a finish on the inside. A faster, less bulky method requires changing the pattern layout so the waistband pattern is cut with one long edge on the selvage. Because the selvage does not ravel, a turned-under edge is not necessary. This method can be stitched entirely by machine. To further eliminate bulk, face waistbands of heavy fabrics with a lightweight fabric or grosgrain ribbon.

Cut a waistband long enough for adequate ease and overlap allowance. The length should equal your waist measurement plus 2¾" (7 cm). The extra amount includes ½" (1.3 cm) for ease, 1¼" (3.2 cm) for seam allowances, and 1" (2.5 cm) for overlap. The width should be twice the desired finished width plus 1¼" (3.2 cm) for seam allowances.

How to Sew a Waistband (selvage method)

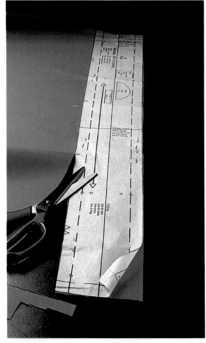

1) Cut waistband on the lengthwise grain, placing the cutting line of one long edge on the selvage.

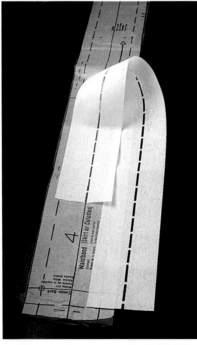

2) Cut length of purchased fusible waistband interfacing according to pattern, cutting off ends at stitching line so interfacing does not extend into seam allowances.

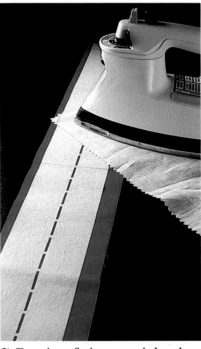

3) Fuse interfacing to waistband, with wider side of interfacing toward selvage edge. Interfacing should be placed so there is a ⅝" (1.5 cm) seam allowance on the notched edge (seam allowance on selvage edge will be narrower).

4) Pin right side of notched edge of waistband to right side of garment, matching notches. Stitch a ⅝" (1.5 cm) seam.

5) Turn waistband up. Press seam allowance toward waistband.

6) Grade the seam allowances to ¼" (6 mm) on the waistband and ⅛" (3 mm) on the garment to eliminate bulk.

7) Fold waistband on interfacing center foldline so waistband is *wrong* side out. Stitch ⅝" (1.5 cm) seam on each end. Trim seam allowances to ¼" (6 mm). Diagonally trim corners.

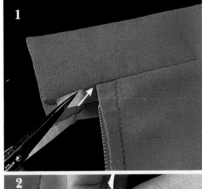
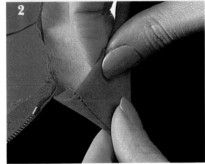

8) Turn waistband right side out. **(1)** On underlap side, diagonally clip from selvage edge to corner (arrow). **(2)** Tuck seam allowance, from edge of underlap to end of clip, up into waistband. Fold clipped corner under at an angle.

9) Pin selvage edge of waistband in place. From right side of garment, stitch in the ditch of waistline seam or topstitch ¼" (6 mm) above the seam, catching selvage edge in stitching. Edgestitch lower edge of underlap (arrow) when using stitch-in-ditch method.

How to Sew a Waistband with Nonroll Woven Waistbanding

1) Cut woven waistband stiffener the length of garment waistband, minus seam allowances at waistband ends. Cut waistband with ⅜" (1 cm) seam allowance on one long edge.

2) Finish one long edge of waistband with zigzag. Stitch waistband to garment, right sides together.

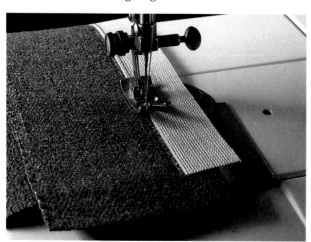

3) Lap stiffener over waistline seam allowances; edgestitch, lining up edge of stiffener with waist seamline. At ends of waistband, stiffener stops at seamlines, not at raw edges.

4) Grade waistband seam. Trim garment seam allowance close to edgestitching. Trim waistband seam allowance to ¼" (6 mm). Press waistband up.

5) Fold waistband along its length, right sides together. Top of waistband should extend slightly beyond stiffener. Stitch across ends. Trim seams.

6) Turn band right side out. Press waistband over stiffener. Pin, baste, or glue in place. From right side, stitch in the ditch, catching finished edge.

How to Attach a Cuff

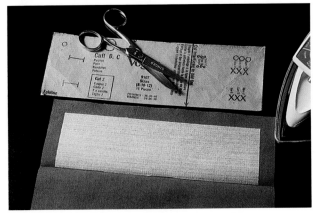

1) Fold cuff pattern in half and cut fusible interfacing from folded pattern, eliminating seam allowances. Fuse interfacing to upper cuff.

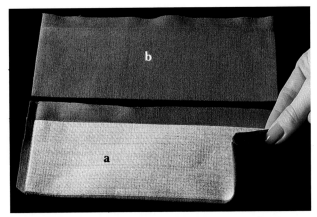

2) Press under seam allowance on interfaced edge. Fold cuff in half lengthwise, right sides together; stitch ends, opening out pressed seam allowance. Trim and grade seams. Press seams open (**a**). Turn cuff right side out (**b**).

3) Pin and stitch wrong side of sleeve to non-interfaced side of cuff, matching markings. Be sure ends of cuff are even with finished placket edges. Do not trim seam allowances.

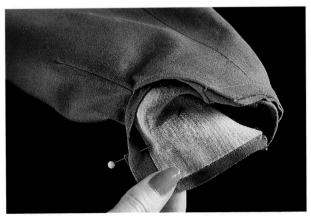

4) Wrap free cuff section around placket opening to front of sleeve as far as it will go. The right side of cuff is on right side of sleeve. Pin about 1" (2.5 cm) from placket opening.

5) Stitch pinned area at each end of cuff exactly on first stitching so first row will not show on outside. Trim seam close to stitching to eliminate bulk.

6) Turn cuff right side out; press. Right side of cuff edge is stitched to sleeve for about 1" (2.5 cm) next to placket opening.

7) Edgestitch folded edge of cuff over seam. Topstitch ¼" (6 mm) from edge of cuff. For a cuff that is not topstitched, attach to right side of sleeve, turn to inside, and slipstitch in place.

Hems

Unless a hem is decorative, it should be virtually invisible from the right side. Use thread the same shade as, or slightly darker than, your fabric.

When hemming by hand, pick up only one or two threads from the outer fabric in each stitch. Do not pull the thread too tight during stitching. This causes the hem to look puckered or lumpy. Press carefully; overpressing creates a ridge along the edge of the hem.

The width of the hem is determined by the fabric and garment style. A hem allowance of up to 3" (7.5 cm) may be given for a straight garment; 1½" to 2" (3.8 to 5 cm) for a flared one. Sheer fabrics, no matter what the style, are usually finished with a narrow, rolled hem. A narrow hem on soft knits helps keep them from sagging. Machine-stitched and topstitched hems are fast and permanent.

Before hemming, let the garment hang for 24 hours, especially if it has a bias or circular hem. Try the garment on over the undergarments you will wear with it. Check to be sure it fits and hangs correctly. Wear shoes, and a belt if the garment is to be belted.

Hemlines are usually marked with the help of a second person using a pin marker or yardstick. Mark the hemline with pins or chalk all around the garment, making sure the distance from the floor to the hemline remains equal. Stand in a normal position and have the helper move around the hem. Pin hem up, and try on the garment in front of a full-length mirror to double check that it is parallel to the floor.

Pants hems cannot be marked from the floor up, as skirts and dresses are. For standard-length pants, the bottom of the pants leg should rest on the shoe in front and slope down slightly toward the back. Pin up the hem on both legs, and try on in front of a mirror to check the length.

Before stitching, finish the raw edges of the hem to keep the fabric from raveling and to provide an anchor for the hemming stitch. Select the hem finish (opposite) and stitch that is appropriate to the fabric and the garment.

Blindstitching by machine makes a fast, sturdy hem on woven and knit fabrics. Many sewing machines have this built-in stitch. A special foot or stitching guide makes blindstitching easy.

Seam binding or lace (above) provides a finish suitable for fabrics which ravel, such as wool, tweed or linen. Lap seam binding ¼" (6 mm) over the hem edge on the right side of the fabric. Edgestitch the binding in place, overlapping ends at a seamline. Use woven seam binding for straight hems, stretch lace for curved hems and knits. Hem light to mediumweight fabrics with the catchstitch, bulky fabrics with the blindstitch.

Hem Finishes and Stitches

Topstitched hem finishes the raw edge and hems the garment all in one step. Turn up hem 1½" (3.8 cm) and pin in place. For ravelly fabrics, pink or turn under raw edge. On right side, topstitch 1" (2.5 cm) from folded edge. Above, a second row of topstitching is applied as a design detail.

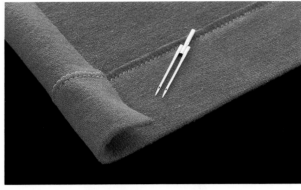

Twin-needle stitched hem is suitable for knits and casual styles. The twin needle produces two closely-spaced parallel lines of stitching on the right side and a zigzag-type stitch on the wrong side. Turn hem up desired amount and stitch through both layers from right side, using seam guide. Trim excess hem allowance after stitching.

Zigzag finish is appropriate for knits and fabrics that ravel, because the stitch gives with the fabric. Stitch close to raw edge with zigzag stitch of medium width and length. Trim close to stitching. Hem with a blindstitch, blind catchstitch or machine blindstitch.

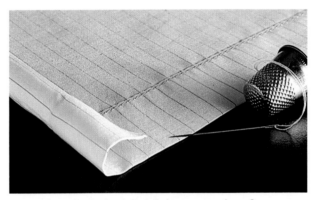

Turned and stitched finish is appropriate for woven lightweight fabrics. Turn raw edge under ¼" (6 mm). Stitch near the edge of the fold. Hem using slipstitch or blindstitch.

Bound hem finish is appropriate for heavy woolens and fabrics that ravel easily. Finish raw edge of hem in double-fold bias tape or Hong Kong finish (page 105). Hem with blindstitch or blind catchstitch. Be careful not to pull hemming thread too tight or fabric will pucker.

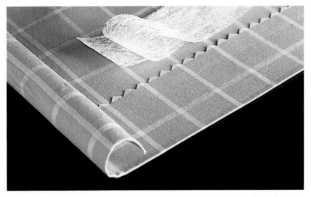

Pinked and fused hem is a fast and easy finish for lightweight woven fabrics. Apply a fusible web strip between the hem and the garment. Steam press, following manufacturer's instructions. Most fusible webs require 15 seconds of heat and steam applied in each section of the hem for permanent bonding.

How to Turn Up a Hem

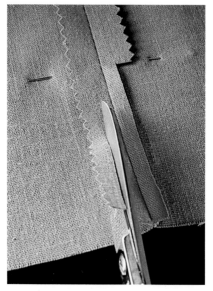

1) Mark garment an even distance from the floor using pins or chalk, and a yardstick or skirt marker. Have your helper move around you so you do not need to shift position or posture. Place marks every 2" (5 cm).

2) Trim seam allowances in hem by half to reduce bulk. Trim seams from bottom of garment to hem stitching line only.

3) Fold hem up along marked line, inserting pins at right angles to the fold at regular intervals. Try on garment to check length.

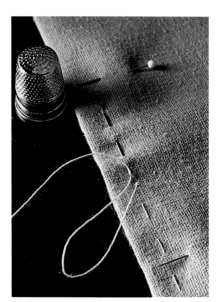

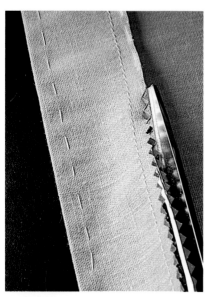

4) Hand-baste ¼" (6 mm) from folded edge. Press edge lightly, easing hem to fit garment.

5) Measure and mark the desired hem depth, adding ¼" (6 mm) for edge finish. Work on ironing board or table, using a seam gauge to ensure even marking.

6) Trim excess hem allowance along markings. Finish raw edge according to fabric type (page 129). Pin finished edge to garment, matching seams and center lines.

How to Sew a Curved Hem

1) Prepare hem as shown opposite, but do not finish raw edge. Curved hems have extra fullness which must be eased to fit garment. Loosen machine tension and easestitch ¼" (6 mm) from edge, stopping and starting at a seamline.

2) Draw up bobbin thread by pulling up a loop with a pin at intervals, easing fullness to smoothly fit garment shape. Do not draw hem in too much, or it will pull against garment when finished. Press hem over a press mitt to smooth out some fullness.

3) Finish raw edge using zigzag stitching, bias tape, seam binding or pinking. Pin hem edge to garment, matching seams and center lines. Hem using machine blindstitch or appropriate hand hemming stitch.

How to Machine Blindstitch

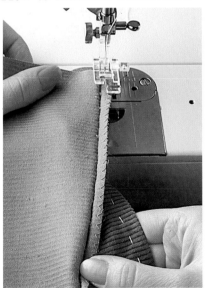

1) Prepare hemline as shown, opposite. Hand-baste hem to garment, ¼" (6 mm) from raw edge. Adjust machine to blindstitch setting and attach blindstitch foot. Select zigzag width and stitch length according to weight and texture of fabric. The stitch taken into the garment is adjustable from ¹⁄₁₆" to ⅛" (1.5 to 3 mm).

2) Place hem allowance face down over feed of machine. Fold bulk of garment back to basting line. The soft fold should rest against the right part of the foot (arrow). Some machines use a regular zigzag foot with a blindstitch hemming guide attached.

3) Stitch along hem close to the fold, catching garment only in zigzag stitch. While stitching, guide hem edge in a straight line and feed soft fold against the right part of the hemming foot or the edge of the guide. Open out hem and press flat.

Three Hems Using Serger with Conventional Machine

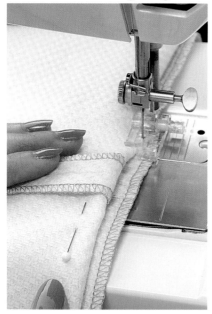

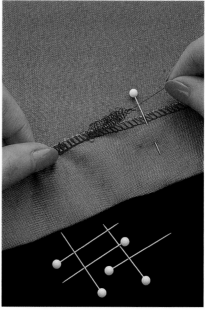

Overedged and blindstitched hem. Mark hem allowance, and grade seams in hem area. Serge hem edge. Fold hem as for blind hem, step 2, below. Pin hem into position, and blindstitch, using a conventional machine, or by hand.

Overedged and topstitched hem. Serge hem edge. Turn up hem; press. Topstitch from right side of garment, using conventional machine. Twin needle may be used for topstitching.

Eased hem. Ease hem fullness by pulling up needle thread. Or adjust differential feed, if available, to the ease setting. Pin hem into position; blindstitch, using a conventional machine, or by hand.

How to Overlock a Blind Hem

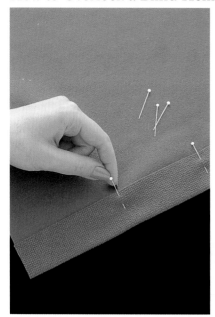

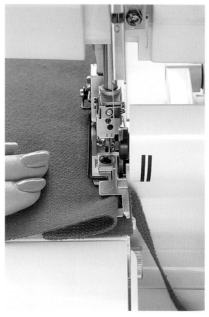

1) Adjust machine for flatlock stitch; use blind hem foot, if available. Set stitch length at 4 mm. Fold up hem; press. On hem side of garment, place pins with the heads toward body of garment.

2) Fold garment over hem allowance, with hem edge extending ¼" (6 mm) beyond fold. Stitch on extended hem edge, with needle *barely* catching fold; remove pins as you come to them.

3) Open hem, and pull fabric flat. Ladder of stitches shows on right side of lightweight fabrics, but is invisible on heavier textured fabrics.

How to Sew a Cover Stitch Hem

Split hem. Adjust machine for cover stitch. Press up hem. Place fabric under raised presser foot, right side up, with fold aligned to desired needle plate guide line. Holding threads, turn handwheel until needles enter fabric at beginning of hem. Stitch to fabric edge at end of hem; raise needles and presser foot. Holding stitches firmly, gently pull threads back. Cut threads, leaving tail; knot. Secure tails, using loop turner or needle.

Circular hem. Adjust machine and stitch hem as for split hem, left; start at back or side seam, and lap first stitches about 1" (2.5 cm). Raise needles and presser foot. Hold stitches behind foot firmly; gently pull fabric slightly back, and then to left. Cut thread tails. Pull out loose threads; secure threads, using fray check or knots as desired. Remove extra needle thread from surface of needle plate.

How to Flatlock a Sport Hem

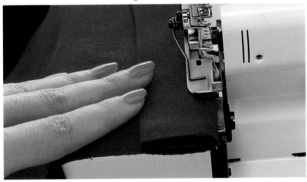

1) Adjust machine for flatlock stitch. Fold up hem, and press. Fold up, and press again, enclosing raw edge; flatlock on fold, taking care to catch hem edge in stitches.

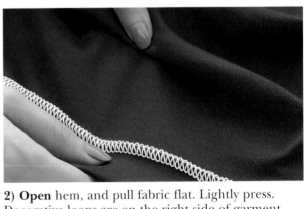

2) Open hem, and pull fabric flat. Lightly press. Decorative loops are on the right side of garment.

How to Flatlock a Fringed Hem

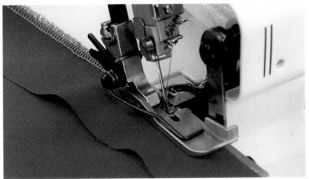

1) Mark placement line, by pulling a thread or using a marking pen, to indicate depth of fringe. Press a crease on marked line. Adjust serger for flatlock stitch. Stitch on fold.

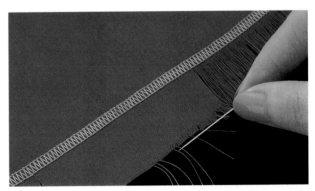

2) Cut fabric up to stitches on grain every 3" (7.5 cm). Remove threads to create fringe. If flatlocking corners, apply liquid fray preventer to intersecting stitches, and use seam ripper to remove stitches in fringe area.

Closures

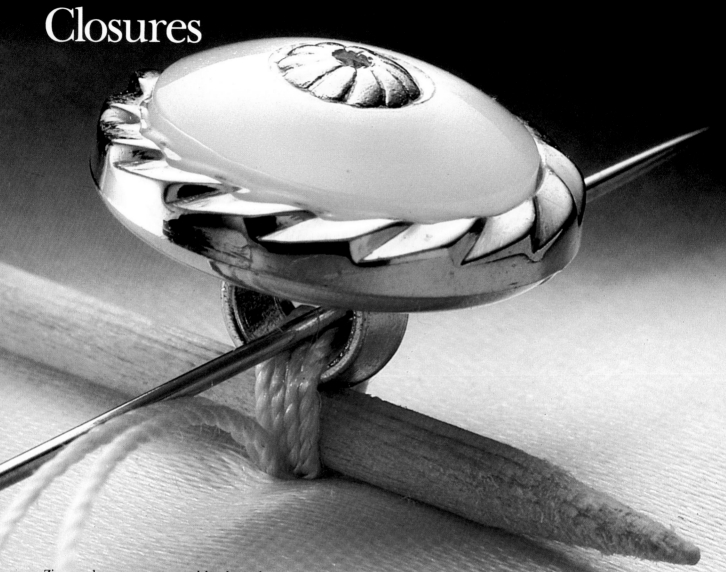

Zippers, buttons, snaps, and hooks and eyes are usually meant to be as inconspicuous as possible, but are sometimes used as decorative details. A stylish button, colorful separating zipper or pearlized gripper snap can make a definite fashion statement.

Select the closure according to the style of garment and amount of strain that will be put on the opening. For example, a heavy-duty hook and eye closure (opposite) can better withstand the strain on a pants waistband than ordinary hooks and eyes. The back of the pattern envelope specifies the type and size of closures to purchase.

Because closures are under strain, it is important to reinforce the garment area where they are placed. Seam allowances or facings provide light reinforcement. Other closure areas should be reinforced with interfacing.

For sewing on buttons, snaps, and hooks and eyes, use an all-purpose thread, and sharps or crewel needles. For heavyweight fabrics or for closures that are under considerable strain, use heavy-duty, or topstitching and buttonhole twist thread.

Hooks & Eyes

Hooks and eyes are strong closures and come in several types. Regular, general-purpose hooks and eyes are available in sizes 0 (fine) to 3 (heavy), in black or nickel finishes. They have either straight or round eyes. Straight eyes are used where garment edges overlap, such as on a waistband. Round eyes are used where two edges meet, such as at the neckline above a centered zipper. Thread loops (opposite) can be used in place of round metal eyes on delicate fabrics or in locations where metal eyes would be too conspicuous. Button loops and belt carriers are made using the same technique, starting with longer foundation stitches.

Heavy-duty hooks and eyes are stronger than regular hooks and eyes, to withstand greater strain. Available in black or nickel finishes, they are used only for lapped areas. Large, plain or covered hooks and eyes are available for coats and jackets. These are attractive enough to be visible and strong enough to hold heavy fabric.

How to Attach Waistband Hooks and Eyes

1) Position heavy-duty hook on underside of waistband overlap, about ⅛" (3 mm) from inside edge. Tack hook in place with three or four stitches through each hole. Do not stitch through to right side of garment.

2) Lap hook side over underlap to mark position of eye. Insert straight pins through holes to mark position. Tack in place with three or four stitches in each hole.

Round hook and eye is used for waistbands which do not overlap. Position hook as for heavy-duty hook. Tack through both holes and at end of hook. Position eye so it extends slightly over inside edge of fabric (garments edges should butt together). Tack in place.

How to Make Thread Eyes

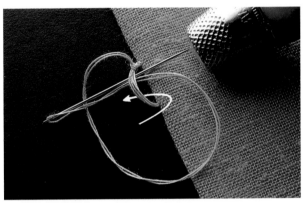

1) Insert needle with double strand of thread at edge of fabric. Take two foundation stitches the desired length of the eye. These are the anchor on which blanket stitch is worked.

2) Work blanket stitch by bringing eye of needle under foundation stitches and through the loop.

3) Bring needle through loop, pulling loop tight against foundation stitches. Work blanket stitch along entire length of foundation stitches.

4) Secure stitching by taking two small backstitches. Trim threads.

Buttonholes

The standards of a well-made buttonhole are:
1) Width is appropriate to the weight of the fabric and size of the buttonhole.
2) Ends are bar-tacked to prevent buttonhole from tearing under stress.
3) Stitches are evenly spaced on each side of the buttonhole.
4) Buttonhole is ⅛" (3 mm) longer than the button.
5) Stitches on each side are far enough apart so that the buttonhole can be cut open without cutting the stitches.
6) Ends have not been cut open accidentally.
7) Interfacing supporting the buttonhole matches the fashion fabric and is not obvious on the cut edges.
8) Buttonhole is on-grain; vertical buttonholes are perfectly parallel to the garment edge, horizontal buttonholes are at perfect right angles to the edge.

Horizontal buttonholes are the most secure, because they are not as apt to let buttons slip out. These buttonholes also absorb any pull against the closure with little, if any, distortion. Horizontal buttonholes should extend ⅛" (3 mm) beyond the button placement line, toward the edge of the garment. Be sure that the space from the center line to the finished edge of the garment is at least three-fourths the diameter of the button. With this spacing, the button will not extend beyond the edge when the garment is buttoned.

Vertical buttonholes are used on plackets and shirt bands. These are usually used with more and smaller buttons to help keep the closure secure. Vertical buttonholes are placed directly on the center front or center back line.

When a garment is buttoned, the button placement lines and center lines of both sides must match perfectly. If the overlap is more or less than the pattern indicates, the garment may not fit properly.

Spaces between buttonholes are generally equal. You may have to change the pattern buttonhole spacing if you have made pattern alterations that change the length or alter the bustline. Respacing may also be necessary if you have chosen buttons that are larger or smaller than the pattern indicates. Buttonholes should be spaced so they occur in the areas of greatest stress. When they are incorrectly spaced, the closing gaps and spoils the garment's appearance.

For front openings, place buttonholes at the neck and the fullest part of the bust. Place a buttonhole at the waist for coats, overblouses and princess-seamed dresses or jackets. To reduce bulk, do not place a buttonhole at the waistline of a tucked-in blouse or belted dress. Buttons and buttonholes should end about 5" to 6" (12.5 to 15 cm) above the hemline of a dress, skirt or coatdress.

To evenly respace buttonholes, mark the locations of the top and bottom buttons. Measure the distance between them. Divide that measurement by one less than the number of buttons to be used. The result is the distance between buttonholes. After marking, try on the garment, making sure the buttonholes are placed correctly for your figure. Adjust as necessary.

How to Determine Buttonhole Length

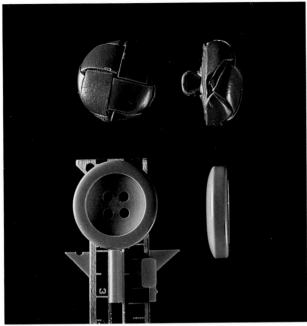

Measure width and height of button to be used. The sum of these measurements plus ⅛" (3 mm) for finishing the ends of the buttonhole is the correct length for a machine-worked buttonhole. The buttonhole must be large enough to button easily, yet snug enough so the garment stays closed.

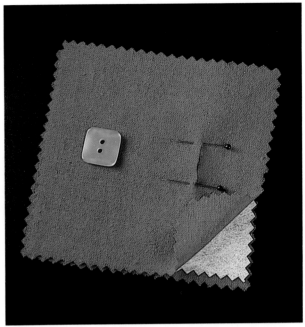

Test proposed buttonhole. First, make a slash in a scrap of fabric the length of the buttonhole minus the extra ⅛" (3 mm). If button passes through easily, length is correct. Next, make a practice buttonhole with garment, facing and interfacing. Check length, stitch width, density of stitching and buttonhole cutting space.

How to Mark Buttonholes

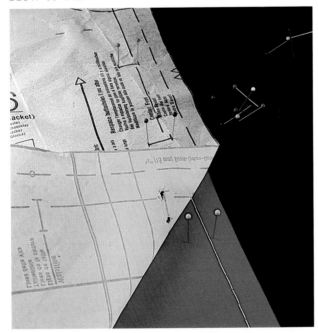

Place pattern tissue on top of garment, aligning pattern seamline with garment opening edge. Insert pins straight down through tissue and fabric at both ends of each buttonhole marking. Remove pattern carefully, pulling tissue over heads of pins.

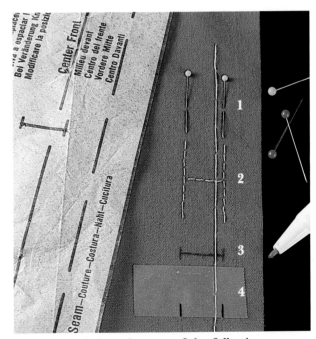

Mark buttonholes using one of the following methods: **(1)** Secure pins. **(2)** Machine or hand-baste between pins and along ends. **(3)** Use a water-soluble marking pen. **(4)** Place a piece of tape above the pins and mark buttonhole length with a pencil; test fabric first to be sure tape does not mar it.

Machine-made Buttonholes

Machine-made buttonholes are appropriate for most garments, especially those which are casual or tailored. There are four types: *built-in* (usually two or four-step), *overedge, one-step* and *universal attachment*. Always make a test buttonhole with appropriate interfacing before making the buttonholes on your garment. The test buttonhole also reminds you at which point your machine begins the buttonhole stitching, so you can position fabric correctly.

1) Built-in buttonholes are made with a combination of zigzag stitching and bar tacks. Most zigzag machines have a built-in mechanism that stitches this type of buttonhole in two or four steps. The four steps are: zigzag forward, bar tack, zigzag in reverse, bar tack. A two-step buttonhole combines a forward or backward motion with a bar tack. Consult your machine manual for specific directions, because each machine varies. The advantage of this buttonhole is that it allows you to adjust the density of the zigzag to suit the fabric and size of the buttonhole. Use spaced zigzag stitches on bulky or loosely woven fabrics, closer stitches on sheer or delicate fabrics.

2) Overedge buttonholes are an adaptation of the built-in or one-step buttonhole. This buttonhole is stitched with a narrow zigzag, cut open and then stitched a second time, so the cut edge is overedged with zigzag stitches. The overedge buttonhole looks like a hand-worked buttonhole. It is a good choice when the interfacing is not a close color match to the fashion fabric.

3) One-step buttonholes are stitched all in one step, using a special foot and a built-in stitch available on some machines. They can be stitched with a standard-width zigzag, or a narrow zigzag for lightweight fabrics. The button is placed in a carrier in back of the attachment and guides the stitching, so the buttonhole fits the button perfectly. A lever near the needle is pulled down and stops the foward motion of the machine when the buttonhole reaches the correct length. All buttonholes are of uniform length, so placement is the only marking necessary.

4) Universal attachment buttonholes are made with an attachment which will fit any machine, including a straight-stitch machine. The attachment has a *template* which determines the size of the buttonhole. This method also offers the advantage of uniform buttonhole length and adjustable zigzag width. The *keyhole* buttonhole, used on tailored garments or heavy fabrics, can be made using this attachment. The keyhole at one end of the buttonhole provides space for the shank.

If buttonholes do not have to be respaced because of pattern alterations, make the buttonholes after attaching and finishing the facings but before joining to another garment section. This way there is less bulk and weight to handle at the machine.

How to Make Buttonholes

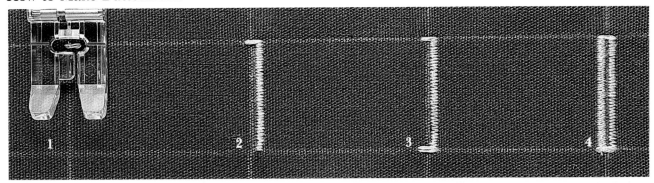

Built-in buttonholes (four-step). Place fabric under buttonhole foot, aligning starting point with needle and centering foot over center marking. (Steps are pictured separately above, but buttonhole is stitched continuously, moving machine to new setting at each step.) **1)** Set dial or lever selector at first step. Slowly stitch 3 or 4 stitches across end to form bar tack. **2)**

Stitch one side. Some machines stitch left side first, others stitch right side. Stitch only as far as marked end. **3)** Stitch 3 or 4 stitches across end to form second bar tack. **4)** Stitch other side to complete buttonhole. Stop sewing when stitching reaches the first bar tack. Return to starting position and make one or two fastening stitches.

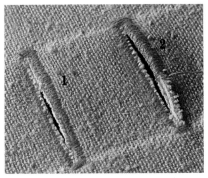

Overedge buttonhole. 1) Stitch buttonhole with narrow zigzag. Cut buttonhole open and trim loose threads. **2)** Reposition buttonhole in exact position as first stitching. Adjust zigzag width to wider stitch. Stitch second time with zigzag going over cut edge of buttonhole.

One-step buttonhole. Place button in attachment carrier. Check machine manual for proper stitch setting. Buttonhole is made the correct length and stitching will stop automatically. Cut open and stitch buttonhole a second time to add an overedge finish.

Universal attachment buttonhole. Attach buttonhole attachment as instructed in manual. Select template of proper size to fit button. For sturdier reinforced buttonhole, stitch around the buttonhole a second time.

How to Open a Buttonhole

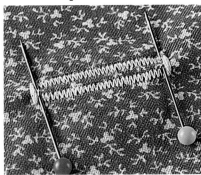

1) Insert straight pins at each end of buttonhole in front of bar tacks to prevent cutting through ends.

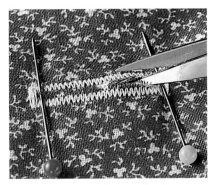

2) Insert point of a small, sharp scissors or seam ripper into center of buttonhole and carefully cut toward one end, then the other.

3) Strengthen the cut edge and prevent raveling by applying liquid fray preventer to the edge. Test on a sample first.

Buttons

More than any other closure, buttons allow you to individualize your garment. Buttons can be decorative as well as functional. There are two basic kinds of buttons, *sew-through* and *shank* buttons, but the variations on these two types are endless.

Sew-through buttons are usually flat, with two or four holes. When they are merely decorative, they can be sewn so they lie directly against the garment. On all other applications, sew-through buttons need a thread shank. A *shank* raises the button from the garment surface, allowing space for the layers of fabric to fit smoothly when it is buttoned.

Shank buttons have their own shanks on the underside. Choose shank buttons for heavier fabrics, as well as when using button loops or thread loops.

When selecting buttons, consider color, style, weight and care.

Color. The color of buttons is usually matched to the fabric, but interesting fashion looks can be achieved with coordinating or contrasting colors. If you are unable to find an appropriate color match, make your own fabric-covered buttons with a kit.

Style. Select small, delicate buttons for feminine garments; clean, classic styles for tailored clothes; novelty buttons for children's clothes. Rhinestone buttons add sparkle to a velvet garment. Try leather or metal buttons with corduroy and wool tweeds.

Weight. Match lightweight buttons to lightweight fabrics. Heavy buttons will pull and distort lightweight fabrics. Heavyweight fabrics need buttons that are bigger or look weightier.

Care. Choose buttons that can be cared for in the same manner as the garment, either washable or dry-cleanable.

The back of the pattern envelope tells you how many and what size buttons to purchase. Try not to go more than ⅛" (3 mm) smaller or larger than the pattern specifies. Buttons that are too small or too large may not be in proper proportion to the edge of the garment. Button sizes are listed in inches, millimeters and *lines*. For example, a ½" button is also listed as 13 mm and line 20; a ¾" button, as 19 mm and line 30.

When shopping for buttons, bring a swatch of fabric with you to assure a good match. Cut a small slit in the fabric so a button on the card can be slipped through, giving you a better idea of how it will look when finished.

Sew on buttons with doubled all-purpose thread for lightweight fabrics, and heavy-duty or buttonhole twist for heavier fabrics. When attaching several buttons, double the sewing thread so you are sewing with four strands at once. This way, two stitches will secure the button.

How to Mark Button Location

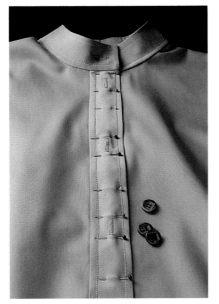 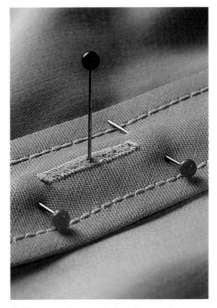 

1) Mark button placement by lapping the buttonhole side of garment over the button side, matching center lines. Pin garment closed between buttonholes.

2) Insert pin straight through buttonhole and into bottom layer of fabric. For vertical buttonholes, insert pin in center of buttonhole. For horizontal buttonholes, insert pin at edge closest to outer edge of garment.

3) Carefully lift buttonhole over pin. Insert threaded needle at point of pin to sew on button. Mark and sew buttons one at a time, buttoning previous buttons for accurate marking.

How to Sew on a Shank Button

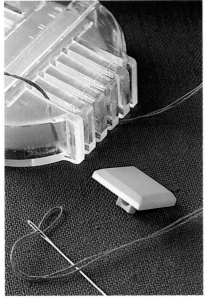  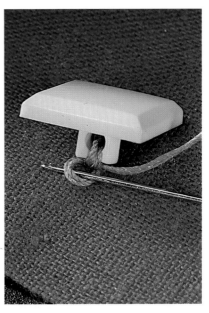

1) Cut a length of thread 30" (76 cm) long and run it through beeswax to strengthen it. Fold thread in half. Thread folded end through a crewel needle. Knot cut ends of thread. Position button at pin mark on the garment center line, placing shank hole parallel to the buttonhole.

2) Secure thread on right side with small stitch under button. Bring needle through shank hole. Insert needle down into fabric and pull through. Repeat, taking four to six stitches through the shank.

3) Secure thread in fabric under button by making a knot or taking several small stitches. Clip thread ends. If a shank button is used on a heavy fabric, it may also need a thread shank. Follow instructions for making a thread shank on a sew-through button, page 142.

How to Hand Sew a Sew-through Button

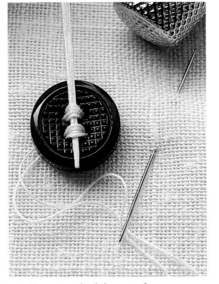

1) Thread needle as for shank button (page 141) and position the button at pin mark. Place holes in button so they line up parallel to buttonhole. Bring needle through fabric from underside and up through one hole in button. Insert needle into another hole and through the fabric layers.

2) Slip a toothpick, match or sewing machine needle between thread and button to form shank. Take three or four stitches through each pair of holes. Bring needle and thread to right side under button. Remove toothpick.

3) Wind thread two or three times around button stitches to form shank. Secure thread on right side under button by making a knot or taking several small stitches. Clip threads close to knot.

How to Machine Sew a Sew-through Button

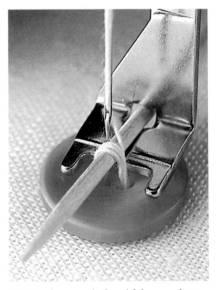

1) Attach button foot and special plate to cover feed, or drop feed. Button will be stitched with close zigzag stitching. Regulate stitch width and tension as directed in machine manual.

2) Position button under foot. Lower needle into center of one button hole by turning handwheel towards you. Lower presser foot. Turn handwheel until needle rises out of button and is just above foot. Insert match or toothpick to form shank.

3) Set zigzag stitch width regulator so that stitch width equals the space between holes in button. Proceed slowly until you are sure you have the correct width. Take six or more zigzag stitches. Secure the stitching as directed in your machine manual.

Snaps

Snaps are available as regular sew-on snaps, gripper-type snaps or snap tape.

Sew-on snaps are suitable for areas where there is little strain, such as at the neckline or waistline to hold the facing edge flat when buttons are used, at the waistline of blouses, or at the pointed end of a waistband fastened with hooks and eyes. Sew-on snaps consist of two parts: a ball and a socket. Select a size that is strong enough to be secure, but not too heavy for the fabric.

Gripper-type snaps are attached with a special plier tool or a hammer. They have more holding power than a sew-in snap and will show on the right side of the garment. Gripper snaps can replace button and buttonhole closures in sportswear.

Snap tape consists of snaps attached to pieces of tape. The tape is stitched to the garment with a zipper foot. Snap tape is used in sportswear, home decorating, and for the inside seam of infant's and toddler's pants.

How to Attach Sew-on Snaps

1) Position ball half of snap on wrong side of overlap section, ⅛" to ¼" (3 to 6 mm) from the edge so it will not show on the right side. Stitch in place through each hole, using single strand of thread. Stitch through facing and interfacing only, not through to right side of garment. Secure thread with two tiny stitches.

2) Mark position of socket half of snap on right side of underlap section. Use one of the following methods: If there is a hole in center of ball half, insert pin from right side through hole and into underlap section. If there is no hole in ball, rub tailor's chalk on ball and press firmly against underlap.

3) Position center of socket half over marking. Stitch in place in same manner as ball half, except stitch through all layers of fabric.

Zippers

Down the back, up the front, on sleeves, pockets or pants legs — zippers provide closings on a variety of fashion features. *Conventional* zippers are most often used. They are closed at one end and sewn into a seam. *Invisible, separating,* and *heavy-duty* zippers are available for special uses.

The pattern specifies the type and length zipper to buy. When selecting a zipper, choose a color that closely matches your fabric. Also consider the weight of the zipper in relation to the weight of the fabric. Choose synthetic coil zippers for lightweight fabrics, because these zippers are lighter and more flexible than metal zippers. If you cannot find a zipper of the correct length, buy one that is slightly longer than you need and shorten it using the directions on the opposite page.

There are several ways to insert a zipper. The one you choose depends on the type of garment and the location of the zipper in the garment. The following pages contain instructions for the *lapped, centered* and *fly-front* applications for conventional zippers, and two methods for inserting separating zippers. There are variations of each of these applications. Methods shown here are quick and easy, featuring timesaving tools such as fabric glue stick and transparent tape.

Close the zipper and press out the creases before inserting it in the garment. If the zipper has a cotton tape and will be applied in a washable garment, preshrink it in hot water before application. This will prevent the zipper from puckering when the garment is laundered. For best appearance, the final stitching on the outside of the garment should be straight and an even distance from the seamline. Stitch both sides of the zipper from bottom to top, and turn the pull tab up to make it easier to stitch past the slider.

Parts of the Zipper

Top stop is the small metal bracket at the top that prevents the slider from running off the tape.

Slider and pull tab is the mechanism that operates the zipper. It locks the teeth together to close the zipper and unlocks the teeth to open the zipper.

Tape is the fabric strip on which the teeth or coil are fastened. The tape is sewn to the garment.

Teeth or coil is the part of the zipper that locks together when the slider runs along it. It may be made of nylon, polyester or metal.

Bottom stop is the bracket at the bottom of the zipper where the slider rests when the zipper is open. Separating zippers have a bottom stop which splits into two parts to allow the zipper to be completely opened.

Separating zippers in jackets and vests can be inserted with zipper teeth covered or exposed. A decorative sport zipper with plastic teeth is lightweight yet sturdy, for active sportswear.

Applications for Conventional Zippers

Lapped application totally conceals the zipper, making it a good choice for zippers which do not perfectly match the fabric color. It is most often used in side seam closings of dresses, skirts and pants.

Centered application is most frequently used for center front and center back closings. Attach facings *before* inserting the zipper. Waistbands should be applied *after* the zipper is inserted.

Fly-front zipper is often found on pants and skirts, and occasionally on coats and jackets. Use the fly-front application only when the pattern calls for it, because it requires the wider underlap and facing included in the pattern.

How to Shorten a Zipper

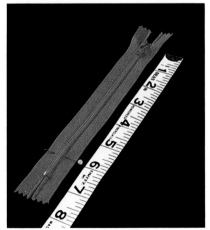

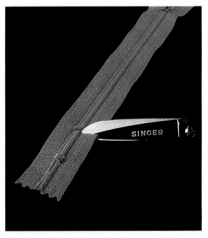

1) Measure desired length along the coil, beginning at top stop. Mark with pin.

2) Machine zigzag across the coil at pin to form new bottom stop.

3) Cut off excess zipper and tape. Insert zipper as usual, stitching slowly across coil at bottom.

How to Insert a Lapped Zipper

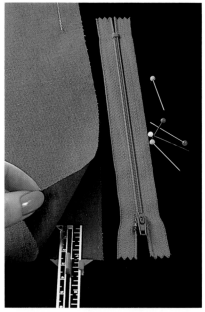

1) Turn the garment to the wrong side. Check seam opening to make sure top edges are even. Length of opening should be equal to length of zipper *coil* plus 1" (2.5 cm). Pin seam from bottom of opening to top of garment.

2) Machine-baste on seamline from bottom of the opening to top of the garment, removing pins as you stitch.

3) Clip basting stitches every 2" (5 cm) to make basting easier to remove after zipper is inserted.

7) Close zipper and turn face up. Smooth fabric away from zipper, forming narrow fold between zipper coil and basted seam.

8) Adjust zipper foot to left side of needle. Starting at bottom of zipper tape, stitch near edge of fold, through folded seam allowance and zipper tape.

9) Turn zipper over so face side is flat against seam. Make sure pull tab is turned up to lessen bulk while stitching. Pin in place.

4) Press seam open. If zipper is in side seam of skirt or pants, press seam over a press mitt or tailor's ham to retain shape of hipline.

5) Open zipper. Place face down on right-hand side of seam allowance (top of garment facing you). Position zipper coil directly on seamline with top stop 1" (2.5 cm) below cut edge. Turn pull tab up. Pin, glue or tape right-hand side of zipper tape in place.

6) Replace presser foot with zipper foot and adjust it to right side of needle. Machine-baste close to edge of coil, stitching from bottom to top of zipper with edge of zipper foot against coil. Remove pins as you stitch.

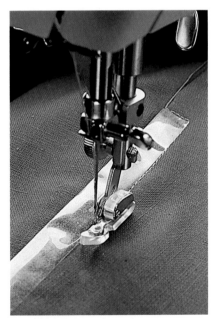

10) Adjust zipper foot to right side of needle. Starting at top of zipper, machine-baste through tape and seam allowance only. This holds seam allowance in place for the final stitching.

11) Topstitch ½" (1.3 cm) from seam on outside of garment. To aid straight stitching, use ½" (1.3 cm) transparent tape and stitch along edge. Starting at seamline, stitch across bottom of zipper, pivot at edge of tape and continue to top cut edge.

12) Remove tape. Pull thread at bottom of zipper to wrong side and knot. Remove machine basting in seam. Press, using a press cloth to protect fabric from shine. Trim zipper tape even with top edge of garment.

How to Insert a Centered Zipper (using glue stick)

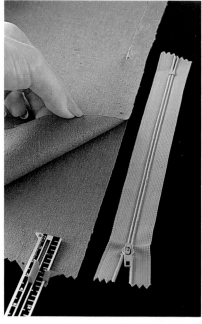

1) Turn garment to the wrong side. Check seam opening to make sure top edges are even. Length of opening should be equal to length of zipper *coil* plus 1" (2.5 cm).

2) Pin seam from bottom of opening to top of garment.

3) Machine-baste on seamline from bottom of opening to top of garment. Clip basting stitches every 2" (5 cm) to make basting easier to remove.

7) Spread garment flat, right side up. Mark bottom stop of zipper with pin. Use transparent or perforated marking tape, ½" (1.3 cm) wide and same length as zipper. Place down center of seamline. Do not use tape on napped or delicate fabrics.

8) Replace presser foot with zipper foot and adjust to left of needle. Topstitch zipper from right side, beginning at seam at bottom of tape. Stitch across bottom of zipper; pivot at edge of tape. Stitch up left side of zipper to top cut edge, using edge of tape as a guide.

9) Adjust the zipper foot to right side of needle. Begin at seam at bottom of tape and stitch across bottom. Pivot and stitch up right side of zipper, using edge of tape as a guide.

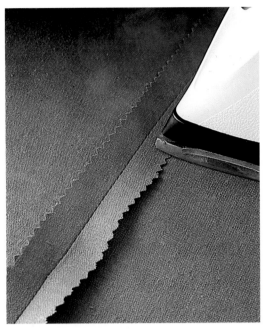

4) Press seam open. Finish raw edges if fabric ravels easily.

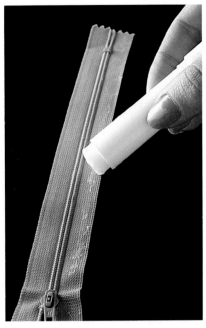

5) Apply glue stick (page 30) lightly on face side of zipper.

6) Place zipper face down on seam, with zipper coil directly on seamline and top stop 1" (2.5 cm) below cut edge (keep pull tab up). Press with fingers to secure zipper. Let glue dry for a few minutes.

10) Pull both threads at bottom to wrong side. Tie all four threads, using pin to pull knot close to zipper. Clip threads.

11) Turn garment to right side. Remove tape. Carefully remove machine basting in seamline.

12) Press, using a press cloth to protect fabric from shine. Trim zipper tape even with the top edge of the garment.

How to Insert a Fly-front Zipper

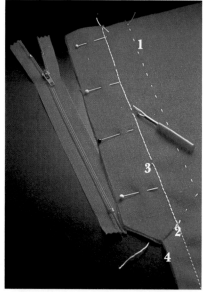

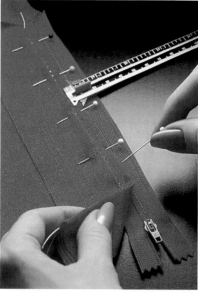

1) Mark zipper topstitching line on right side with hand basting or non-permanent marking (**1**). Stitch front crotch seam, backstitching at marking for end of zipper placket (**2**). Machine-baste seam closed (**3**). Clip basting stitches every 2" (5 cm). Clip seam allowances below fly facings (**4**). Press facings open.

2) Fold right-hand fly facing (top edge facing you) under ¼" to ½" (6 mm to 1.3 cm) from center front. Place folded edge along coil with top stop 1" (2.5 cm) below top edge. Pin or baste in place.

3) Replace presser foot with zipper foot and adjust to left of needle. Stitch close to the fold, starting at bottom of zipper.

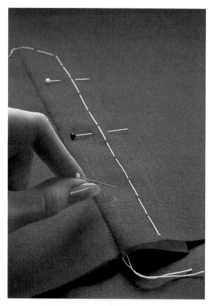

4) Turn zipper face down over *left* fly facing. Turn pull tab up and bulk of garment out of the way. Adjust zipper foot to right of needle. Starting at top of zipper, stitch through tape and fly facing, ¼" (6 mm) from zipper coil.

5) Spread garment flat, wrong side up. Pin left fly extension to garment front. Turn garment to right side and repin fly facing. Remove pins from inside.

6) Stitch on right side along marked topstitching line, with zipper foot to right of needle. Begin at seam at bottom of zipper and stitch to top of garment, removing pins as you come to them. Pull threads to inside and knot. Remove basting and marking. Press using a press cloth.

How to Insert a Covered Separating Zipper

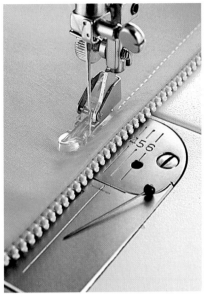

1) Use basting tape, pins or glue to hold closed zipper, face up, under faced opening edges. Position pull tab ⅛" (3 mm) below neck seamline. Edges of the opening should meet at center of zipper, covering the teeth.

2) Open zipper. Turn ends of zipper tape under at top of garment. Pin in place.

3) Topstitch ⅜" (1 cm) from each opening edge, sewing through fabric and zipper tape. Stitch from bottom to top on each side, adjusting zipper foot to correct side.

How to Insert an Exposed Separating Zipper

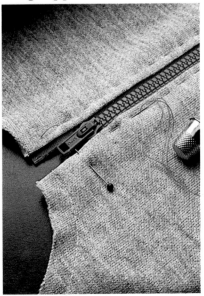

1) Pin faced opening edges to closed zipper so that edges are close to but not covering zipper teeth, with pull tab ⅛" (3 mm) below neck seamline.

2) Baste zipper in place with tape ends extending above neck seamline. Turn ends of zipper tape under at top of garment if facing is already attached. Open zipper.

3) Topstitch close to opening edges on right side of garment, using zipper foot and stitching from bottom to top on each side. To hold zipper tape flat, add another line of stitching ¼" (6 mm) from first stitching line on each side.

Tailoring

Tailoring differs from dressmaking in a number of ways. The term *tailored* applies to fashions styled like menswear, such as a suit jacket. It also describes certain methods of construction and pattern design. The undercollar and collar on a tailored jacket, for example, are cut from two different pattern pieces to shape the collar. In dressmaking, both collar layers are usually cut from the same pattern piece. Details such as a welt pocket, notched collar, and full lining are typical in patterns for tailored fashions.

Tailoring also calls for extensive use of interfacings for building in shape. Entire garment sections, not just the details, are backed with interfacing when tailored. Two layers of interfacing may be used for shaping the roll line on jacket lapels. Because different kinds of interfacings have distinctive effects, a single tailored jacket may require several types of interfacing.

Fusible interfacings have eliminated most of the time-consuming handwork that was once the trademark of tailoring. With fusibles you can tailor

expertly with just a little practice. However, it's important to choose the right fashion fabric and interfacing for the tailoring task at hand.

Using Fusible Interfacings

Four types of fusible interfacings may be used for tailoring; often all four are used in one garment. *Fusible tricot*, a knitted interfacing, adds body and support to the fabric without causing stiffness. Use it to stabilize garment sections such as sleeves, hems, front facings, and the upper collar. *Fusible hair canvas*, a woven interfacing, is firm and resilient. Use it for the jacket front and undercollar when the fabric needs strong support. *Weft insertion fusible* is a knitted interfacing with extra yarns inserted crosswise. In a medium weight, it is a softer alternative to hair canvas and is used to stabilize fashion details, such as vents on jacket hems and the roll lines of lapels and undercollars. In a lighter weight, it is an alternative to fusible tricot. *Crisp,*

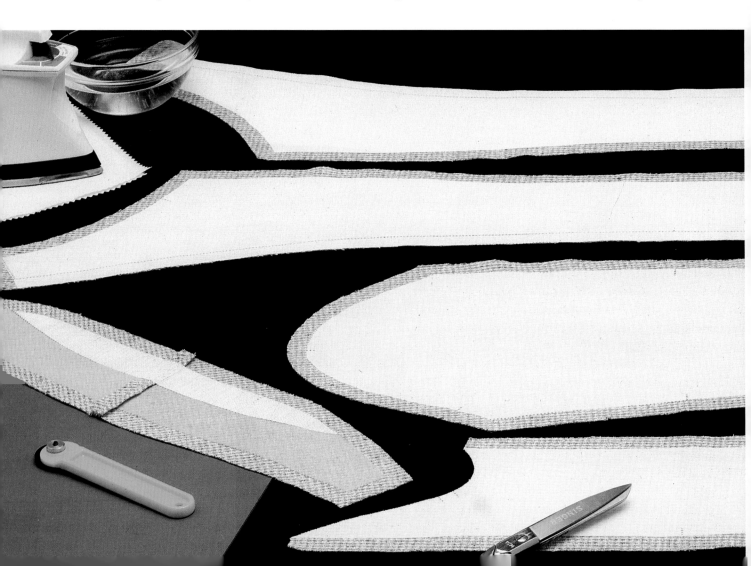

nonwoven fusible interfacing is used to keep small details, such as pocket flaps, firm and smooth.

Test fusible interfacings by making a sample when tailoring. Because entire sections of the garment will be interfaced, the sample should be large enough to drape over your hand, at least 6" (15 cm) square (larger if you can spare the fabric). The ideal method for testing fusible interfacings is to fuse 6" (15 cm) squares of different types of interfacing on a long panel, leaving plain fabric in between. The contrast in feeling between interfaced and non-interfaced areas clearly shows the effect of each interfacing.

Choosing Tailoring Fabrics

When tailoring with fusible interfacings, you'll be more satisfied if you begin with a durable fabric of good quality. Natural fiber fabrics, such as wool, cotton, silk, and linen, respond well to fusing. Many fabrics made from synthetic fibers and blends, such as polyester and rayon, fuse nicely, too. However, some synthetics and metallic fibers are too heat sensitive for fusible interfacings.

Textured fabrics, such as tweeds and linen weaves, tailor well; their surfaces give the fusible adhesive something to grip for a strong bond. On the other hand, some fabrics with tight weaves and smooth surfaces, such as fine polyester gabardines, resist smooth fusing and should be used with sew-in interfacing.

Preshrink tailoring fabrics to prepare them for the extra steam used when fusing interfacings and to prevent shrinkage of the garment. Thorough steam-pressing preshrinks fabric effectively without sacrificing the fresh, new look. Steam-press fabric at home, or have a drycleaner do it for you. A faster and easier preshrinking method is tossing the fabric into a clothes dryer with a few damp towels. Tumble for 7 to 10 minutes at a medium-high heat. Remove immediately; lay flat to dry. Steam-press if necessary.

Sequence for Tailoring a Jacket

The first step in tailoring a jacket is to fuse interfacing onto the major sections. Make pockets next. Then sew the jacket together and make a notched or shawl collar. Finish the sleeves, including the sleeve hems, and set them in. Shape the shoulders with shoulder pads and sleeve heads. Hem the jacket, and sew the lining as the final step.

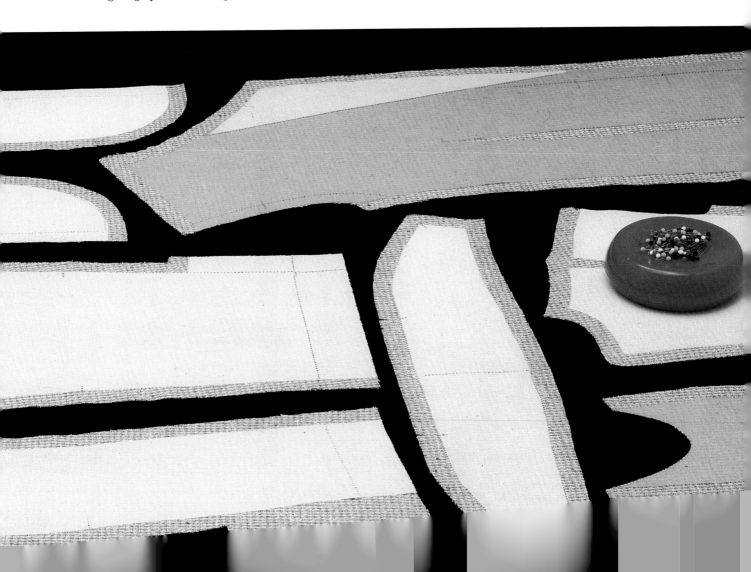

Interfacing the Jacket Sections

In one session, fuse interfacing to the jacket front, facing, back, collar, undercollar, and sleeves. Grouping the work is an efficient way to prepare major jacket sections for the steps that follow. After fusing, let the sections cool and dry on a flat surface. Wait overnight before handling medium to

heavyweight woolens and textured tweeds. Wait one or two hours for fabrics of lighter weight.

Fusible interfacing is cut on the seamline rather than the cutting line in all places except at the armhole. Stitch interfacing in the seam at the armhole to support the sleeve. For lightweight fabrics, use the cutting line at the hem instead of the hem foldline.

How to Interface a Jacket Front and Facing

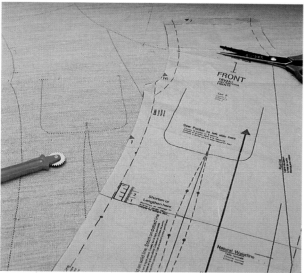

1) Trace seamlines of jacket front and side front pattern pieces on fusible weft insertion or hair canvas. Transfer all pattern markings to interfacing, including lapel roll line and dart stitching lines; it is unnecessary to mark fashion fabric.

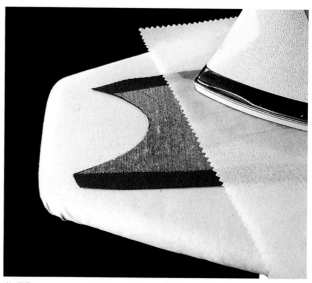

2) Cut out any darts on dart stitching lines to eliminate bulk. Dart in fashion fabric will be stitched along cut edge of interfacing.

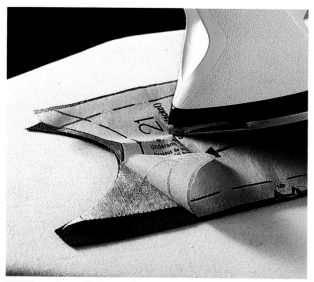

3) Place interfacing, adhesive side down, on wrong side of jacket sections. Place pattern on top to position darts and edges of interfacing at seamlines. Using dry iron, tack interfacing in place to prepare for permanent fusing. Set pattern piece aside.

4) Place press cloth on interfacing. Begin at center of section, then fuse each end. To avoid disturbing fused sections, fuse remaining areas by alternating from one side to the other. Never slide iron, which could cause layers to shift.

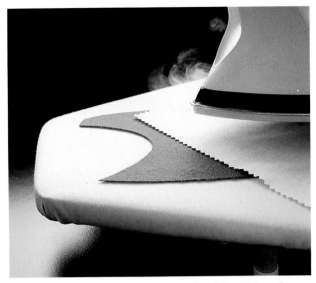

5) Turn jacket section over to right side. Using dry press cloth to protect right side of fabric, press thoroughly with steam iron. Lay flat to allow fused sections to cool and dry completely.

6) Fuse tricot knit interfacing or lightweight nonwoven interfacing to front facings after trimming seam allowances at front of facings. Interfacing extends to outer edge of facing.

Shaping Lapels

Layer. Add second layer of interfacing to lapel area only. Use weft insertion fusible interfacing, and cut it to fit from roll line to seamline of lapel; roll line should be placed on straight grain of interfacing to stabilize bias grain of jacket at roll line.

Hinge. When using fusible hair canvas, use a hinged roll line for a sharper edge on bulky or heavyweight fabrics. To make a hinge, cut interfacing on lapel roll line before fusing interfacing to jacket front.

Tape. Use narrow twill tape ¼" to ½" (6 mm to 1.3 cm) shorter than lapel roll line to contour roll line; shorten tape ½" (1.3 cm) for full bust. Place one edge of tape next to roll line; zigzag both tape edges to jacket, easing interfacing to fit tape.

Fold fused lapel on roll line, and press a crease. Do not press crease at lower 2" (5 cm) of lapel roll line; gently steam this area instead. Lay lapel over tailor's ham for pressing. Leave lapel on ham until lapel is completely cool and dry.

How to Interface a Jacket Back with Fusible Interfacing

1) Cut interfacing for jacket back from same interfacing used for jacket front, or use lighter weight interfacing. Cut and mark as for jacket front interfacing, page 154, steps 1 and 2.

2) Fuse interfacing to jacket back, using same technique as for interfacing jacket front, pages 154 and 155, steps 3 to 5. Fuse interfacing to both jacket back sections before stitching center back seam.

How to Interface a Jacket Back and Hem

1) Cut partial jacket back interfacing from lightweight woven fabric when garment does not need a fused interfacing for the entire back. Stitch darts separately in interfacing and garment. Press interfacing darts toward armhole and garment darts toward center back.

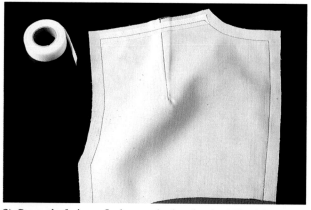

2) Staystitch interfacing to jacket back, ½" (1.3 cm) from raw edges. Include narrow twill tape stay in staystitching at shoulders to prevent bias shoulder seam from stretching.

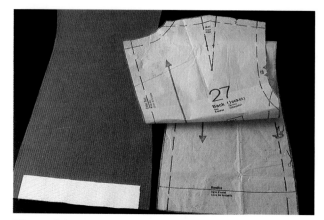

Hem without vent. Cut fusible knit or nonwoven interfacing crosswise to fit shape of hem from hem fold to raw edge; cut fusible weft insertion on the bias. Fuse as for jacket front interfacing, pages 154 and 155, steps 3 to 6.

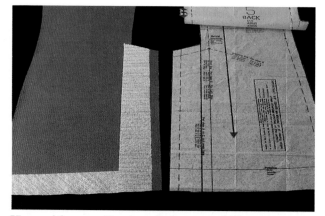

Hem with vent. Cut interfacing to stabilize vent underlap and overlap. Place straight grain of interfacing on lap foldlines.

How to Interface and Shape a Jacket Undercollar

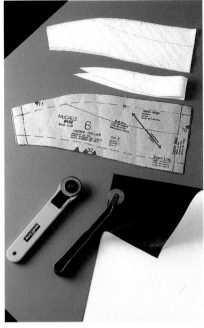

1) Cut undercollar from fusible weft insertion or hair canvas on bias grain. To cut collar stand interfacing, trace undercollar pattern from roll line to neckline seam; place center back seam on straight grain fold.

2) Transfer all pattern markings to both layers of interfacing. Fuse interfacing to undercollar; stitch center back seam. Fuse stand after stitching seam.

3) Fold undercollar on roll line, and press a sharp crease. Pin as pressed around tailor's ham, and steam. Leave in place on ham until completely cool and dry.

How to Interface Sleeves

1) Use lightweight fusible interfacing for comfort and appearance. Cut interfacing on seamlines of sleeve pattern. At sleeve hem, use cutting line instead of seamline. Transfer all pattern markings to sleeve interfacing.

2) Fuse interfacing to sleeve sections before sewing seams.

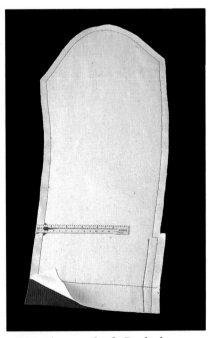

Alternative method: Back the jacket sleeves with batiste. Transfer pattern markings to batiste. Staystitch batiste to sleeve, ½" (1.3 cm) from raw edges. Machine-baste along hem and vent foldlines.

Tailoring a Notched Collar

A notched collar takes its name from the angle of the jacket collar where it joins the jacket lapels. The seams that meet there form a *notch,* or V-shaped cutout, on each side of the neckline. The seam is the *gorge* line. A crisp, flat, even notch is a hallmark of fine tailoring. The key to this detail is an artful combination of stitching and pressing, plus careful trimming of enclosed seam allowances to reduce bulk.

Several pattern pieces are needed to make a notched collar. The undercollar, interfaced and shaped, is the first section to be sewn to the jacket. Next, sew the upper collar to the facing; a portion of this facing becomes the outside of the lapels when the collar is finished. After sewing the final seam, which attaches the collar/facing section to the jacket, press and edgestitch or topstitch, using techniques on page 161 to shape and stitch the notches.

How to Sew a Notched Collar

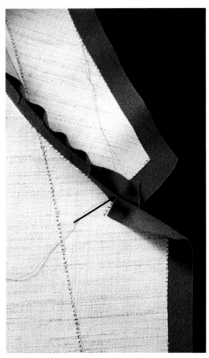

1) Staystitch jacket ½" (1.3 cm) from neckline raw edge. Clip to staystitching. This releases curved neckline seam allowance so it lies flat for easier sewing.

2) Match pattern markings to line up undercollar and jacket neckline edge. Stitch undercollar to jacket neckline up to pattern markings on lapels (arrow); clip to marking.

3) Press seam open over tailor's ham. Trim seam allowances to ¼" (6 mm) to reduce bulk.

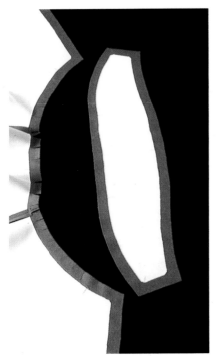

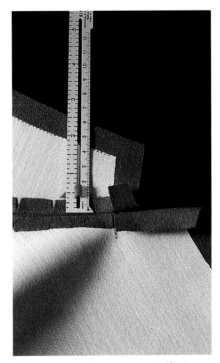

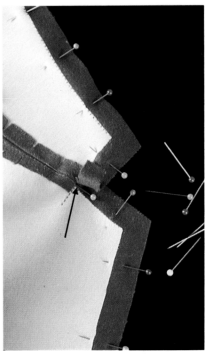

4) Staystitch facing ½" (1.3 cm) from neckline edge. Clip to staystitching. Stitch collar to facing neckline up to pattern markings on lapels; clip to marking.

5) Press seam open over tailor's ham. Trim seam allowances to ⅜" (1 cm), slightly wider than undercollar to reduce bulk.

6) Pin collar/facing section to undercollar/jacket section, pinning through seams at collar notches (arrow) to be sure the seams line up precisely.

(Continued on next page)

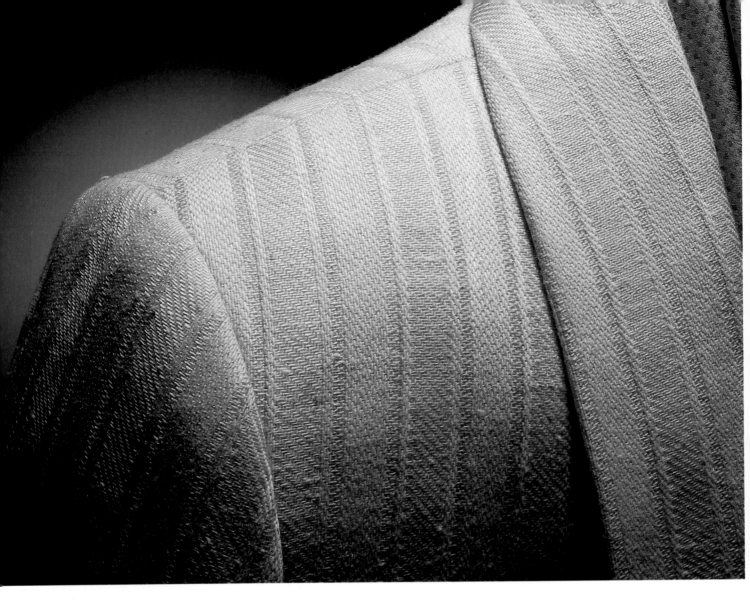

Shaping the Shoulders

Jackets need inside support for firm, smooth shape at the shoulders. In tailoring, the two important shaping aids are shoulder pads and sleeve heads.

Shoulder pads can be custom-made to fit the jacket armhole, using the jacket pattern pieces. To fit your figure, adjust the size and thickness of the shoulder pad. If one shoulder is higher than the other one, the pad can be made thicker to compensate for the difference. If your shoulders are sloping, use a thicker pad than the pattern suggests. For square shoulders, use a thinner shoulder pad.

On tailored garments such as jackets and coats, the front of the shoulder pad is wider than the back to fill in the hollow area below the shoulder and to create a smooth line. The back is narrower than the front to fit around the shoulder blades. For a full bust, make the shoulder pad slightly shorter in front. Whenever you try on the jacket or coat for fitting, slip the shoulder pads in place. The shape

and size of the shoulder pads can make a big difference in the way the shoulder and sleeve fit.

To build the pads to the desired thickness, cut graduated layers of a thin filler, such as polyester fleece or cotton/polyester quilt batting. These fillers add lift without being too soft. For the upper layer of a shoulder pad, use fusible hair canvas. The goat's hair fibers in the canvas grip the jacket fabric, helping to secure the pad to the garment. Also, the strong, resilient canvas makes the shoulder pads firm and wrinkle free.

Sleeve heads are strips of filler that support the sleeve caps on a tailored jacket to boost the caps and smooth out any wrinkles where the sleeve was eased to fit the armhole. Sleeve heads also improve the way the jacket sleeves drape. The same filler used for shoulder pads (fleece or quilt batting) can be used to make sleeve heads. Necktie interfacing cut on the true bias grain can also be used.

How to Make a Custom Shoulder Pad

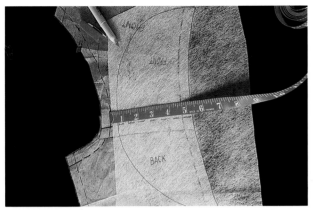

1) Lap jacket front and back patterns at shoulder seam. Trace armhole between front and back notches. End shoulder pad pattern ½" (1.3 cm) from neck seam edge, about 5" (12.5 cm) from armhole. Mark shoulder seam on pad pattern. Label armhole front and armhole back.

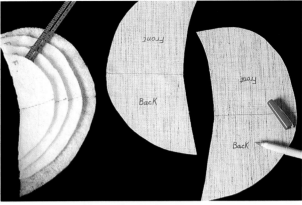

2) Cut pattern from fusible hair canvas. Transfer shoulder seam markings. Mark front and back of armhole on canvas. Also cut four layers of filler, gradually reducing layers by about ¾" (2 cm) in size, to make ½" (1.3 cm) thick pad. Adjust sizes and numbers of layers to make pad desired thickness.

3) Stitch around armhole edge and across shoulder marking with running stitches to hold filler layers together. Add more rows of stitches about 1" (2.5 cm) apart, fanning rows out from armhole edge.

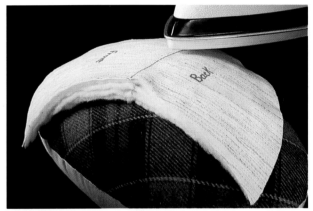

4) Fuse hair canvas to widest layer of fleece, placing pad over tailor's ham to press pad to shape of shoulder. Tack pad to jacket by hand, placing canvas layer next to jacket.

How to Make a Sleeve Head

1) Cut strip of filler 1⅞" (4.7 cm) deep and the length of jacket sleeve cap. Sleeve cap is eased area of set-in sleeve, between pattern markings. Match one long edge of sleeve head to raw edge of armhole seam allowance.

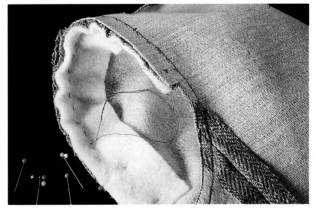

2) Stitch sleeve head to seamline around sleeve cap, using running stitches. When sleeve is turned right side out, sleeve head folds into two layers. Top layer extends beyond bottom layer to prevent ridge on outside of jacket.

Tailored Hems

Tailored hems on jackets and jacket sleeves are best put in with a catchstitch. These are small horizontal stitches made in a zigzag pattern. With a blind catchstitch, the stitches do not show from the inside or the outside of the jacket because they are worked between the hem edge and the jacket or sleeve. The hem is not held tightly against the garment; it should be sewn loosely with some play at the raw edge. A tailored hem should not show a ridge on the outside of the jacket after pressing, even if a bulky fabric is used.

Determine hem lengths on jackets and sleeves before cutting out the pattern pieces. Although the depth can vary, the standard hem on a jacket is 2" (5 cm) deep. The standard sleeve hem is 1½" (3.8 cm) deep. Hem a jacket after completing the collar or

before sewing in the lining. For easier handling, sew sleeve hems before setting the sleeves into the jacket.

Trimming. Trim seam allowances within the hem to half their width, from raw edge of hem to hemline only. This reduces bulk and prevents bumps where seams cross hemline.

Edge finishing. Lining covers the hem edge when a jacket is completed, so finishing this edge may not be necessary. Finish the edge only if the fabric ravels or stretches. Use a nonbulky zigzagged, overlocked, or stitched-and-pinked finish. If you have fused the interfacing, the edge is stabilized adequately and needs no further finishing.

Pressing. Press the hem before sewing. If a jacket hem is very curved, use a line of easestitching along the raw hem edge to help ease in fabric fullness.

How to Sew a Tailored Hem

1) Turn hem up and press at hem foldline. Open out pressed hem and trim seam allowances to half width from raw edge of hem to foldline. Baste hem in place close to fold.

2) Press, letting steam penetrate fabric to ease extra fullness in smoothly. To avoid a ridge on right side, do not press over upper edge of hem.

Catchstitch for lined garments. Work loosely over hem edge from left to right. Make stitch in hem, catching one or two threads; then make a stitch just outside hem edge, catching a single thread of garment. Alternate stitches in zigzag pattern.

Blind catchstitch for unlined garments. Finish raw edge with appropriate edge finish. Baste hem in place close to finished edge. Fold hem edge down and loosely catchstitch between hem and garment. Stitching is not visible.

How to Hem a Jacket Vent

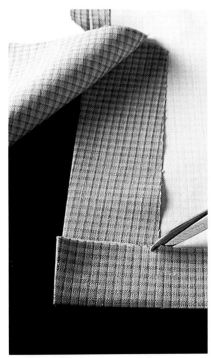

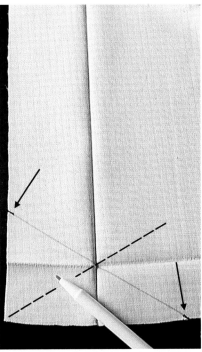

1) Arrange vent in finished position. Clip seam so underlap lies flat. From inside of jacket, vent underlap is on top with seam allowance pressed back; overlap on bottom has self-facing folded back.

2) Press hem into position on overlap. Press fold at hem and at vent self-facing to prepare for mitering. Clip vent facing and hem allowance where two edges meet.

3) Open out corner. Mark stitching line from clips (arrows) through corner point where pressed lines meet. Fold through corner (dotted line), with right sides together, matching clip marks.

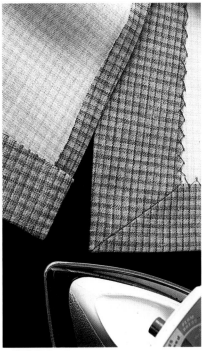

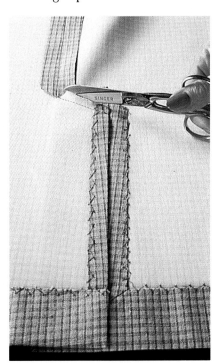

4) Stitch on marked line. Trim seam to ¼" (6 mm). Press seam open; turn to right side.

5) Fold hem to outside on vent underlap, right sides together. Stitch seam from hem fold to top of hem. Trim to ¼" (6 mm) and press open; turn right side out. Catchstitch hem and vent in place.

6) Arrange vent in finished position. Stitch across top of vent from inside through all layers. Grade seam.

Lining a Jacket

A lining is cut and sewn along the same style lines as a jacket, but has extra details designed to add comfort. A pleat in the center back of the lining allows for wearing ease across shoulders and upper back. A pleat also is formed between the lining and hems. This is a *jump hem,* and it allows you to move comfortably while wearing the jacket without straining the stitches to the breaking point.

Some jacket patterns provide separate pattern pieces for the lining, and others furnish cutting lines for the lining on the jacket pattern itself. If the same pattern is used for the sleeve and the sleeve lining, cut the sleeve lining ½" (1.3 cm) higher at the underarms. This allows the lining to rest above the jacket underarm seams and prevents binding at the armholes. When a separate sleeve lining pattern is provided, this may have been done for you. Check by placing the sleeve and sleeve lining pattern pieces with one on top of the other, matching the underarm seamlines.

Cut the jacket and sleeve lining ½" (1.3 cm) longer than the finished length after hemming. After the lining is applied to jacket and sleeve hems, the finished edges of the lining will fall just below the halfway point on the jacket and sleeve hems. If you shortened or lengthened the jacket or sleeves, make the same adjustments on the lining pattern pieces.

How to Line a Jacket

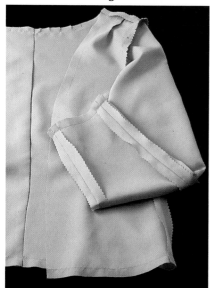

1) Stitch lining sections together, including sleeves. Reinforce armhole seam with two rows of stitching. Fold and machine-baste center back pleat at top and bottom of lining. Staystitch ½" (1.3 cm) from neckline, sleeve, and lower edges of lining; clip to staystitching at neckline.

2) Turn jacket facing out. With right sides together, stitch lining to facing. On each side in front, leave seam unstitched for twice the depth of hem. [Leave 4" (10 cm) unstitched if jacket hem is 2" (5 cm) deep.] Clip seam allowance at curves. Press seam as stitched.

3) Match seam allowances of lining and jacket at shoulder **(a)** and underarm **(b)** seams; tack in place. Turn lining right side out. Smooth sleeves into position on inside of jacket. Lightly press facing/lining seam allowances toward lining, using a press cloth.

How to Line a Jacket with a Hem Vent

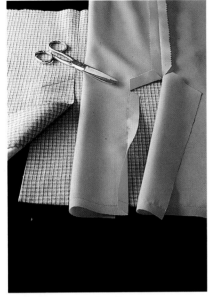

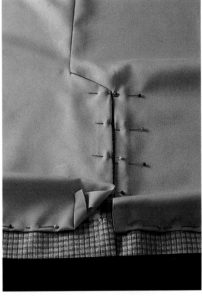

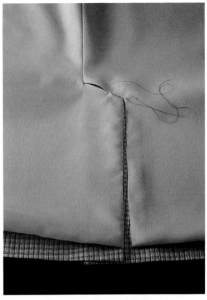

1) Stitch center back seam to marking at top of vent; clip into seam so left side of vent lies flat. Staystitch right side of vent on seamline across top and on foldline. Clip into corner to fold under raw edge on staystitching. Attach lining to jacket facing, following steps 1 to 3, opposite.

2) Match center back seams of lining and jacket at vent opening. Fold under ⅝" (1.5 cm) seam allowance across top of left vent lining and down side. Pin lining to side edges of vent on jacket; leave top edge unpinned. Match raw edge of lining to jacket hem edge, forming pleat at bottom of vent.

3) Sew lining to hems, following steps 4 and 5, below. Slipstitch vent lining along vent side edges. Stitch across top of vent lining. To prevent lining from pulling at top of vent, slipstitches should not go through to jacket fabric.

4) Trim raw edges of front facing to neaten them, if necessary. Whipstitch raw edges to hem. Turn lining under on staystitching line at lower edge. Pin so raw edge of lining is even with top edge of jacket hem.

5) Slipstitch lining fold to jacket hem, sewing through jacket hem allowance only. At front edges, fold lining hem down to form pleat, and slipstitch to facing on each side.

6) Sew lining to each sleeve hem, following steps 4 and 5. Sew jump hem around entire sleeve, even if sleeve hem has vent; sleeve vents are decorative and not meant to open and close. Press sleeve lining hem over seam roll.

Lining a Skirt

Few patterns provide linings for skirts and pants, but adding a lining makes garments hang better and is easy to accomplish. The method given here is for a slip lining, which is free-hanging and attached at the waistline; the skirt or pants and the lining are hemmed separately. An advantage of a slip lining is that the garment is easy to press because you can lift the whole lining out.

Unlike jacket and coat linings, skirt and pants linings are usually worn next to your skin. In warm or humid climates, fabrics made from rayon, cotton, or cotton blends may feel more comfortable than those made from polyester and similar synthetic fibers.

Tips for Lining Skirts & Pants

Cut the lining from the major front and back pattern pieces. Omit small pattern pieces such as the waistband, facings, and pockets. For a gathered skirt in a lightweight fabric, the skirt and lining may be treated as one layer of fabric. For a heavier weight gathered skirt, cut the lining from a pattern for a simple A-line skirt, or make small pleats or released tucks instead of gathers in the lining. Or pleat out the fullness from the tissue pattern before cutting the lining, allowing some ease for movement. Any of these methods eliminates bulk at the waistline.

Omit any seam extensions for in-seam pockets when you cut out a lining. Straighten the cutting lines on the front and back pattern pieces to change the pocket openings to plain seams. If the garment has slanted pockets, lap the front pattern pieces to cut the lining without pockets.

Shorten the pattern pieces so the lining will be 1" (2.5 cm) shorter than the skirt or pants after hemming. If you plan to make a 1" (2.5 cm) hem in the lining, cut the lower edge of the lining at the hemline of the skirt or pants.

Transfer pattern markings at the zipper opening and the waist to the lining sections after cutting. These markings will help you position the lining inside the skirt or pants.

Assemble the skirt or pants, including the zipper and pockets, before attaching the lining. All stitching on the garment should be completed except for the waistband and the hem. Press seams open. Unless the fabric ravels easily, it is not necessary to finish the seams.

How to Line a Skirt

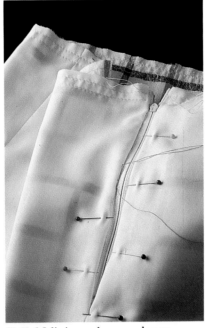

1) Stitch lining seams, leaving seam open at zipper; press open. Slip lining over skirt, wrong sides together, matching seams. Machine-baste together on waist seamline, folding lining under at zipper edge.

2) Fold lining edges under to expose zipper coil and allow easy opening and closing of zipper. Pin and slipstitch lining to zipper tape.

3) Apply waistband. Hem lining so it is 1" (2.5 cm) shorter than skirt. Sew lining hem by hand or machine, as desired.

Darts, Ease, or Pleats in Linings

Darts. Pin tucks in the skirt or pants lining, matching the dart markings. Darts in skirt or pants are pressed toward center front and back. Press tucks in lining in opposite direction to reduce bulk.

Eased or slightly gathered area. Slip lining over skirt, wrong sides together. Machine-baste at waistline seam. Gather lining and skirt as if they were one layer of fabric, pulling up ease to fit waistband.

Pleat-front skirts or pants. Machine-baste pleats separately in lining and garment. Press lining pleats flat in opposite direction of skirt pleats. Slip lining over skirt, wrong sides together. Machine-baste at waistline.

Sewing Activewear

Elasticized Waistbands

Elasticized waistbands are comfortable to wear and easy to sew. They complement the stretch of knit fabrics. Some elasticized waistbands are "cut on," which means the waistbands are cut as an extension of the garment at the waistline edge, while others are a separate waistband piece. Choose an application technique according to the fabric, the garment style, and the type of elastic you are using.

Two techniques for cut-on waistbands are included: one with a casing and one with topstitching. Both are appropriate for garments made from lightweight to mediumweight fabrics. Cut-on waistbands with casings (a) give a casual look. Firm braided or woven elastics are well suited for this technique. Because the elastic is not caught in the waistline seam, it can easily be adjusted for a better fit, if necessary. Cut-on waistbands with topstitching (b) give a variety of looks, depending on the type of topstitching. Use an elastic with good stretch and recovery qualities so the elastic will stretch to the circumference of the garment opening, yet retain its fit. Drawstring elastic (c) may be used for this method.

Two additional techniques are included for waistbands that use a separate waistband piece: smooth waistbands and shirred waistbands. When sewing garments from lightweight or mediumweight knits, you may cut the waistband from self-fabric. When sewing bulky fabrics, such as sweatshirt fleece, choose matching ribbing for the waistband or, for a more decorative effect, a contrasting fabric.

Smooth separate waistbands (d) give the smooth appearance of a traditional waistband when the garment is worn. This waistband style is suitable for a slim-fitting garment made from lightweight or mediumweight knit fabric with moderate stretch. Use a firm 1" or 1¼" (2.5 or 3.2 cm) elastic.

Shirred separate waistbands (e) complement fuller garment styles, such as full skirts, and are especially attractive when used with wider elastics. Shirred waistbands may be topstitched or not, depending on the look you prefer. Firm elastic is recommended for this type of waistband.

In general, cut elastics 2" to 3" (5 to 7.5 cm) less than your waist measurement. Cut soft, lightweight elastics, such as knit elastics, 3" to 5" (7.5 to 12.5 cm) less than your waist measurement. Cut very firm elastics, such as nonroll waistband elastic, equal to, or 1" (2.5 cm) less than, your waist measurement. Mark the elastic, and pin it around your waistline before cutting it. Check to see that the elastic fits comfortably around your waist and pulls over your hips easily.

Multiple rows of topstitching can cause elastic to lose some of its recovery. If you are using a method that calls for topstitching, you may want to cut the elastic up to 1" (2.5 cm) shorter than the guidelines, to ensure a snug fit.

Tips for Sewing Elasticized Waistbands

Preshrink elastics for casing applications before measuring. Elastics that will be stitched on do not require preshrinking.

Use longer stitches, about 8 to 9 stitches per inch (2.5 cm), when stitching through the elastic; the stitches will appear shorter when elastic is relaxed. A stitch length that is too short weakens and stretches out the elastic.

Steam the finished waistband after construction, holding the iron above the fabric, to help the elastic return to its original length.

Two Ways to Join the Ends of the Elastic

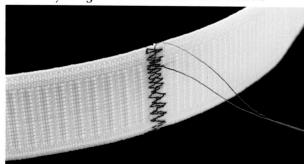

Butted method. Butt ends of elastic. Stitch back and forth, using 3-step zigzag stitch or wide zigzag stitch, catching both ends of elastic in stitching. This method is recommended for firm elastics.

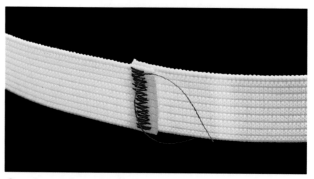

Overlapped method. Overlap ends of elastic ½" (1.3 cm). Stitch back and forth through both layers, using wide zigzag stitch or 3-step zigzag stitch. Use for soft elastics, such as knitted elastic.

How to Sew a Cut-on Waistband with a Casing

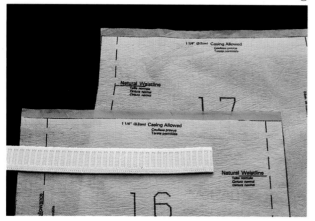

1) Extend garment pattern pieces above waistline twice the width of the elastic plus ⅝" (1.5 cm). Cut out garment sections, and stitch together.

2) Overlock raw edge at waist, if desired. Fold edge of fabric to wrong side, an amount equal to width of elastic plus ½" (1.3 cm). Edgestitch close to fold.

3) Join ends of elastic (page 170). Position elastic within folded casing area. Stitch next to elastic, using straight stitch and zipper foot; do not catch elastic in stitching. Shift fabric around elastic as necessary while stitching.

4) Stretch waistband to distribute fabric evenly. From right side of garment, stitch in the ditch through all waistband layers, at center front, center back, and side seams, to secure elastic.

Alternate method. 1) Follow steps 1 and 2, above. Mark elastic to desired length; do not cut. Position elastic within folded casing area. Stitch next to elastic, using straight stitch and zipper foot, leaving 2" (5 cm) unstitched; do not catch elastic in stitching.

2) Pull elastic through to marking; secure, using safety pin. Try on garment to check fit; adjust elastic, if necessary. Cut and join ends of elastic (page 170). Complete waistband stitching. Stitch in the ditch as in step 4, above.

How to Sew a Cut-on Waistband with Topstitching

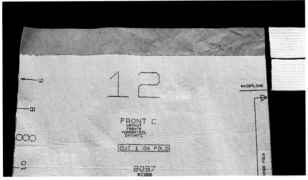

1) Extend garment pattern pieces above waistline twice the width of the elastic. Cut out garment sections, and stitch together. Join ends of elastic (page 170).

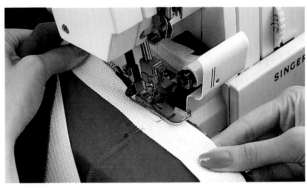

2) Divide elastic and garment edge into fourths; pin-mark. Pin elastic to wrong side of garment, with edges even, matching pin marks; overlock or zigzag, stretching elastic to fit between pins. If using overlock machine, guide work carefully or disengage knives to avoid cutting elastic.

3) Fold elastic to wrong side of garment so fabric encases elastic. From right side of garment, stitch in the ditch through all waistband layers, at center front, center back, and side seams, to secure elastic.

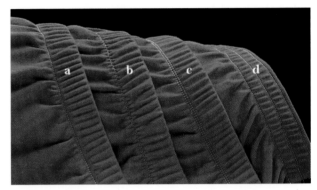

4) Topstitch through all layers of waistband, stretching elastic as you sew. Straight-stitch or narrow zigzag close to lower edge of casing, using long stitches **(a)**; zigzag close to lower edge, using medium-to-wide stitches **(b)**; double-needle topstitch close to lower edge **(c)**; or stitch three or more evenly spaced rows of straight stitching or double-needle stitching **(d)**.

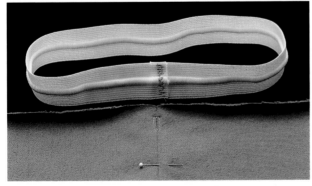

Drawstring-elastic method. 1) Extend pattern pieces as in step 1, above. Join ends of drawstring elastic, using overlapped method (page 170). Stitch garment sections together, leaving ½" (1.3 cm) opening in center front seam in drawstring area; topstitch around opening to secure.

2) Follow step 2, above. Stitch again at lower edge of elastic, using zigzag stitch. Fold elastic to wrong side of garment so fabric encases elastic. Stitch ¼" (6 mm) from upper and lower edges of elastic, through all layers, using straight stitch and stretching elastic to fit. Pull drawstring through center front opening. Cut drawstring, and knot ends.

How to Sew a Smooth Separate Waistband

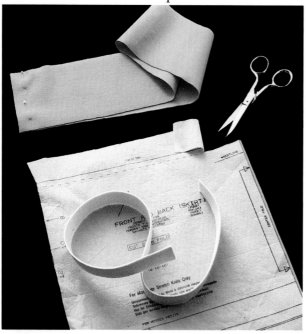

1) Mark cutting line on garment section pattern pieces ⅝" (1.5 cm) above waistline. Cut waistband on crosswise grain, twice the width of elastic plus 1¼" (3.2 cm); length of waistband is equal to your waist measurement plus 3¼" (8.2 cm). Pin ends of waistband together with ⅝" (1.5 cm) seam allowances; check fit over hips.

2) Join ends of waistband; press seam open. Divide waistband and garment edge into fourths; pin-mark. Pin waistband to right side of garment, with raw edges even, matching pin marks. Stitch ⅝" (1.5 cm) seam, using straight stitch or narrow zigzag stitch; if using straight stitch, stretch fabric as you sew.

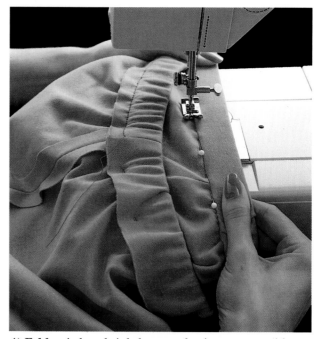

3) Join ends of elastic (page 170). Divide elastic and garment edge into fourths; pin-mark. Place elastic on seam allowance of waistband; pin in place, with lower edge of elastic just above seamline. With elastic on top, stitch through both seam allowances, using wide zigzag or multiple zigzag stitch; stretch elastic to fit between pins. Trim seam allowances.

4) Fold waistband tightly over elastic to wrong side of garment; pin. Stitch in the ditch along seamline from right side of garment, stretching elastic; catch waistband in stitching on wrong side of garment, but do not catch elastic. Trim waistband seam allowance to ¼" (6 mm) from stitching.

How to Sew a Shirred Separate Waistband

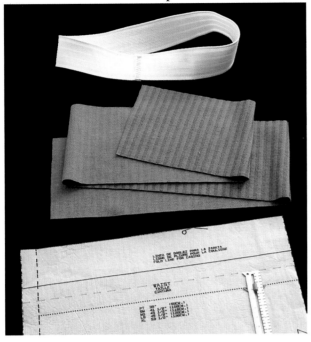

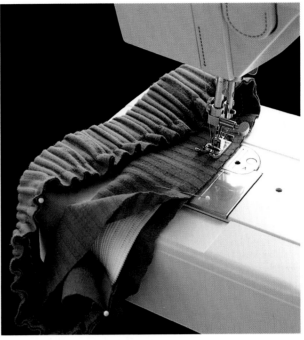

1) Mark cutting line on garment section pattern pieces ⅝" (1.5 cm) above waistline. Cut waistband on crosswise grain, twice the width of elastic plus 1¼" (3.2 cm); length of waistband is equal to your hip measurement plus 1¼" (3.2 cm). Join ends of elastic (page 170).

2) Join ends of waistband in ⅝" (1.5 cm) seam; press seam open. Divide the waistband and garment edges into fourths; pin-mark. Fold the waistband in half lengthwise, wrong sides together, encasing elastic. Baste ½" (1.3 cm) from raw edges, avoiding pins; shift fabric around elastic as necessary.

3) Pin waistband to right side of garment, matching pin marks; if garment is very full, gather waistline edge before attaching waistband. Stitch just inside basting stitches, stretching waistband to fit garment between pins. Trim seam allowances to ¼" (6 mm). Overlock raw edges, if desired.

4) Stretch waistband to distribute fabric evenly. From right side of garment, stitch perpendicular to the waistline through all waistband layers, at the center back and side seams, to secure the elastic. If desired, topstitch through all layers as on page 173, step 4.

Ribbed Edges

The most common use for ribbing is to finish the edges of knit sportswear garments. Ribbing, which has great crosswise stretch and recovery, enables garment openings to stretch easily when you are getting dressed and return to a neat, comfortable fit during wear. Ribbing is available as yardage and as prefinished ribbed bands.

Ribbing yardage ranges in width from 28" to 60" (71 to 152.5 cm), or 14" to 30" (35.5 to 76 cm) tubular, and is available in several weights. To use ribbing yardage, cut a crosswise strip of the fabric, fold it in half lengthwise, and apply it so the fold becomes the finished edge.

Prefinished ribbed bands have one finished edge and are applied as a single layer. They are available in various widths and lengths. They also come in different weights and styles.

Ribbing can be used as an edge finish for several styles of necklines, including turtleneck, mock turtleneck, crewneck, and scoop-neck. It is also used on sleeves, lower edges of T-shirts and sweatshirts, and waistlines of pants and skirts. The cut width and cut length of the ribbing varies, depending on where it will be used and the style you want.

If you use ribbing yardage, the cut width of the ribbing is equal to twice the desired finished width plus ½" (1.3 cm) for seam allowances. If you use prefinished ribbed bands, the cut width is equal to the desired finished width plus one ¼" (6 mm) seam allowance.

Many patterns designed for knits indicate what length to cut the ribbing, or they provide a pattern piece to be used as a guide for the ribbing pieces. The cut length for ribbing can also be determined by measuring the garment opening at the seamline, as shown below.

For straight, close-fitting edges, the cut length can be determined by pin-fitting the ribbing on the body. On any straight edges that do not require a close fit, such as the lower edge of a skirt, cut the ribbing just slightly shorter than the garment edge.

To sew ribbed edges, you may use either the flat or the in-the-round method of construction. Flat construction is the fastest method; however, the seams may be noticeable at the edges of the ribbing. For a better-quality finish, the in-the-round method is usually preferred. With this method, the ribbing seams are enclosed for a neater appearance.

If matching ribbing is not available, self-fabric, cut on the crosswise grain, can be substituted for ribbing yardage. Use a knit fabric that stretches at least 50 percent crosswise; for example, 10" (25.5 cm) of knit must stretch to at least 15" (38 cm).

How to Determine the Cut Length

Measure seamline of garment opening by standing tape measure on edge. For necklines, cut ribbing as on page 177. For other garment openings, ribbing is usually cut two-thirds of the measurement plus ½" (1.3 cm). If self-fabric is substituted for ribbing, cut it three-fourths of the measurement plus ½" (1.3 cm).

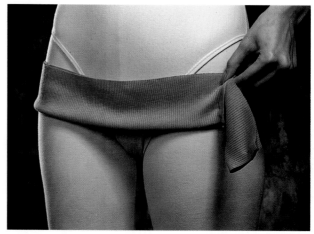

Pin-fit ribbing or self-fabric around body for straight, close-fitting edges, such as at hiplines, wrists, and ankles. Fold ribbing crosswise for double thickness, and pin ribbing so it lies flat, without gaping; do not distort the ribs. Add ½" (1.3 cm) for seam allowances.

Types of Ribbed Necklines

Crewneck garments (**a**) usually have ribbing with a finished width of 1" to 1¼" (2.5 to 3.2 cm); the neckline seam falls ¾" (2 cm) below the natural neckline. Cut the ribbing two-thirds of the neckline measurement plus ½" (1.3 cm).

Turtleneck garments (**b**) have ribbing with a finished width of 4" to 6" (10 to 15 cm). The neckline seam falls at the natural neckline. Cut the ribbing the length of the neckline measurement plus ½" (1.3 cm).

Mock turtleneck garments (**c**) have ribbing with a finished width of 2" to 2¼" (5 to 6 cm). The neckline seam falls ½" (1.3 cm) below the natural neckline. Cut the ribbing three-fourths of the neckline measurement plus ½" (1.3 cm).

Scoop-neck garments (**d**) have rounded necklines, with the edge of the ribbing falling lower than the natural neckline in the front and, sometimes, in the back. Cut the ribbing two-thirds of the neckline measurement plus ½" (1.3 cm). The finished width of the ribbing varies from ¾" to 1" (2 to 2.5 cm).

Self-fabric may be used instead of ribbing. For turtlenecks, cut the self-fabric the length of the neckline measurement plus ½" (1.3 cm); for crew necks, mock turtlenecks, and scoop necks, cut it three-fourths of the neckline plus ½" (1.3 cm).

How to Sew Ribbed Edges (flat method)

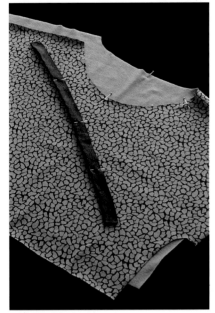

1) Cut garment pieces, allowing ¼" (6 mm) seam allowances at garment openings. Leave one seam unstitched. If using ribbing yardage, fold ribbing in half lengthwise, wrong sides together. Divide ribbing and garment opening into fourths; pin-mark.

2) Pin ribbing to right side of garment, matching pin marks. With ribbing on top, stitch ¼" (6 mm) seam, using narrow zigzag or overlock stitch; stretch ribbing to fit garment opening as you sew. Lightly press seam toward garment.

3) Stitch remaining garment seam, matching ribbing seam and ends carefully. If desired, topstitch close to seamline as in step 3, below.

How to Sew Ribbed Edges (in-the-round method)

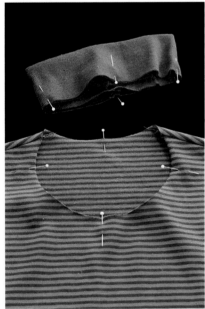

1) Join ends of ribbing in ¼" (6 mm) seam. If using ribbing yardage, fold ribbing in half lengthwise, wrong sides together. Divide ribbing and garment opening into fourths; pin-mark.

2) Pin ribbing to right side of garment, matching pin marks. With ribbing on top, stitch ¼" (6 mm) seam, using narrow zigzag or overlock stitch; stretch ribbing to fit garment opening as you sew. Lightly press seam toward garment.

3) Topstitch close to seamline, if desired, stitching through garment and seam allowances, using single or double needle. If single needle is used, stretch fabric slightly as you sew.

How to Apply Lapped Ribbing to a V-Neckline

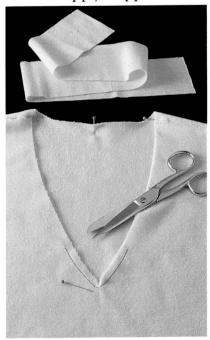

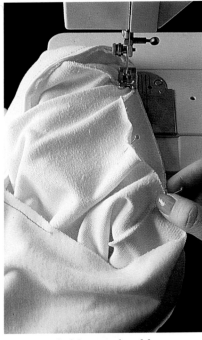

1) Cut ribbing slightly longer than the cut edge of neckline. With short stitches, staystitch on the seamline 2" (5 cm) on either side of the V. Clip carefully to the V. Fold ribbing in half lengthwise.

2) Pin ribbing to right-hand side of neckline in ¼" (6 mm) seam; leave 1" (2.5 cm) for lapping. With garment on top, begin stitching at center front. Stretch ribbing slightly as you sew.

3) Stop stitching at shoulder seam. Measure back neckline between shoulder seams. Mark ribbing with pin at point equal to two-thirds the measured length. Match pin mark to shoulder seam.

4) Stitch ribbing to garment across back neckline and down left-hand side of neckline, stretching ribbing slightly. Stop stitching before reaching point of V, leaving an opening equal to width of ribbing. Remove garment from machine.

5) Turn ribbing seam to inside. Lay garment out flat. Tuck the extensions inside the seam opening with right-hand side overlapping left. Pin ribbing at center front in lapped position.

6) Fold front of garment out of the way. From wrong side, stitch opening closed; pivot at point of V, and stitch free end of ribbing to right-hand seam allowance. Trim extensions close to stitches.

Variations for Ribbed Edges

Ribbed edges can be varied in a number of ways to add detailing and interest to garments. Although these techniques give a variety of looks, they all use basic in-the-round construction.

Double ribbing (a), used at the neckline and the lower edges of sleeves, gives the look of two shirts in one. For this effect, two pieces of ribbing are cut to different widths and applied in one step to the garment opening.

A lapped neckline (b) features ribbing overlapped at the center. For women's and girls' garments, the right

end of the ribbing laps over the left; for men's and boys' garments, the left end laps over the right.

A contrasting self-fabric insert (c) can accent the center front of a ribbed neckline or waistline. For added detailing, decorative topstitching can be added to the insert.

Striped ribbing (d) is made by stitching two or three pieces of ribbing together for a multicolor trim. This ribbed trim is especially suitable for mock turtlenecks and the lower edges of sleeves and T-shirts.

How to Apply Double Ribbing

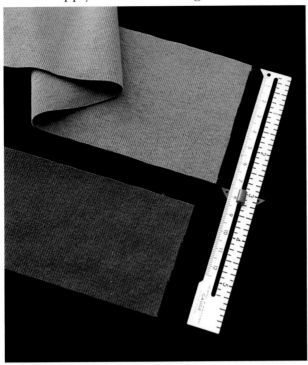

1) Cut two pieces of ribbing to length determined for garment opening (page 177). Cut one ribbing piece 3" (7.5 cm) wide for a finished width of 1¼" (3.2 cm); cut the other piece 2½" (6.5 cm) wide for a finished width of 1" (2.5 cm).

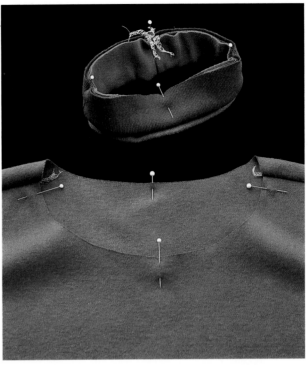

2) Stitch ends of each ribbing piece in ¼" (6 mm) seam. Fold each piece in half lengthwise, wrong sides together. Pin narrow ribbing over wide ribbing, with raw edges even and seams matching. Divide ribbing and garment opening into fourths; pin-mark.

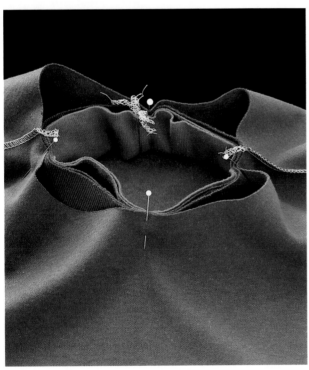

3) Pin double ribbing to garment, matching pin marks, with right sides together, raw edges even, and ribbing seams at center back of neckline or underarm seam of sleeve. Narrow ribbing will be next to garment.

4) Stitch neckline in ¼" (6 mm) seam, with ribbing on top, using overlock stitch or narrow zigzag; stretch ribbing to fit garment opening as you sew. Lightly press seam toward garment. Edgestitch, using single, double, or triple needle, if desired.

How to Apply Lapped Ribbing

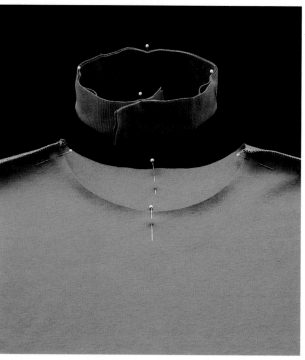

1) Cut ribbing to desired cut width by 2" (5 cm) longer than length determined for garment opening (page 177). Fold in half lengthwise. Measure 1" (2.5 cm) from each end; pin-mark.

2) Lap ends, matching pin marks; this is center front. Divide ribbing into fourths; repeat for garment opening, with one pin at center front.

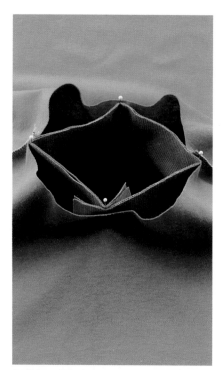

3) Pin ribbing to right side of garment, matching pin marks and center fronts, with raw edges even. (Woman's garment is shown.)

4) Curve ends of ribbing into seam allowance, so folded ends overlap and taper to raw edges.

5) Release center pin so garment neckline relaxes to natural curve. Repin at center front. Trim excess fabric. Stitch as on page 181, step 4.

How to Apply Ribbing with a Self-fabric Insert

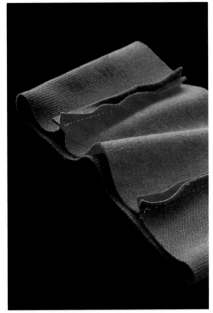

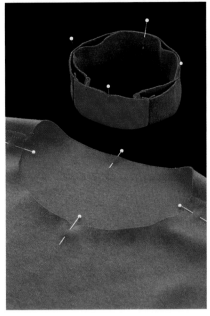

1) Cut ribbing to desired cut width by 3" (7.5 cm) shorter than length determined for garment opening (page 177). Cut insert fabric to same width as ribbing by 3½" (9 cm) long. Stitch insert to ribbing at short ends in ¼" (6 mm) seams, forming a circle.

2) Fold ribbing/insert in half lengthwise, wrong sides together. Divide ribbing/insert into fourths; pin-mark, with one pin marking center front at middle of insert. Divide garment opening into fourths; pin-mark, with one pin at center front.

3) Pin ribbing/insert to garment, with right sides together and raw edges even; match center fronts and pin marks. Stitch as on page 181, step 4. Topstitch through all layers of insert, if desired.

How to Apply Striped Ribbing

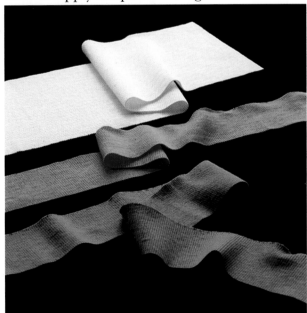

1) Cut strips to length determined for garment opening (page 177). The cut width of each strip is desired finished width of strip plus ½" (1.3 cm) for seam allowances; also add finished width of pieced strip to color at outer edge to allow for back of ribbing. Join long ends of strips, right sides together, in ¼" (6 mm) seams; lightly press to one side.

2) Join short ends in ¼" (6 mm) seam; lightly press. Fold in half lengthwise, wrong sides together. Divide ribbing and garment opening into fourths; pin-mark. Pin ribbing to garment, matching pin marks, with right sides together, raw edges even, and ribbing seam at center back of neckline or underarm seam of sleeve. Stitch as on page 181, step 4.

Swimsuits & Leotards

Patterns for swimsuits and leotards are usually closely fitted for comfort and easy motion. A wide range of pattern styles is available. Styles with princess seams are slenderizing. So are patterns with a center panel of a contrasting color; to minimize hips, use a dark color for the side panels. High-cut leg openings on swimsuits and leotards give the appearance of longer legs and a slimmer torso. For a full-busted figure, choose a pattern with a bustline shaped by darts or seams. To fill out a slender figure, use a pattern with shirring, draping, or ruffles. Or choose a simple pattern style and a splashy printed fabric to enhance a slender figure.

By sewing your own swimsuits and leotards, you can make garments that meet your needs. Add a full-front lining to a swimsuit, if desired; this is especially important for light-colored and light-weight fabrics. Or you may line just the crotch area or add a bandeau lining in the bust area. Purchased bra cups may be sewn into the bandeau if firmer support is desired.

Two-way stretch fabric stretches to fit the contours of many different figure types. Select the pattern according to the bust measurement to avoid extensive fitting adjustments at the bustline. If you require different pattern sizes for the hips and the bust, choose a multisize pattern, following the cutting lines for the appropriate sizes and blending the lines in the waistline area.

Adjusting the Pattern

For one-piece swimsuits and leotards, measure your torso length as shown, below, and compare it to the torso lengths given in the chart at right; do not measure the pattern pieces for this comparison, because they will measure less than the actual body measurement. If your torso measurement falls within the range given for your bust size, no pattern adjustment is needed.

If your torso measurement is different from the length given in the chart, first adjust the pattern front an amount equal to one-fourth the difference, then adjust the pattern back the same amount. The total pattern adjustment is only one-half the difference between your torso measurement and the chart; the two-way stretch fabric will be stretched when it is worn, automatically giving you the rest of the length needed. If each pattern piece has two adjustment lines, divide the total amount of adjustment needed equally among all four lines.

Linings can limit the stretch of the swimsuit fabric, so if you are going to line the front of a swimsuit, add an extra ½" (1.3 cm) of length to the front and back pattern pieces.

Comparison of Bust Size and Torso Length

Bust size	Torso length
30" (76 cm)	52" to 54" (132 to 137 cm)
32" (81.5 cm)	53" to 55" (134.5 to 139.5 cm)
34" (86.5 cm)	54" to 56" (137 to 142 cm)
36" (91.5 cm)	55" to 57" (139.5 to 145 cm)
38" (96.5 cm)	56" to 58" (142 to 147 cm)
40" (102 cm)	57" to 59" (145 to 150 cm)
42" (107 cm)	58" to 60" (147 to 152.5 cm)
44" (112 cm)	59" to 61" (150 to 155 cm)

How to Adjust the Torso Length on the Pattern

1) Measure from indentation at breast bone in front; bring tape measure between your legs to prominent bone at back of neck. Keep the tape measure snug to duplicate fit of finished garment. It is helpful to have someone help you take this measurement.

2) Determine the difference between your torso measurement and the torso length given in the chart, above, that corresponds to your bust size. The pattern needs to be adjusted an amount equal to one-half the difference; distribute this amount equally among the pattern adjustment lines.

3) Adjust the pattern, adding or subtracting length to the pattern by spreading or overlapping front and back pattern pieces on the adjustment lines. In the example shown here, front and back pieces are lengthened ¼" (6 mm) on each adjustment line for a total adjustment of 1" (2.5 cm).

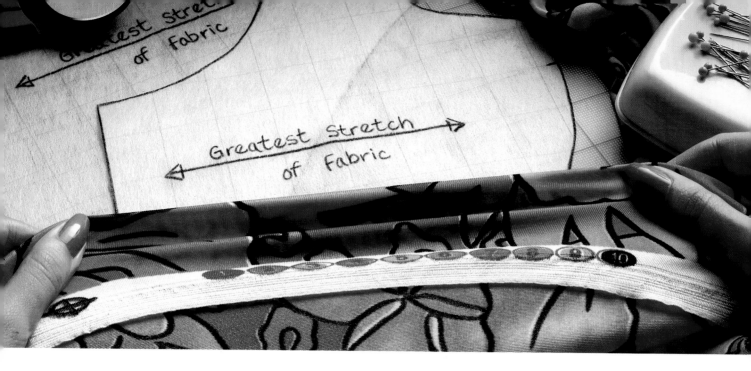

Sewing Swimsuits & Leotards

Before laying out a swimsuit or leotard pattern, determine which direction of the fabric has the greater amount of stretch. Nylon/spandex knits usually stretch more in the lengthwise direction; cotton/spandex, in the crosswise. For a comfortable fit, lay out the pattern on the fabric so the greater amount of stretch will encircle the body.

Swimsuits and leotards are fast and easy to sew. Most styles have only a few seams and edge finishes. Stitch the side seams and crotch seam first; then try on the garment and adjust the fit as needed.

If a one-piece swimsuit or leotard is too long in the torso, shorten it at the shoulder seams; if this raises the neckline, the neck opening can be trimmed as necessary. If the armholes are too small, causing the garment to bind under the arms, enlarge them by trimming the openings. Leg openings should fit smoothly; if they are too large, take in the side seams at the lower edge, tapering the seams gradually. Stitch the shoulder seams after the fitting, and apply the elastic (pages 188 and 189).

How to Sew a Basic One-piece Swimsuit or Leotard

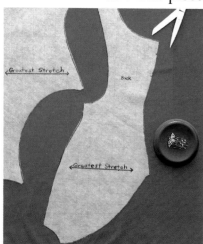

1) **Determine** whether the fabric stretches more on lengthwise or crosswise grain. Lay out pattern on fabric so the greater amount of stretch will encircle the body.

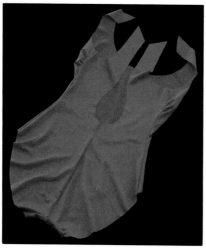

2) **Stitch** center back seam; then stitch crotch seam, applying crotch lining if desired. Stitch side seams. Check garment for fit, opposite.

3) **Apply** full-front lining, if desired. Stitch shoulder seams. Apply elastic to garment openings (pages 188 and 189).

How to Sew a Basic Two-piece Swimsuit

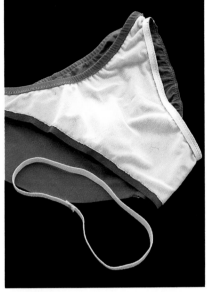

1) Lay out the pattern as in step 1, opposite. Stitch seams, and machine-baste lining to wrong side of swimsuit top, basting a distance equal to width of elastic from raw edges; trim lining close to the stitching. Center boning, if used, on side seam allowance, positioned so the ends will curve away from body. Stitch over previous stitches along inner edge of boning.

2) Apply elastic to edges of swimsuit top (pages 188 and 189). Make straps; stitch to garment, using narrow zigzag stitch. Pull right end through swimsuit hook, folding ½" (1.3 cm) to wrong side; zigzag across end. Fold left end ½" (1.3 cm) to wrong side; zigzag in place. Garment details, such as center front detail, are sewn following pattern.

3) Stitch center back seam of the swimsuit bottom. Apply full-front lining, if desired. Apply elastic to upper edge and leg openings of swimsuit bottom (pages 188 and 189).

Adjusting for a Good Fit

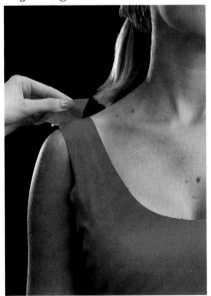

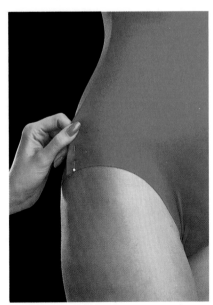

1) Adjust shoulder seams for snug fit if garment is too long in torso. Adjust neck opening if shoulder adjustment raised the neckline, marking adjustment with chalk, then trimming on marked lines.

2) Adjust armhole openings if the garment binds under the arms, marking the adjustment with chalk, then trimming away excess fabric.

3) Adjust side seams, if necessary, so leg openings fit snugly before the elastic is applied.

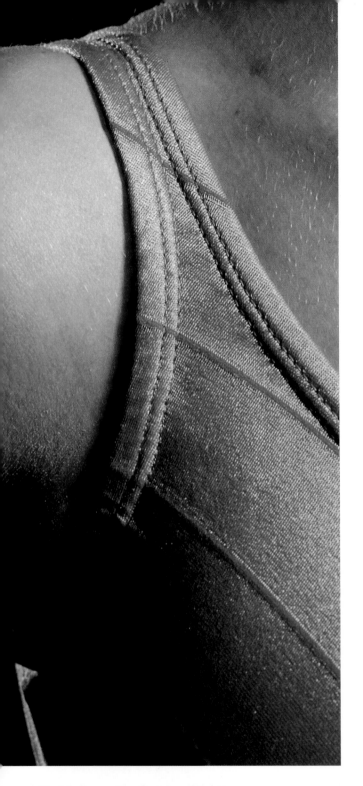

Elasticized Edges

To stabilize edges and to ensure a snug fit on swimsuits and leotards, use elastic at necklines, armholes, waistlines, and leg openings. Elasticized edges also allow you to slip the garment on and off easily. Although elasticized edges do self-adjust to your figure, do not depend on them to solve fitting problems.

If you have not adjusted the neckline, armhole, or leg openings, cut the elastic to the lengths specified by the pattern. If you have changed the size of the openings, follow the guidelines given in the chart below. Most patterns print the cutting information for the elastic on the guide sheet or provide a cutting guide on the pattern tissue. If using a pattern with several views, be sure to cut the elastic for the style you have chosen; for example, a high-cut leg opening requires longer elastic than a standard leg opening.

Cotton braided swimwear elastic or transparent elastic may be used. Both types of elastic, with excellent stretch and recovery, are chlorine-resistant and salt-resistant. Most patterns call for ⅜" (1 cm) elastic for adults' swimwear and ¼" (6 mm) elastic for children's.

Guidelines for Cutting Elastic

Type of Edge	Length to Cut Elastic
Leg opening	Measurement of leg opening minus 2" (5 cm) for adult's garment or minus 1" (2.5 cm) for child's.
Upper edge of two-piece swimsuit bottom	Measurement of upper edge minus 2" to 3" (5 to 7.5 cm), depending on desired fit. Check to see that elastic fits comfortably over hips.
Armhole	Measurement of armhole.
Neckline	Measurement of neckline. Or for a snug fit on V-necked, low, or scoop necklines, use elastic 1" to 3" (2.5 to 7.5 cm) shorter than neckline.

How to Apply Elastic

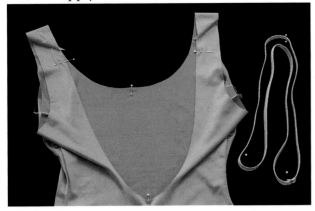

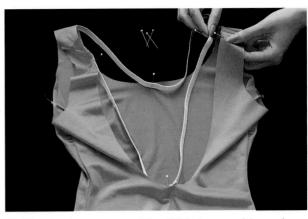

Neckline or waistline openings. 1) Join ends of elastic, using overlapped method (page 170). Divide elastic into fourths; pin-mark, with one pin next to joined ends of elastic. Divide garment opening into fourths; pin-mark. Seams may not be halfway between center front and center back.

2) Pin elastic to wrong side of fabric, matching edges and pin marks. Place joined ends at center back of neckline or waistline.

3) Stitch outer edge of elastic to the garment, using overlock or narrow zigzag stitch; stretch elastic to fit between pins. If using overlock machine, guide work carefully or disengage knives to avoid cutting elastic.

4) Fold elastic toward inside of garment, encasing it in garment fabric.

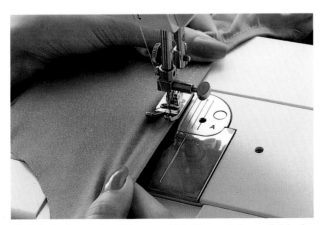

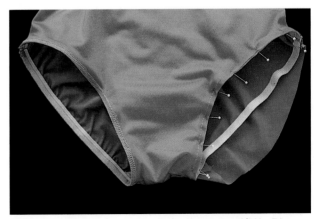

5) Stitch through all layers, ¼" (6 mm) from folded edge, using long straight stitches or narrow zigzag stitches, stretching as you sew. Or topstitch, using double needle.

Leg openings. Join ends of elastic (page 170). Pin elastic to leg opening, with joined ends at side seam, keeping elastic relaxed on garment front; remaining elastic will stretch to fit the back of leg opening. Follow steps 3 to 5, stretching elastic as you sew.

Sewing for Children

Sewing children's clothes can be quite economical and need not be time-consuming. Because children's garments require less fabric than garments for adults, the fabric cost is usually minimal. You may be able to use fabric from other sewing projects to construct a garment, or part of a garment, for a young child.

Most children's clothing designs follow simple lines, have few pieces, and are easy to sew. They are a good starting point for a beginning sewer or for a sewer whose skills need updating.

Planning for Safety

Build safety into children's garments. Avoid loose strings or excess fabric that may get tangled, especially for infants. Beware of long skirts or gowns that may cause a child to trip, or very full sleeves that may catch on objects. Limit tie belts and drawstrings to short lengths, and securely fasten buttons and trims. Use fire-retardant fabrics for sleepwear.

Customizing Clothes for Children

Creative touches can make a garment special to a child. Use a child's crayon drawing as a guide to colors and shapes for a machine-embroidered design. Or let children color or paint fabric before you cut out the pattern. Some children may enjoy designing their clothes by drawing the garment they would like and then having you match the color and general style. Simple, original appliqués can reflect a favorite hobby or special toy.

Involve the child in selecting patterns, fabrics, and notions. For young children learning to identify colors, primary colors of red, yellow, and blue are popular. Look at colors of a favorite toy and the colors a child often chooses for painting or drawing. Consider the coloring of the child's hair, eyes, and skin; select colors that compliment them.

Features for Self-dressing

To encourage self-dressing, choose garments with loose-fitting necklines and waistlines and with manageable fasteners. Make closures easy to see and reach on the front or side of a garment. Hook and loop tape can be used for closures on most types of garments. Young children can easily unfasten simple, large, round buttons and snaps, but may have difficulty closing them with small hands. They also enjoy smooth-running zippers with large teeth and zipper pulls. Pull-on pants that have elastic waists are easier for young children to pull on and off. Children can be frustrated by trying to fasten hooks and eyes, tiny buttons, and ties.

Tips for Planning Garments for Growth and Comfort

Add ribbing cuffs to lower edges of sleeves or pants legs so you can turn up built-in room for growth.

Choose pants patterns in a style that can be cut off for shorts when outgrown in length.

Use elastic waists on generously sized pants or skirts for comfort during growth spurts.

Allow extra crotch and body length in one-piece garments to prevent them from becoming uncomfortable as the child grows.

Add elastic suspenders with adjustable closures.

Choose dress and jumper patterns with dropped waist or no waist for comfort and maximum length of wear.

Use knit fabrics for easier sewing and maximum stretch for growth and comfort.

Consider patterns with pleats, gathers, and wide shapes that allow for growth without riding up.

Select patterns with raglan, dolman, and dropped sleeves to offer room for growth and less restriction of movement.

Select oversized styles for comfort.

Receiving Blankets & Hooded Towels

Receiving blankets and hooded towels can be made large enough to accommodate the growth of the child. Choose soft, warm, and absorbent woven or knit fabrics. Select from flannel, interlock, jersey, thermal knit, terry cloth and stretch terry. Two layers of lightweight fabric can be used with wrong sides together. Round all corners for easy edge application.

Cut a 36" (91.5 cm) square blanket or towel from 1 yd. (.95 m) of 45" or 60" (115 or 152.5 cm) wide fabric. When using 45" (115 cm) wide fabric, the mock binding and hood require an additional ¼ yd. (.25 m). Cut a 1½" (3.8 cm) wide binding strip on the lengthwise or crosswise grain, 2" (5 cm) longer than the distance around the item; piece, as necessary. Press binding in half, with wrong sides together.

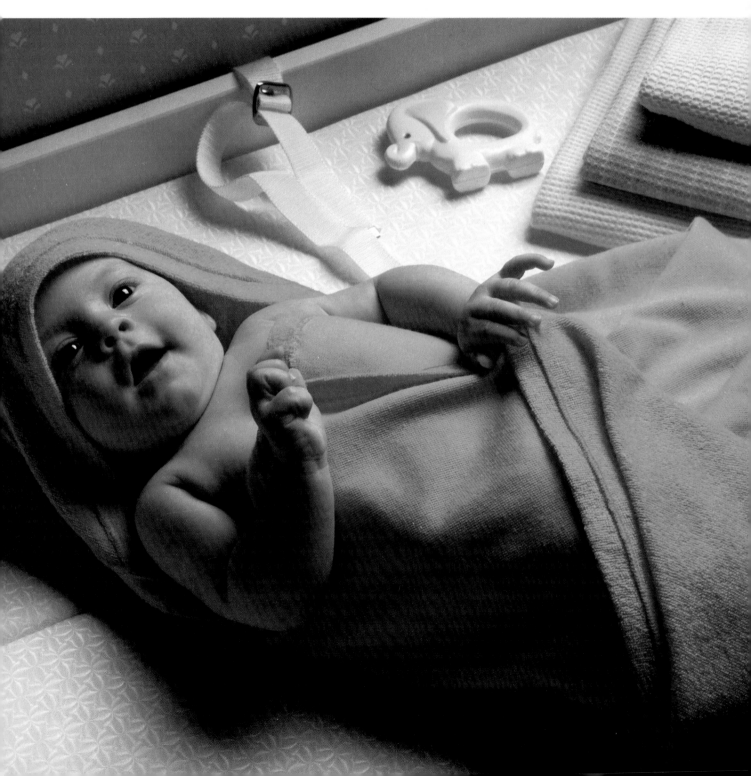

How to Finish Edges with a Mock Binding

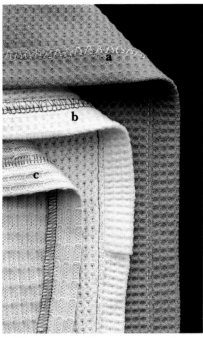

1) Use overedge stitch or serge binding to right side of fabric, starting 1½" (3.8 cm) from end of binding. Stitch to within 2" (5 cm) of start of binding, stretching fabric slightly at corners; do not stretch binding. (If flatlock stitch on serger is used, stitch *wrong* sides together.)

2) Fold 1" (2.5 cm) of binding to inside; lap around first end of binding. Continue stitching binding to fabric, stitching over previous stitches for 1" (2.5 cm) to secure the ends.

3) Turn seam allowance toward blanket or towel; topstitch through all layers of overedged **(a)** or serged **(b)** seam, to hold seam allowances flat. If flatlock **(c)** stitch is used, pull binding and fabric flat.

How to Sew a Hooded Towel

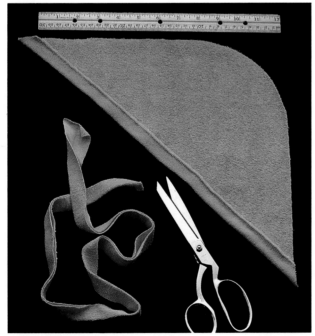

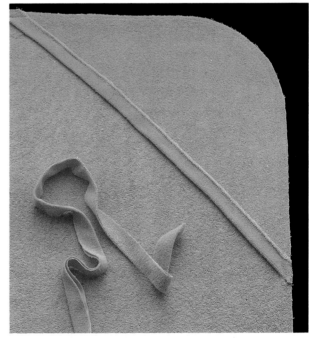

1) Cut a right triangle with two 12" (30.5 cm) sides from matching or contrasting fabric. Round right angle corner, and finish diagonal edge with mock binding, above.

2) Position wrong side of the hood to right side of the towel. Stitch triangle to one rounded corner of towel, ¼" (6 mm) from matched edges. Finish outside edges, above.

Bibs

Infant bibs are quick and easy to make. Create durable bibs from terry cloth or knit fabric or from fingertip towels, and customize the bibs with simple appliqué techniques and bias tape. Increase absorbency by using a double layer of fabric. Back a fabric bib with soft, pliable plastic to protect clothing; finish edges with wide double-fold bias tape. Or use a fingertip towel with prefinished edges.

Custom Bibs

Attach a toy or pacifier to a bib with a snap-on strip **(1)**. Stitch together the edges of a 12" (30.5 cm) strip of wide double-fold bias tape, and fold under the ends of the strip. Attach one end to the bib with the ball half of a gripper snap. Attach the socket half of the gripper snap to the other end of the tape. Slip the toy or pacifier onto the tape; snap securely to the bib.

A purchased squeaker can be inserted between the appliqué and bib **(2)** before you stitch the appliqué (page 201).

A fingertip towel makes an absorbent, washable bib. Fold the towel for double absorbency under the chin **(3)**, and attach double-fold bias tape around the neck edge.

How to Make a Pullover Bib

1) Use fingertip towel. Cut 5" (12.5 cm) circle with center of circle one-third the distance from one end of towel. Cut 3" (7.5 cm) wide ribbing, with length two-thirds the circumference. Stitch short ends to form circle, using ¼" (6 mm) seam allowance.

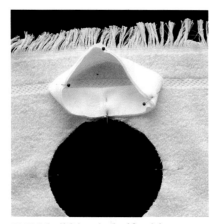

2) Fold ribbing in half, with wrong sides together. Divide ribbing and neck edge into fourths; pin-mark. Matching pins, and with seam at center back, pin ribbing to neck edge, with raw edges even. Stitch ¼" (6 mm) seam, stretching ribbing to fit neckline.

3) Fold seam allowance toward bib. Edgestitch to bib through all layers.

How to Make a Tie-on Bib

1) Press wide double-fold bias tape to follow curve of outer edge of bib. Glue-baste tape over raw edge of bib, positioning the wider tape edge on the wrong side; edgestitch in place.

2) Cut bias tape 30" (76 cm) longer than neck curve. Center bias tape over the neck edge; glue-baste. Edgestitch from one end of tie around neckline to other end. Bar tack bias tape at edge of bib (arrow) by zigzagging in place; tie knot at each end.

Alternative. Cut fingertip towel as for pullover bib, opposite. Fold so neck opening forms a half circle. Zigzag raw edges together with wide stitch. Apply bias tape for ties and neck finish, step 2, left.

Adding Durability

Build in durability as you construct children's garments. Seams and knees are subject to the most stress during dressing and active play, but both areas can be strengthened easily as you sew the garment.

Seams are most vulnerable at the crotch, shoulder, neck, and armhole. Strengthen the crotch and armhole seams with double-stitched, mock flat-fell, or edgestitched seams. Reinforce shoulder and neckline seams with decorative twin-needle seam finish, stitching before crossing with another seam. Machine-stitch hems for added strength in activewear.

The knee area wears out faster than any other part of a child's garment and is difficult to reach for repairs. Flat construction techniques allow you to reinforce knee areas as you construct the garment.

Patches

Tightly woven fabrics make the most durable patches. Interface, pad, or quilt patches for extra durability and protection at the knee, especially for crawling toddlers. Fuse the patch to the garment to make the application easier and to strengthen the patch.

Double-knee and decorative patches are cut according to the child's size. For infants, cut the patch 3½" × 4" (9 × 10 cm); for toddlers, 3¾" × 5" (9.5 × 12.5 cm); for children, 4½" × 6" (11.5 × 15 cm).

Round the corners of decorative patches to simplify application and to eliminate sharp corners that could catch and tear.

How to Add Decorative Knee Patches

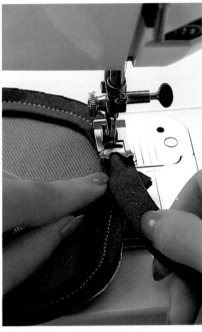

1) Cut two patches to size (opposite); round corners. Iron paper-backed fusible web to back of patches. Cut two strips of fabric for piping 1" × 24" (2.5 × 61 cm); cut on bias for woven fabrics or crosswise grain for knits.

2) Press strips in half lengthwise, wrong sides together. Stitch to right side of each patch, raw edges even, with ¼" (6 mm) seam allowance.

3) Curve ends of piping into seam allowance, so folded ends overlap and taper to raw edge. Trim piping even with raw edge of patch.

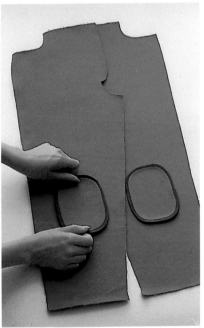

4) Trim seam allowance to ⅛" (3 mm). Press seam allowance to wrong side of patch, pulling piping out from patch. Remove paper backing from fusible web.

5) Fuse one patch to front of pants leg, parallel to hemline with center of patch slightly below center of knee. On the other pants leg, align second patch with first; fuse.

6) Stitch patch to garment, stitching in the ditch. Finish pants according to pattern directions.

Adding Grow Room

Build in grow room when you construct children's clothing, to get the maximum amount of wear from the garments. Without this extra room, a child going through a rapid growth spurt may be unable to wear a garment that is well liked and in good condition. The easiest place to add grow room is at the lower edge or sleeve hem. Rolled-up lined cuffs can be gradually lowered as the child grows. To add a coordinated look, select a lining fabric to match a shirt or other part of the ensemble. Cut lining on the straight grain or bias; add interest with a plaid or stripe. When sewing a garment that has straps, add extra length to the straps, and use overall buckles for easy length adjustment.

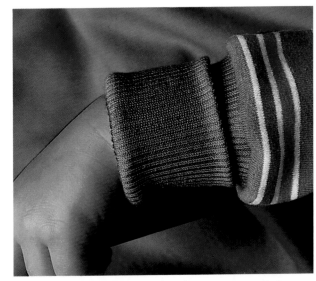

Ribbing. Make ribbing twice the recommended finished width. Fold the ribbing up, and gradually unroll it to add length as the child grows. Add ribbing to outgrown sleeves or pants legs by opening the hem and using the hemline for the new stitching line.

Inserts and trims. Planning carefully for balanced finished proportions, cut off the lower edge of the garment. Cut an insert of coordinating fabric, lace, or eyelet 1" (2.5 cm) wider than desired length, to allow for ¼" (6 mm) seam allowances on insert and garment. Stitch upper edge of insert to garment, then stitch lower section of garment to insert. Trims with finished edges can be stitched to the right or wrong side of a garment at the hemline for added length.

How to Add Lined Cuffs

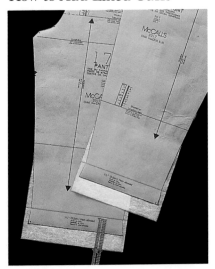

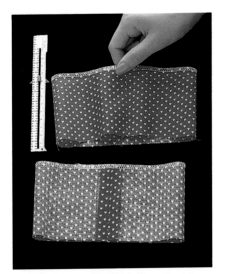

1) Adjust pattern at hem; lengthen hem allowance to 2½" (6.5 cm). Straighten side seams above original hemline for 4" (10 cm) to eliminate taper. Cut out garment; assemble according to pattern directions, but do not hem.

2) Cut two cuffs 3½" (9 cm) wide, and 1" (2.5 cm) longer than the circumference of finished sleeve or pants leg. Stitch short ends of cuff, right sides together, using ½" (1.3 cm) seam; press open. Serge upper edge, or turn under ¼" (6 mm), and press.

3) Stitch cuff to garment, with right sides together and raw edges even, using ¼" (6 mm) seam; match cuff seam to inseam. Turn cuff at stitching line, and press to wrong side of garment; topstitch at lower and upper edges. Fold cuff to right side.

Appliqués

Appliqués are a traditional method for decorating children's garments. Select from three basic types of appliqués; purchase iron-on or sew-on appliqués, or design your own. For a fast and easy decorative touch, fuse purchased iron-on appliqués to a garment, following the manufacturer's directions. Purchased sew-on appliqués may be fused to the garment using fusible web. You may wish to topstitch to secure the appliqué through many launderings.

You may want to design your own custom-made appliqués. Look at magazines, ready-to-wear garments, or coloring books for ideas. Fruit, animals, numbers, toys, hearts, and rainbows are all popular shapes for children's appliqués. Consider cutting motifs from printed fabrics.

Before assembling the appliqué, plan the work sequence. Smaller pieces may need to be positioned on and stitched to larger pieces before applying appliqué to the garment, and some pieces may overlap other pieces.

Embellish the appliqués with bows, buttons, ribbons, pom-poms, fabric paint, or cord. Cut ends of cord may be placed under appliqué pieces before fusing. Trims may be stitched or glued in place, using permanent fabric glue.

Tips for Appliqués

Practice stitching an appliqué on a test piece before working with the garment piece.

Select a colorfast fabric for an appliqué that is compatible with garment fabric in weight and care requirements; preshrink all fabrics.

Remember that it is easiest to stitch around large, simple shapes with few corners.

Leave a fabric margin in a geometric shape around intricate motifs cut from printed fabrics.

Apply paper-backed fusible web to the wrong side of the appliqué fabric before cutting out the shape.

Add durability to a garment by applying an appliqué with fusible web at knees or elbows.

Add ½" (1.3 cm) to sides of appliqué pieces that will go under another piece; trim to reduce bulk when final placement is determined.

Remember that shapes drawn on paper backing of fusible web will be reversed on the garment; draw mirror images of letters or numbers.

Apply tear-away stabilizer to the wrong side of a garment for smooth satin stitching at the edge of an appliqué.

Use a special-purpose presser foot with a wide channel to prevent buildup of satin stitches.

Apply an appliqué to garment before joining seams. It is easier to apply an appliqué while fabric is flat.

How to Make and Apply an Appliqué

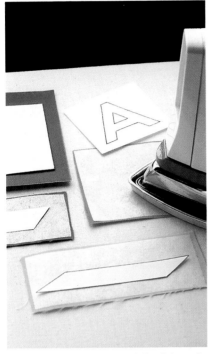

1) **Apply** paper-backed fusible web to wrong side of appliqué fabric, following manufacturer's directions. Allow fabric to cool.

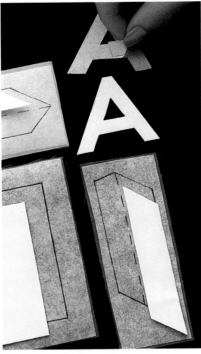

2) **Draw** design on fabric or paper backing; add ½" (1.3 cm) to sides of appliqué pieces that go under another piece. Cut out design and remove paper backing.

3) **Position** appliqué pieces on the garment fabric. Trim appliqué pieces under other pieces to reduce bulk; leave scant ¼" (6 mm). Fuse appliqué pieces to garment.

4) **Cut** tear-away stabilizer 1" (2.5 cm) larger than appliqué. Glue-baste to the wrong side of garment, under appliqué. Zigzag stitch around appliqué, using short, narrow stitches.

5) **Decrease** the upper tension, and adjust stitches for short, wide zigzag; satin stitch around appliqué edges to cover all raw edges. Remove tear-away stabilizer.

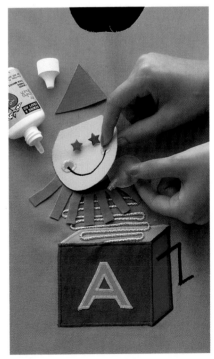

Appliqué with squeaker. Apply fusible interfacing to wrong side of appliqué. Place squeaker under appliqué; glue appliqué in place at edges. Complete appliqué as in steps 4 and 5, left.

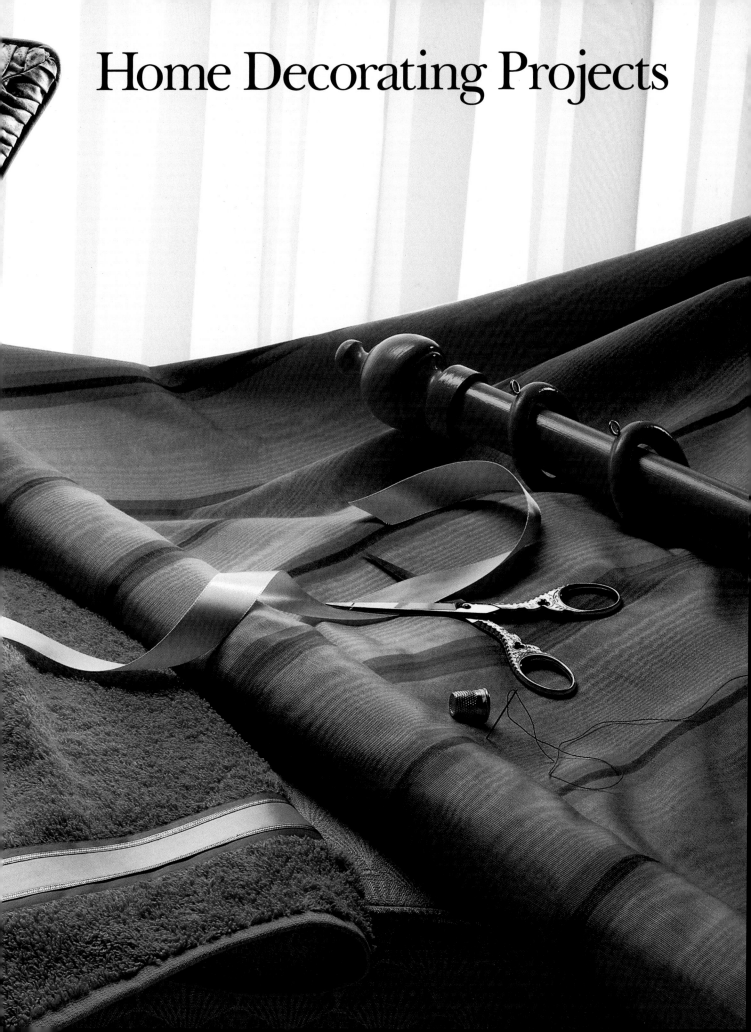

Home Decorating Projects

Fabric Selection

It pays to use good quality fabrics for home decorating projects. A good quality decorator fabric usually lasts longer and results in a finer finished look. Some of the most popular home decorator fabrics are shown here and on the next pages to help you with your selection.

As a rule, the tighter the weave or higher the thread count (number of threads per inch), the stronger the fabric. Most decorator fabrics have a higher thread count than garment fabrics.

Many decorator fabrics have a stain-resistant finish. To test, drop a small amount of water on the sample. If the water beads up instead of soaking in, the fabric will repel stains. This is more of a concern for cushions, pillows, slipcovers, and upholstery than for window treatments. Also, make sure that the dyes do not rub off when the fabric is handled or rubbed between your fingers.

Consider the end use, and be sure that the fabric is appropriate to the function. A decorative top treatment for a curtain, for example, will receive little wear; if a simple style is selected, it can be changed easily to update a look. Fabric for such a project does not get the heavy use that a chair cushion does; nor is it used as long as the average drapery. Remember that the average drapery may hang in a room anywhere from eight to fifteen years.

When comparing costs for large amounts of fabric, consider that prints may cost more than solid fabrics because you will need more fabric to match the motifs. The larger the repeat, the more likely you are to waste fabric when matching.

Lightweight open weaves are often used for window treatments because they let in the sunlight yet offer more privacy than undraped windows. Casement fabrics (1) are loosely woven, with uneven yarns and open areas. The variation in the weave creates a design in the fabric. Polyester, cotton, or linen fibers may be used. Laces and eyelets (2) may look delicate and fragile, but are easy to sew and provide a light, airy look. Wide borders and finished edges eliminate hemming. Sheers (3) vary in fiber content but are usually polyester for a sheer, transparent look. Imported sheers can be up to 118" (295 cm) wide with embroidered or decorative hems.

Fiber Content

Cotton is a basic, strong, all-purpose fiber for home furnishing fabric. It dyes well for vibrant colors and has good wearability. It may be used as a blend with many other fibers.

Linen is strong, but it will wrinkle. If wrinkling is a concern, crush a handful of fabric tightly in your fist and release it to see if wrinkles are retained. Decorator fabrics usually do not have crease-resistant finishes.

Rayon and acetate are often used together or in blends for a rich, silky appearance. Acetate may stretch in draperies and may spot if it gets wet.

Polyester is used alone or combined with other fibers to add stability. With all synthetics, use a low iron temperature when pressing.

Decorator Fabric vs. Garment Fabric

Decorator fabrics can be more expensive than garment fabrics, but garment fabrics may not have all the features you need. Normally, garment fabrics are not treated with stain-resistant finishes, and they usually have a lower thread count so they are not as durable. Use garment fabrics if the item will get little or no wear and your goal is simply to create an effect. Some garment fabrics are not heavy enough for a drapery, but may be acceptable as a curtain, valance, or dust ruffle.

If using garment fabric, preshrink it. If repeated washing will be necessary for an item, do not sew it with materials that cannot be washed, such as buckram or linings.

Mediumweight basics are versatile multipurpose fabrics used for window treatments, cushions, cornices, and fabric screens. Chintz (**1**) is a glazed, plain-weave cotton or cotton-blend fabric. This tightly woven fabric is available in solid colors or prints that are often large, traditional florals. Warp sateen (**2**) is a cotton or cotton blend that has a softer hand than chintz but feels heavier. Warp threads float on the surface to create a smooth surface. This fabric is multipurpose for draperies, bedspreads, cushions, and slipcovers. Antique satin (**3**) varies in fiber content and quality. It is a very drapable, mediumweight solid fabric, which has slubs and a sheen.

Borders, Stripes & Wide Fabrics

Fabrics with borders or wide stripes have many possibilities for coordinating color and design within a room. By removing a border from one fabric and applying it to another, or applying it in an unusual way, you can create an entirely new fabric. You can also manipulate striped fabrics to change their appearance by using them diagonally, mitering to the center, or cutting them apart to create a border on a coordinating fabric.

Estimate the amount of border that it will take for the project or decorative effect. It is possible to get several yards of border from a few yards of striped fabric cut into strips. Doing this is usually more economical than buying a bordered fabric. When cutting the stripes, allow ½" (1.3 cm) seam allowance on each side of the stripe for application.

Railroading Wide Fabrics

To eliminate seams, *railroad* a fabric. To railroad a fabric, turn the fabric on its side so that the normal width of the fabric becomes the length. This technique can often be used on valances, cornices, and dust ruffles, but is particularly practical for short curtains and seamless sheer draperies when fabric is extra wide.

The advantage of making draperies without seams is that there is no unevenness or puckering where widths of fabric are joined. In sheer fabrics, having no seams has the additional advantage of eliminating shadows at the seams. Railroading may require less fabric, and it saves time because there are no seams to sew.

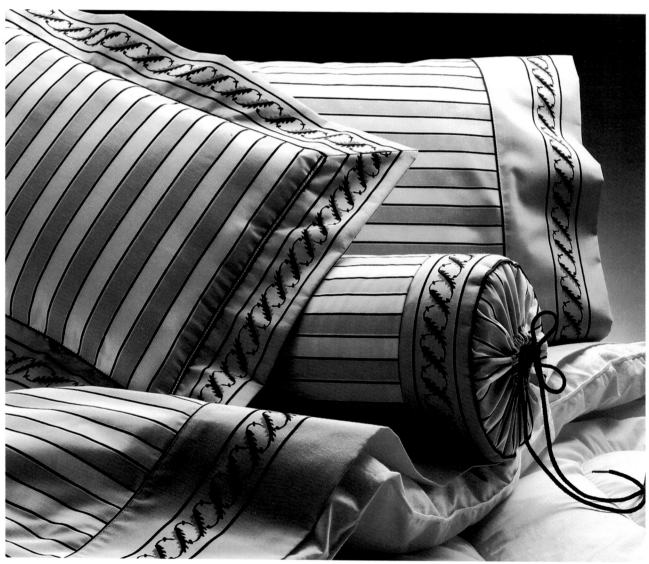

Coordinate bedroom accessories with bordered sheets and pillowcases. Miter the border from a sheet for a flange edge on pillow shams. Also use the border to trim a neckroll pillow.

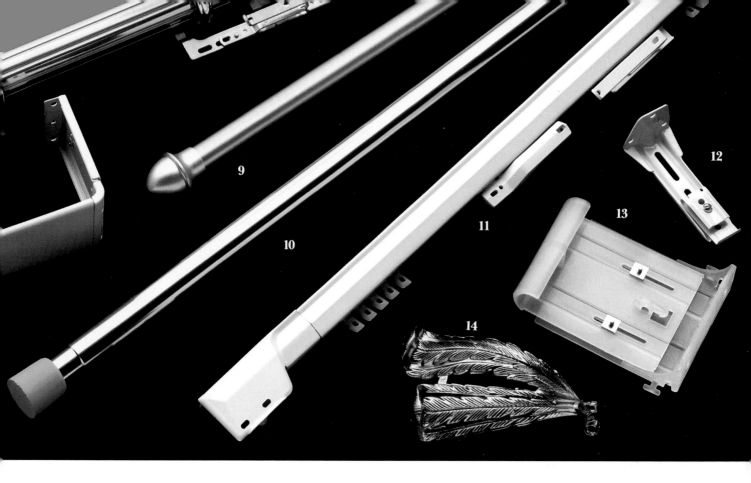

12) Support brackets should be placed every 12" to 20" (30.5 to 51 cm), depending on the weight of draperies. On multi-paneled windows, align brackets with the frame between panels.

13) Tieback holders fit behind the last fold of draperies to prevent crushing and to hold the folds in clean, graceful lines. The projection of the holder can be adjusted from 5" to 8" (12.5 to 20.5 cm).

14) Holdbacks have projection arms or stems used to hold draperies back from the window.

Basic Terms to Know

a) Drapery return is the measurement from the last pleat of the drapery panel to the wall.

b) Projection, or clearance, is the measurement from the wall to the back of the master slides.

c) Length measurement for conventional traverse rods is from end bracket to end bracket. For decorative rods, it is from end ring to end ring.

d) Master slides are attached to the draw cord to push or pull the leading edge of each drapery panel.

Overlap is the area where drapery panels overlap in the center of a two-way traverse rod. Standard overlap is about 3½" (9 cm) per panel.

Stackback is the amount of space occupied by open draw draperies. This space depends on the panel width, pleat spacing, and fabric bulk but is usually one-third the rod width. Allow for one-half the amount on each side of the window.

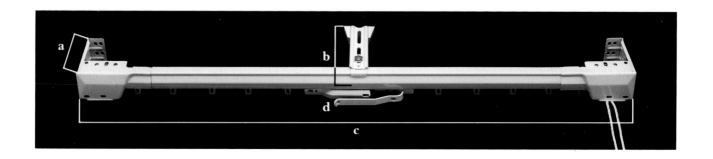

Matching Prints

Prints require careful planning. To avoid wasting fabric or making costly errors, cut, match, and stitch carefully. Prints must be positioned to please the eye, and they must be sewn to match at every seam. Start matching a print at eye level so if the match does become imperfect, it will be off at the top or bottom of the panel, where it is less noticeable.

Start a full print at the bottom of a curtain or panel. If the print is behind a sofa or piece of furniture, position a full print at the top of the furniture line.

Match motifs across drapery or curtain panels. Be sure that motifs on all curtain panels match at eye level when there are several windows in the same room or area.

Because most decorator fabrics have a stabilizing finish applied to the surface, it is not advantageous to pull a thread to straighten a crosswise end. Cut decorator fabrics at right angle to the selvages, or follow a printed motif.

Two Ways to Cut Crosswise Ends

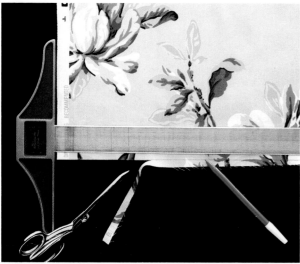

Use T-square or right angle to straighten crosswise ends. Place the T-square or right angle parallel to selvage. Mark cutting line; cut on marked line with shears or rotary cutter.

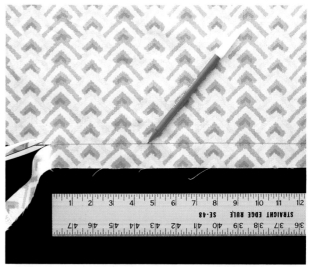

Follow a design line that runs across fabric on crosswise grain. Cut along design with shears or rotary cutter.

How to Match Prints Traditionally

1) Match motifs from wrong side by placing point of pin through matching designs. Pin at close intervals to prevent shifting.

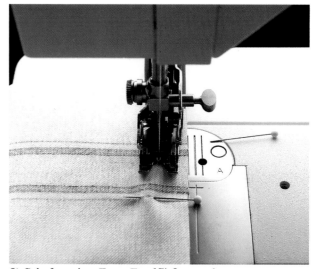

2) Stitch, using Even Feed™ foot to keep seam aligned. Remove pins as you come to them.

How to Match Prints As You Sew

1) **Position** panels with right sides together, matching the selvages.

2) **Fold** selvage back at top of panel until pattern matches on both panels.

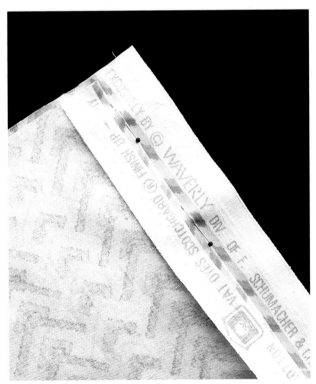

3) **Pin** next to the fold at point where the design matches; turn fabric over to the right side to check matching. No other pins are necessary.

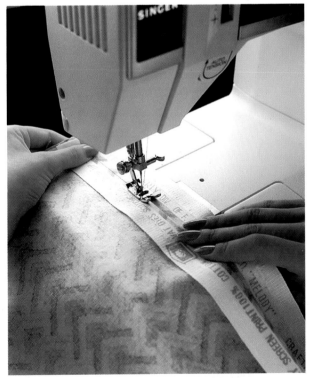

4) **Stitch** from right side as close to the fold as possible. Keep fabric taut while lining up motif as pinned. Continue sewing without additional pins, matching the motifs as you stitch. Trim off selvages.

Seams & Hems

All seams in home decorating sewing are ½" (1.3 cm) unless otherwise indicated. When cutting fabric, remember to add the seam allowances to the finished size of the item you are sewing. Use a seam appropriate to the fabric when none is specified.

Avoid placing a seam in the center of wide items such as bedcovers, top treatments, or round table toppers. Split the panels and put the seams on sides so you will have a wide, full panel in the center. On cloud, Austrian, and pleated valances, hide the seams with a scallop or pleat.

Plain seams, stitched with right sides together and pressed to one side, are used if the item is to be lined. If the item is not lined, finish raw edges with a zigzag or multistitch zigzag. Or overlock the seam allowances together.

French seams are appropriate on sheer fabrics and unlined curtains, draperies, table toppers, and dust ruffles. Because all raw edges are enclosed, this seam is especially stable for washable items.

Overlocked or serged seams are timesaving and practical for home decorating because the seam is stitched and overedged at the same time. The overlock machine is a supplement to a conventional sewing machine.

Double bottom and side hems are standard for window treatments. The longer the panel and lighter weight the fabric, the deeper the hem should be. Use double 4" (10 cm) hems on curtains or draperies that are longer than window length. Be careful not to place a hem in front of the window; when light comes through the curtain, the hem or lining edges should not be visible. Double side hems are usually 1" or 1½" (2.5 or 3.8 cm).

How to Sew a French Seam

1) Pin *wrong* sides of fabric together. Stitch a scant ¼" (6 mm) seam. Press seam allowance to one side.

2) Turn fabric panels so right sides are together to enclose trimmed seam allowance. Stitch ⅜" (1 cm) from folded edge, enclosing first seam. Press to one side.

Overlock Hems

Rolled edge sewn with 3-thread overlock stitch is durable and neat on lightweight fabrics. Use it on tablecloths, napkins, and ruffles that otherwise require narrow hem. Contrasting thread can be used for decorative detail.

Satin edge is sewn with short, narrow 3-thread or 2-thread overlock. This method is good on textured fabrics, because it is less bulky than rolled edge. Use woolly nylon thread for better coverage.

Overlock Seams

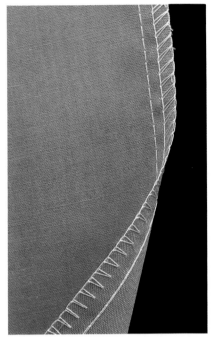

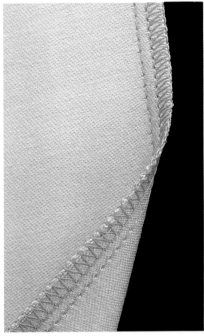

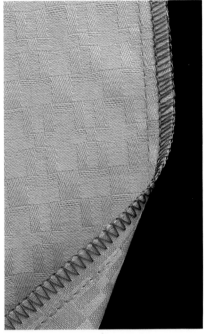

4-thread overlock seam is durable, nonstretch, self-finished seam. Use for long straight seams.

3-thread overlock seam is an alternative for 4-thread seam. Use with conventional straight stitches, if necessary, to reinforce and to prevent stretching.

2-thread overlock stitch is fast, neat technique for finishing plain seams or raw edges of fabrics that ravel. Edges may be overlocked either before or after seam is stitched.

How to Sew a Double-fold Hem

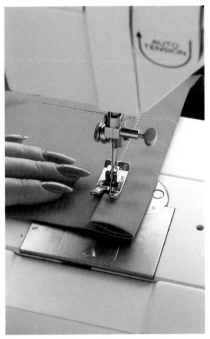

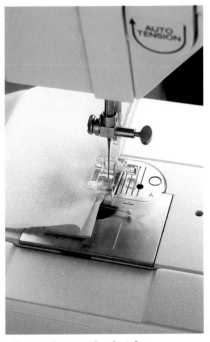

1) Turn under hem allowance. Press the fold. Turn under hem allowance again; press in place.

2) Straight-stitch on folded hem edge, using 8 to 10 stitches per inch (2.5 cm). When stitching several layers of bulky fabric, lighten pressure slightly and stitch slowly.

Alternative method. After pressing hem, fold back to right side, leaving a fold of fabric about ⅛" (3 mm) from hem edge. Set machine to blindstitch. Adjust zigzag stitch to take tiny bite.

Casings & Headings

A casing or *rod pocket* is the hem along the upper edge of the curtain or valance. The curtain rod is inserted through the casing so that the fullness of the curtain falls into soft gathers.

Before cutting the curtains, decide on the casing style. A simple casing places the curtain rod at the uppermost edge of the curtain.

For simple casings, add to the cut length an amount equal to the diameter of the rod plus ½" (1.3 cm) to turn under and ¼" to 1" (6 mm to 2.5 cm) ease. The amount of ease depends on the size of the rod and thickness of the fabric.

A heading is a gathered edge above the casing. It finishes the curtain more decoratively than a simple casing. Curtains with headings do not require cornices or valances.

For casings with headings, use the formula for a simple casing, adding to it an amount twice the depth of the heading. Headings may be from 1" to 5" (2.5 to 12.5 cm) deep. The depth of the heading

must be determined before the curtains are cut. The heading depth should be appropriate for the length of the curtain: in general, the longer the curtain, the deeper the heading.

Wooden, brass or plastic poles may be covered with a *shirred pole cover*. The exposed pole between the curtain panels is covered with a casing made from a shirred tube of matching fabric (above). The casing may be plain or have a heading the same height as the curtain heading. Wide poles and casings are more than decorative. They often are used to conceal a shade heading, the plain heading on shirred curtains, or the traverse rod of sheer or lightweight curtains.

Wide casings are used on the flat *Continental*™ *rod* or *cornice rod*. These rods are 4½" (11.5 cm) wide. A cornice rod is actually two regular curtain rods attached with a spacer between them.

Finish lower and side hems of curtains before sewing casings and headings.

How to Sew a Simple Casing

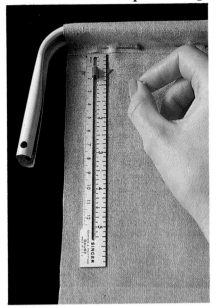

1) Determine casing depth by loosely pinning a curtain fabric strip around the rod. Remove rod and measure the distance from the top of the strip to the pin. Add ½" (1.3 cm) to be turned under.

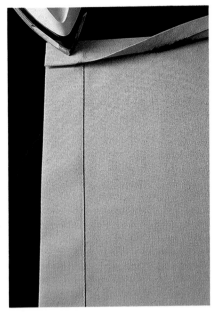

2) Press under ½" (1.3 cm) along upper cut edge of curtain panel. Fold over again and press to form a hem equal to amount measured in step 1.

3) Stitch close to folded hem edge to form casing, backstitching at both ends. If desired, stitch again close to the upper edge to create a sharp crease appropriate for flat or oval curtain rods.

How to Sew a Casing with a Heading

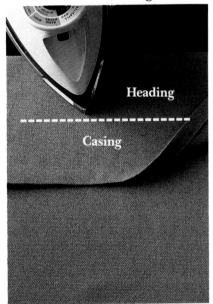

1) Determine the depth of the casing as directed in step 1, above. Determine the depth of heading, opposite. Press under ½" (1.3 cm) along upper cut edge of the curtain panel. Fold and press again to form hem equal to casing plus heading depth.

2) Stitch close to folded edge, backstitching at both ends. Mark heading depth with a pin at each end of panel. Stitch again at marked depth. To aid straight stitching, apply a strip of masking tape to the bed of the machine at heading depth, or use seam guide.

3) Insert rod through casing and gather curtain evenly onto rod. Adjust heading by pulling up the folded edge so the seam is exactly on the lower edge of the rod. A wide heading may be made to look puffy and more rounded by pulling the fabric out on each side.

Lining Curtains

Linings add body and weight to curtains to help them hang better. A lining also adds opaqueness, prevents fading and sun damage to curtain fabric, and provides some insulation.

Curtains may be lined the traditional way or lined to the edge with coordinating fabric to create a custom look.

Select linings according to the weight of the curtain fabric. White or off-white sateen is the most often used lining fabric. Specially treated linings that resist staining and block out light are also available.

✂ Cutting Directions

For a lined curtain with a casing, cut the curtain as directed on pages 208 and 209. For lining with 2" (5 cm) double-fold hem, cut lining the finished length of curtain plus 2½" (6.5 cm); cut lining 6" (15 cm) narrower than cut width of curtain. Seam and press widths, aligning curtain and lining seams if possible.

For curtains lined to the edge, cut curtain and lining the finished length plus amount for double-fold hem and ½" (1.3 cm) for seam at upper edge. Cut panels the finished width plus 1" (2.5 cm) for side seams.

How to Line Curtains

1) Turn, press and stitch 2" (5 cm) double-fold hem in lining. Turn and press double-fold hem in curtain. Tack weights inside fold of curtain hems at seams and stitch curtain hems.

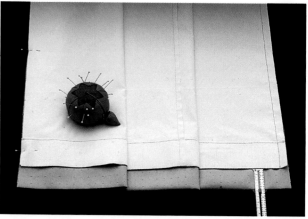

2) Place lining on curtain, right sides together, so lining is 1½" (3.8 cm) above curtain hem. Pin and stitch ½" (1.3 cm) seams on sides.

3) Turn curtain right side out. Center lining so side hems are equal width. Press side hem with seam allowance toward center. Continue to the top edge of the curtain.

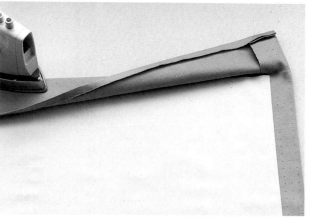

4) Press ½" (1.3 cm) seam allowance across upper edge of curtain. Fold upper edge of curtain down an amount equal to depth of casing and heading. Lining ends at foldline.

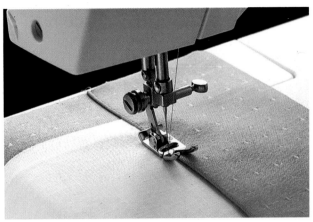

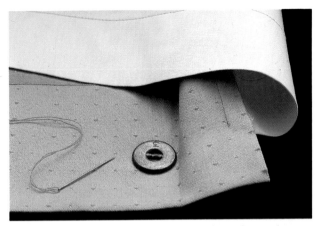

5) Stitch close to the folded edge to form casing. For curtains with headings, stitch the heading the desired depth.

6) Hand-tack weights along lower edge of curtain inside side hems.

7) Turn side hems back diagonally below lining to form a miter. Slipstitch miter in place.

8) Make French tacks about 12" (30.5 cm) apart between hem and lining, using double thread. Take two stitches near top of hem and directly across in lining, leaving 1" (2.5 cm) slack in thread. Make blanket stitch over thread; secure with knot in lining.

How to Line Curtains to the Edge

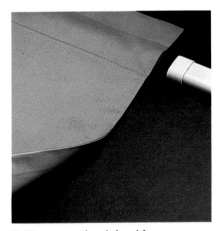

1) Cut curtain and lining the same size. Turn, press and stitch equal lower hems in curtain and lining. Place right sides of curtain and lining together with lower hems even. Pin sides and upper edge.

2) Mark casing and heading depth on lining. Join lining and curtain with ½" (1.3 cm) seam on sides and upper edge, leaving opening on both sides at casing line. Diagonally trim upper corners. Press the upper seam open.

3) Turn curtain right side out. Press seams flat. Stitch casing and heading. Insert curtain rod in casing. Hang curtain and fold lining to right side so contrasting fabric shows; secure with tieback.

Tab Top Curtains

Fabric tabs are an attractive alternative to conventional casings or curtain rings. Tab top curtains used with a decorative curtain rod create a traditional country look, a contemporary tailored look or a casual cafe look. They are also ideal for stationary side panels. Tabs give top interest to a curtain, and can be made with contrasting fabric, decorative ribbon or trim.

Only one and one-half to two times the fullness is needed for tab top curtains. Allow ½" (1.3 cm) seam allowance at the upper edge of the curtain instead of the usual casing allowance. When determining the finished length, allow for the upper edge of the curtain to be 1½" to 2" (3.8 to 5 cm) below the rod. This determines the length of the tabs. Determine number of tabs needed by placing a tab at each edge of the curtain, and space the remaining tabs 6" to 8" (15 to 20.5 cm) apart.

How to Sew Tab Top Curtains

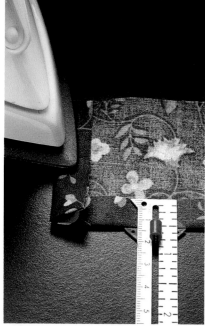

1) Cut a 3" (7.5 cm) facing strip equal in length to the width of the curtain panel. Press under ½" (1.3 cm) on one long side and each short end. Press double-fold lower and side hems of curtain. Stitch lower hem only.

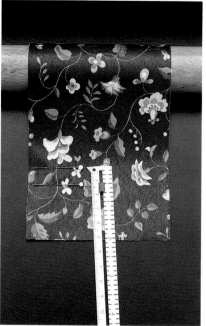

2) Measure tab length by pinning a strip of fabric over the rod and marking the desired length with a pin. Add ½" (1.3 cm) for seam allowance. Cut tabs to measured length, and two times the desired width plus 1" (2.5 cm).

3) Fold each tab in half lengthwise, right sides together. Stitch ½" (1.3 cm) seam along cut edge; sew from one tab to the next, using continuous stitching (arrow). Turn tabs right side out. Center seam in back of each tab; press.

4) Fold each tab in half so raw edges are aligned. Pin or baste tabs in place on right side of curtain, aligning raw edges of tabs with upper edge of curtain. Place end tabs even with side hem foldline of curtain.

5) Pin facing to upper edge of curtain, right sides together, so raw edges are aligned and tabs are sandwiched between facing and curtain. Stitch ½" (1.3 cm) seam, with curtain side hems extended.

6) Press facing to wrong side of curtain so tabs extend upward. Fold curtain side hems under facing, covering seam allowance; grade. Stitch side hems. Slipstitch facing to curtain. Insert curtain rod through tabs.

Tiebacks

Tiebacks are a decorative way to hold curtains open. Make them straight or shaped, ruffled or plain. Use matching or contrasting solids, coordinating prints or bordered fabrics. Interface all tiebacks to add stability.

An easy way to make tiebacks the proper length is to complete and hang the curtains before sewing the tiebacks. Cut a strip of fabric that is 2" to 4" (5 to 10 cm) wide; experiment by pinning it around the curtains to determine the best tieback length. Slide the strip up and down to find the best location for tiebacks. Mark the wall for positioning cup hooks, which will be used to fasten the tiebacks. Remove the strip and measure it to determine the finished size.

✄ Cutting Directions

For straight tiebacks, cut a piece of heavyweight fusible interfacing the finished length and two times the finished width. To cut fabric, add ½" (1.3 cm) on all sides for seams.

For shaped tiebacks, cut a strip of brown paper for pattern, 4" to 6" (10 to 15 cm) wide and slightly longer than the tieback. Pin the paper around the curtain and draw a curved shape around the edge of the paper. Experiment by pinning and trimming the paper to get the effect you want. Cut two pieces of fabric and heavyweight fusible interfacing for each tieback. Cut interfacing same size as pattern. To cut fabric, add ½" (1.3 cm) on all sides for seams.

YOU WILL NEED

Decorator fabric for tiebacks.

Heavyweight fusible interfacing.

Brown paper for pattern.

Fusible web strips, length of finished tieback width.

Two ⅝" (1.5 cm) brass or plastic rings for each tieback.

Two cup hooks.

How to Sew Straight Tiebacks

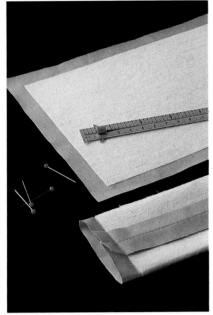

1) Center fusible interfacing on wrong side of tieback and fuse. Press the short ends under ½" (1.3 cm). Fold tieback in half lengthwise, right sides together. Stitch ½" (1.3 cm) seam, leaving short ends open. Press open.

2) Turn tieback right side out. Center seam down back and press. Turn pressed ends inside. Insert fusible web at each end and fuse. Or slipstitch closed.

3) Hand-tack ring on back seamline at each end of tieback, ¼" (6 mm) from edge **(a)**. Or press corners diagonally to inside to form a point; slipstitch or fuse corners in place. Attach ring **(b)**.

How to Sew Shaped Tiebacks

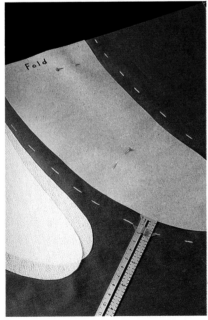

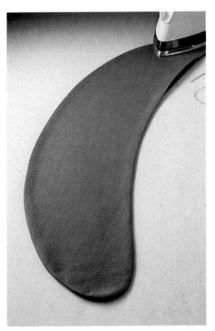

1) Position pattern on fold to cut fabric and interfacing. Center interfacing on wrong side of each tieback piece and fuse.

2) Pin tieback pieces, right sides together. Stitch ½" (1.3 cm) seam, leaving 4" (10 cm) opening on one long edge for turning. Grade seam allowances; notch or clip curves at regular intervals.

3) Turn tieback right side out; press. Insert fusible web at opening and fuse. Or slipstitch closed. Hand-tack rings at each end of tieback ¼" (6 mm) from the edge.

223

Bound Tiebacks

Binding emphasizes the graceful line of a curved tieback and allows you to pick up an accent color from the room decor or from the curtain fabric. Shaped tiebacks are easier to bind than straight tiebacks because the bias binding will ease around curves.

✂ Cutting Directions

Cut two pieces of fabric and two pieces of fusible interfacing from the pattern; do not add seam allowances to tieback. Make bias tape as on page 270. Cut the tape 1" (2.5 cm) longer than the distance around the tieback.

How to Bind Shaped Tiebacks

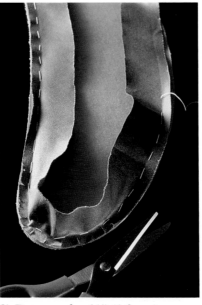

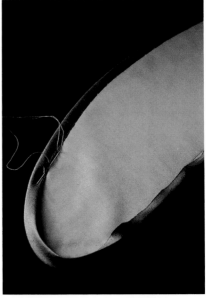

1) Position pattern on fold to cut fabric and interfacing. Fuse interfacing to wrong side of tieback. Pin wrong sides of tieback together.

2) Press under ½" (1.3 cm) on one end of bias strip. Starting with pressed end, baste strip to tieback, right sides together, clipping to ease around curves. Stitch strip ½" (1.3 cm) from edge.

3) Press bias strip over edge of tieback. Turn under cut edge of bias strip to meet seamline; slipstitch. Hand-tack rings to ends of tieback.

Ruffled Tiebacks

Adding ruffled tiebacks changes the appearance of the curtains and the look of a window. Make ruffles from a matching or coordinating fabric in a width that suits the length of the curtain. Purchased pregathered lace or eyelet ruffles may be used to reduce sewing time.

✂ Cutting Directions

Cut ruffle the desired width plus 1" (2.5 cm) for seams, and two and one-half times the finished length.

Cut a straight tieback and interfacing (page 222). The tieback should be in proportion to the ruffle width, usually less than half as wide.

How to Sew Ruffled Tiebacks

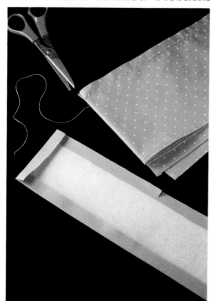

1) Fuse interfacing to wrong side of tieback. Press under ½" (1.3 cm) on one long side and both ends of tieback. Stitch a ¼" (6 mm) hem on one long side and both ends of ruffle. Fold ruffle and tieback into fourths; mark folds with snips.

2) Zigzag over a cord (page 243). Pin wrong side of ruffle to right side of tieback, matching snips and raw edges. Pull up gathering cord until ruffle fits tieback. Distribute gathers evenly and pin. Stitch ruffle ½" (1.3 cm) from edge.

3) Fold tieback in half lengthwise, wrong sides together. Pin the folded edge over ruffle seam. Edgestitch across ends and along gathered seam. Hand-tack the rings to ends of tieback.

Pinch-pleated Draperies

Pinch-pleated draperies are a popular treatment for windows because draperies open to let in light, and close for privacy. The pleats are spaced at intervals to control the fullness of the drapery. The more fabric that is pleated into the drapery panels, the fuller the draperies become.

Although pleater tapes are a quick solution for some draperies, the fullness, spacing, and depth of the pleats are limited when you use these tapes. The only way to have total control over the fullness and position of the pleats is the traditional buckram heading used in drapery workrooms.

Before you can determine the size of the drapery panels, you must determine the hardware and the mounting. For conventional rods, measure from ½" (1.3 cm) above the top of the rod to the desired finished length. For draperies that are mounted on decorative rods, measure from the pin holes in the rod to the desired finished length.

Remember to include stackback when mounting the rods. This is the amount needed at the side of the windows for the drapery to clear the window when the drapery is open to its fullest. Actual stacking space will vary with the weight of the fabric, the fullness, and whether or not the drapery is lined, but it can be estimated at one-third the window width measurement. For center-pull draperies, allow for half the stacking space on each side of the window.

✂ Cutting Directions

Measure the window, and follow the guidelines for curtains and draperies (pages 208 and 209). There are two basic measurements to consider: finished length and finished width. Determine yardage and cut the lengths for drapery and lining, using the chart on the opposite page. These directions are for a pair of draperies.

YOU WILL NEED

Decorator fabric for draperies.

Lining fabric for lined draperies.

Conventional traverse rod, ringless decorator traverse rod, or wood pole set.

Buckram, 4" (10 cm) wide; length equal to width of panels before pleating.

Determine Yardage

Drapery Length*	
1) Desired length as measured from rod	
2) 8" (20.5 cm) for heading	+
3) 8" (20.5 cm) for double hem	+
4) Cut drapery length	=
Drapery Width	
1) Rod width (from end bracket to end bracket on conventional rods; from end ring to end ring on decorative rods)	
2) Returns	+
3) Overlap [standard is 3½" (9 cm)]	+
4) Finished drapery width	=
Drapery Widths per Panel	
1) Finished width times 2, 2½, or 3 (fullness)	
2) Width of fabric	÷
3) Fabric widths needed: round up or down whole width	=
4) Divide widths by 2	÷
5) Number of widths per panel	=
Total Drapery Fabric Needed	
1) Cut drapery length (figured above)	
2) Fabric widths needed (figured above)	×
3) Total fabric length	=
4) Number of yd. (m) needed: total fabric length divided by 36" (100 cm)	yd. (m)

Lining Length	
1) Finished length of drapery (from top of heading to hem)	
2) 4" (10 cm) for double hems	+
3) Cut lining length	=
Lining Width	
1) Number of widths per panel (figure as for drapery widths per panel, above)	
2) Multiply widths by 2	×
3) Total fabric widths	=
Total Lining Fabric Needed	
1) Cut length (figured above)	
2) Fabric widths (figured above)	×
3) Total fabric length	=
4) Number of yd. (m) needed: total fabric length divided by 36" (100 cm)	yd. (m)

* For fabrics requiring pattern match, see page 212.

Drapery Pleats

Use the drapery pleat worksheet to determine the number and size of pleats and spaces per panel; this should be done after panels are sewn together and hemmed. The recommended amount of fabric required for each pleat is 4" to 6" (10 to 15 cm). The recommended space between pleats is 3½" to 4" (9 to 10 cm), approximately the same amount as the center overlap. If the worksheet calculation for the pleat size or the space between pleats is greater than the recommended amount, add one more pleat and space; if the calculation is smaller than the recommended amount, subtract one pleat and space.

Drapery Pleat Worksheet

Finished Panel Width	
1) Finished drapery width (figured left)	
2) divided by 2	÷
3) Finished panel width	=
Space between Pleats	
1) Number of widths per panel (figured left)	
2) Times number of pleats per width*	×
3) Number of pleats per panel	=
4) Number of spaces per panel (one less than pleats)	
5) Finished panel width (figured above)	
6) Overlap and returns (figured left)	−
7) Width to be pleated	=
8) Number of spaces per panel (figured above)	÷
9) Space between pleats	=
Pleat Allowance	
1) Flat width of hemmed panel	
2) Finished panel width (figured above)	−
3) Pleat allowance	=
Pleat Size	
1) Pleat allowance (figured above)	
2) Number of pleats in panel	÷
3) Pleat size	=

*Figure 5 pleats per width of 48" (122 cm) fabric, 6 pleats per width of 54" (140 cm) fabric. If you have a half width of fabric, figure 2 or 3 pleats in that half width. For example, for 48" (122 cm) fabric, 2½ widths per panel = 12 pleats.

How to Sew Unlined Pinch-pleated Draperies

1) Seam widths together as necessary. (Remove selvages to prevent puckering.) Use French or serged seams. Turn under and blindstitch or straight-stitch double 4" (10 cm) bottom hems.

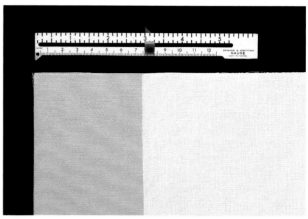

2) Cut 4" (10 cm) wide buckram 6" (15 cm) shorter than width of panel. On wrong side of drapery panel, place buckram even with top edge and 3" (7.5 cm) from the sides.

3) Fold heading over twice, encasing buckram in fabric. Press; pin or hand-baste in place.

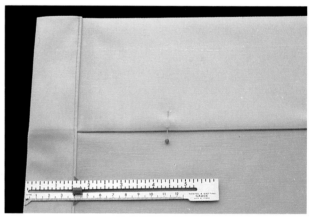

4) Turn under and blindstitch or straight-stitch double 1½" (3.8 cm) side hems. Determine size of pleat and space between pleats from worksheet (page 227).

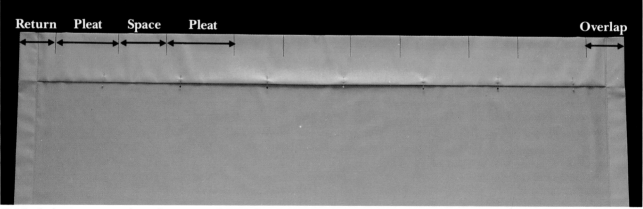

Return   Pleat   Space   Pleat   Overlap

5) Mark the returns and overlaps on each panel; then mark the pleats and spaces. Make sure there is a pleat just before the return and next to overlap. Pleat size can vary slightly to accommodate excess width, and pleats can be adjusted as necessary to hide seams in pleats. Keep the spaces uniform.

6) Fold individual pleats by bringing two pleat lines together and pinning. Crease buckram on the fold.

7) Stitch on pleat line from top of heading to ½" (1.3 cm) below heading; backstitch to secure.

8) Divide into three even pleats. Crease the fold of the pleat with one hand while opening the pleat at the top of the heading.

9) Press fold straight down to meet the pleat stitching line. Two pleats form at the sides.

10) Pinch outer folds up to meet center fold. Finger press three pleats together, making sure they are all even.

11) Tack pleats with machine bar tack in center of pleat, ½" (1.3 cm) from bottom of buckram. Set machine for widest stitch, and stitch 4 to 5 times.

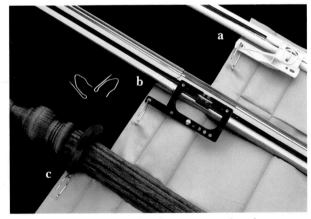

12) Insert drapery hooks. On a conventional traverse rod **(a)**, top of hook is 1¾" (4.5 cm) from upper edge of drapery. On a ringless decorator traverse rod **(b)**, hook is ¾" to 1" (2 to 2.5 cm) from upper edge. On a wood pole set **(c)**, hook is ½" (1.3 cm) from upper edge.

How to Sew Lined Pinch-pleated Draperies

1) Stitch drapery fabric, following step 1, page 228. Sew lining widths as necessary, using plain or serged seams. (Remove selvages to prevent puckering.) Turn under and stitch a 2" (5 cm) double bottom hem.

2) Place drapery on table or large flat surface. Lay lining on top of drapery, with *wrong* sides together and hem of lining ¾" (2 cm) above the hem of the drapery.

3) Trim 3" (7.5 cm) from each outside edge of lining. Trim lining so it is 8" (20.5 cm) from top edge of drapery.

4) Follow step 2, page 228. Then fold heading over *twice*, folding buckram over lining at the top. Press; pin or hand-baste.

5) Fold double 1½" (3.8 cm) side hems over the lining.

6) Blindstitch side hems (page 215). Finish draperies, following steps 5 to 12, pages 228 and 229.

Dressing Draperies

Window treatments need hand-dressing, or training, to keep them looking their best and most attractive. Before hanging draperies, press them with a warm, dry iron to remove any wrinkles. After draperies are hung, if wrinkles still exist, press with a warm, dry iron over a hand-held roll of paper towels.

If fabric is particularly hard to train into pleats, you may want to finger press. Place the front edge of the drapery between the thumb and index finger, and follow the front edge of the pleat all the way to the hemline. Finger pressing creates a light crease and helps train the drapery and tailor the pleat.

Roman shades may also need to be raised and then tied in position for a few days to set the folds. Then when the shade is raised again after being lowered, the pleats will naturally fold into the right position.

How to Dress Draperies

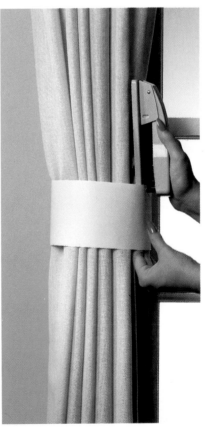

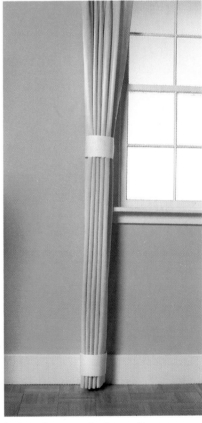

1) Draw draperies into the stacked position. Starting at top, guide pleats into soft folds. If lined, catch lining in folds. Make sure depth of folds is even. Use grain of fabric as guide to keep pleats perpendicular to floor.

2) Staple a piece of paper or tie a piece of muslin around the pleats halfway between top and hem to hold them in place. Do not fasten so tightly that wrinkles appear.

3) Staple second piece of paper at the hemline. The draperies should hang straight from the rod. Leave tied for 5 to 7 days. Humidity will encourage the setting process.

Roman Shade

Roman shades have a tailored appearance that complements many styles of decor. Use them alone or add cornices, curtains or draperies.

Like roller shades, Roman shades are flat and smooth when down. When pulled up, they take up more space at the top because they pleat crisply instead of rolling. If you want the raised shade to clear the window completely, mount it at the ceiling. This also adds apparent height to the window. A system of evenly-spaced cords and rings on the back of the shade causes the shade to pleat when pulled. A weight bar near the bottom of the shade adds stability and aids smooth tracking.

The choice of fabric affects the look of the finished shade. Sturdy, firm fabrics work best for the pleats of these shades. Lightweight, softer fabrics may be used, but the shades will be less crisp-looking. Roman shades are usually lined. This gives added body to the shade, prevents fabric fading and gives windows a uniform appearance from the outside.

You may need to seam fabric or lining to create enough width for the shades. Be sure to consider these seams when measuring for construction. Additional fabric may be needed to match a print, plaid or other design.

To make measuring and construction easier and more accurate, use a folding cardboard cutting board on your work surface.

✂ Cutting Directions

Determine width and length of finished shade. Cut decorator fabric for shade 3" (7.5 cm) wider and 3" (7.5 cm) longer than finished shade.

Cut lining with width equal to finished width of shade; length equal to finished length plus 3" (7.5 cm).

Cut facing strip from lining fabric, 5" (12.5 cm) wide; length equal to finished width of shade plus 2" (5 cm).

YOU WILL NEED

Decorator fabric for shade.

Lining fabric for lining and facing strip.

Mounting board, 1" × 2" (2.5 × 5 cm), cut to size for inside or outside mounting. Paint ends of board or cover with matching fabric.

Screw eyes or pulleys, large enough to hold all the pull cords. Number should equal the number of vertical rows.

Shade cord for each vertical row of rings. Each cord must be long enough to go up the shade, across the top and partway down the side for pulling.

Plastic rings, ½" (1.3 cm), equal to number of vertical rows multiplied by number of horizontal rows. Or use ring tape with 6" (15 cm) spaces the length of the shade times the number of vertical rows plus 6" (15 cm) for each row.

Weight rod, one ⅜" (1 cm) brass rod or ½" (1.3 cm) rustproof flat bar, cut ½" (1.3 cm) shorter than finished width of shade.

White glue or liquid fray preventer.

Awning cleat.

Staple gun or tacks.

Drapery pull (optional).

How to Make a Roman Shade

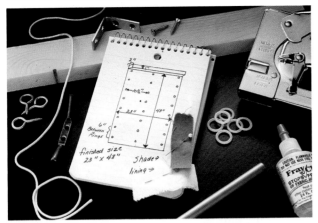

1) **Sketch** the shade to use as a guide for ring locations, page 234, step 7. Cut shade fabric; seam for width, if necessary. If fabric ravels, finish side edges with zigzag stitch or liquid fray preventer.

2) **Place** shade fabric wrong side up on work surface. Mark finished width. Press 1½" (3.8 cm) side hems.

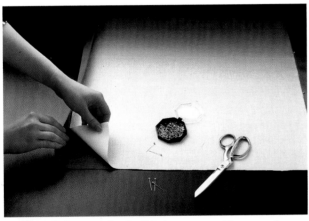

3) **Place** lining on shade fabric, wrong sides together. Slip lining under side hems. Smooth and press lining. Pin in place; slipstitch, if desired.

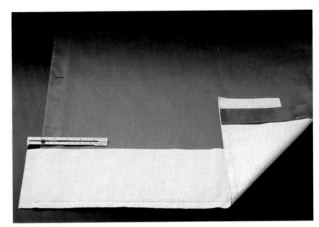

4) **Center** and pin facing strip on right side of shade, even with lower edge, with 1" (2.5 cm) extending at each side. Stitch ½" (1.3 cm) from lower edge. Press toward wrong side of shade.

5) **Fold** and press facing extensions to back of shade so they do not show on the right side. Fuse or stitch in place.

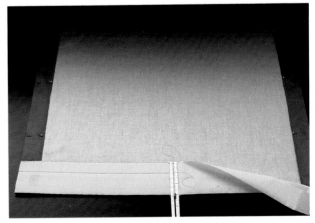

6) **Turn** under raw edge of facing 1½" (3.8 cm); turn under again 3" (7.5 cm). Stitch along folded edge. Stitch again, 1" (2.5 cm) from first stitching to form pocket for weight rod.

(Continued on next page)

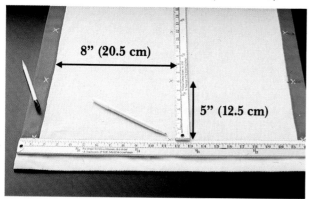

7) Mark locations for rings with horizontal and vertical rows of X's. First, mark outside vertical rows 1" (2.5 cm) from shade edges so rings hold side hems in place. Space vertical rows 8" to 12" (20.5 to 30.5 cm) apart across shade. Position bottom row just above the rod pocket. Space horizontal rows 5" to 8" (12.5 to 20.5 cm) apart.

8) Pin through both layers of fabric at center of ring markings, with pins parallel to bottom of shade. Fold shade in accordion pleats at pins to position shade for machine or hand stitching of rings. If using ring tape, omit steps 9a and 9b.

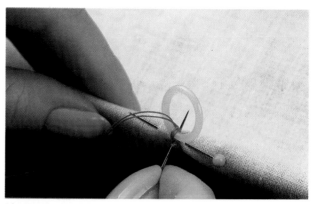

9a) Attach rings by placing fold (pin in center) under presser foot with ring next to fold. Set stitch length at 0, and zigzag at widest setting. Secure ring with 8 to 10 stitches, catching small amount of fold in each stitch. Lock stitches by adjusting needle to penetrate the fabric in one place (width setting at 0) for 2 or 3 stitches.

9b) Tack rings by hand if zigzag stitch is not available. Use double thread. Secure with 4 or 5 stitches in one place, through both fabric layers. Reinforce all rings in bottom row with extra stitches; they hold the weight of the fabric.

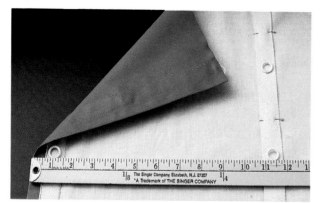

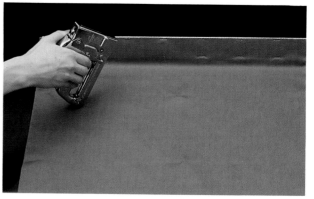

9c) Use ring tape instead of rings, if desired. Turn under ½" (1.3 cm) at bottom of tape and place at top of rod pocket. Pin tape to shade in vertical rows, lining up rings horizontally. Stitch both long edges and bottom of tape with zipper foot, stitching all tapes in same direction.

10) Staple or tack shade to top of mounting board. If shade is mounted outside of window frame, paint or wrap the board with lining fabric before attaching shade. This gives the shade a finished look.

(Continued on next page)

How to Make a Roman Shade (continued)

11) Insert screw eyes on mounting board to line up with vertical rows; place one screw eye above each row. On heavy or wide shades, use pulleys instead of screw eyes.

12) Tie a nonslip knot in bottom ring. Apply white glue to knot and ends of cord to prevent knot from slipping. Thread cord through the vertical row of rings.

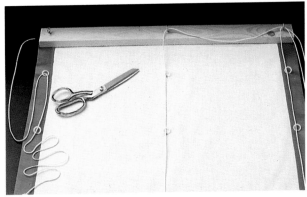

13) Cut lengths of cord, one for each row of rings. Each cord will be a different length; cords go up the shade, across the top and partway down one side. String cord through rings and screw eyes, with excess cord at one side for pulling.

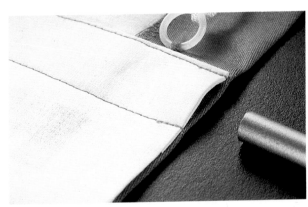

14) File ends of weight rod or cover ends with tape. Insert rod into rod pocket and slipstitch ends closed. A galvanized or iron rod, painted to resist rusting, can be used instead of a brass rod.

15) Mount shade. Adjust cords with shade lowered so the tension on each cord is equal. Tie cords in a knot just below screw eye. Braid cords and secure at bottom with a knot or drapery pull.

16) Center awning cleat on edge of window frame or on wall. Wind cord around cleat to secure shade position when the shade is raised.

Stitched-tuck Shade

Narrow stitched tucks along each fold line add interest to this tailored version of the Roman shade. Read about Roman shades on pages 232 to 235 before beginning this project.

To determine the number of tucks, subtract 3" (7.5 cm) for the hem from finished length of shade. Divide this number by 3" (7.5 cm), the approximate spacing between tucks, to get the number of tucks. Round this figure to the nearest whole number. To determine the spacing between tucks, divide the finished length of shade by the number of tucks (as determined above). Rings will be placed on alternate tucks, beginning with the bottom tuck.

✄ Cutting Directions

Cut decorator fabric and lining as for Roman shade (page 232), adding ½" (1.3 cm) for each tuck to the length of both fabrics. Also cut facing strip from lining fabric, 5" (12.5 cm) wide; length equal to finished shade width plus 2" (5 cm).

YOU WILL NEED

Decorator fabric for shade.

Lining fabric for lining and facing strip.

Notions: mounting board, plastic rings, screws eyes or pulleys, shade cord, weight rod, white glue, awning cleat and staple gun, as for Roman shade.

How to Make a Stitched-tuck Shade

1) Follow directions for Roman shade, pages 233 and 234, steps 1 to 7, except space horizontal rows as figured above. Draw horizontal lines across wrong side of shade at ring locations. Baste lining and outer fabric together on each line.

2) Remove water-soluble pen markings. Fold and press sharp crease exactly on each basting line, right sides together. Bring opposite folds together, accordion pleat style, and press crease in each fold. Machine-baste as in step 1.

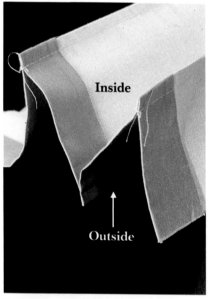

3) Stitch tucks ¼" (6 mm) from creased edges on right side and wrong side of shade. Complete the shade following the directions for a Roman shade, pages 234 and 235, steps 9a to 16. Do not use ring tape.

Hobbled Shade

The hobbled shade falls into soft folds, held in place by twill tape. Read about Roman shades (pages 232 to 235) before beginning this project.

To determine the number of folds, double the finished length of the shade and subtract 3" (7.5 cm); then divide this number by 7" (18 cm), the approximate spacing between the folds. Round this figure to the nearest whole number. To determine the actual spacing between the folds, divide twice the finished length of the shade minus 3" (7.5 cm) by the number of folds.

✂ Cutting Directions

Cut decorator fabric and lining as for Roman shade (page 232), doubling the length for both fabrics. Cut facing strip from lining fabric, 5" (12.5 cm) wide; length of facing strip is equal to finished shade width plus 2" (5 cm). Cut twill tape, with length equal to finished length of shade plus 3" (7.5 cm).

YOU WILL NEED

Decorator fabric for shade.

Lining fabric for lining and facing strip.

Twill tape, ½" (1.3 cm) wide.

Notions: mounting board, plastic rings, screw eyes or pulleys, shade cord, weight rod, white glue, awning cleat and staple gun, as for Roman shade.

How to Make a Hobbled Shade

1) Follow steps 1 to 7 on pages 233 and 234, except space horizontal rows on shade as figured above for actual spacing between folds. Mark tapes at intervals halfway between rings on shade, beginning at top of rod pocket.

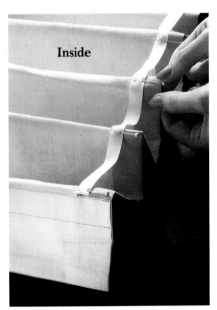

2) Pin tapes to the shade, lining up marks on tapes with marks on shade. The excess fabric between the markings forms folds on the right side of the shade.

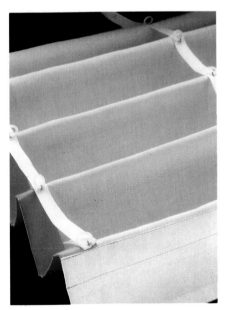

3) Tack the rings in place, catching the tape and both layers of the fabric at each ring. Complete shade following directions for Roman shade, pages 234 and 235, steps 10 to 16.

Top Treatments

Top treatments give curtains, draperies, or shades a custom look that sets the window apart from the ordinary. They include valances, poufs, swags and jabots, and cornices. They may be used alone, to allow the maximum light or view through a window, or with any curtain or drapery to cover an unattractive rod, or simply as a decorative accent.

Top treatments are used not only with curtains and draperies, but also with shower curtains, mini-blinds, pleated shades, vertical blinds, and shutters to soften the overall appearance or to coordinate fabric or color within a room.

A top treatment can be a useful camouflage. It can help to extend the visual height of a window or can make it appear shorter, depending on the style and placement. Valances and cornices can make windows that are at different levels in a room appear uniform. When wall space is limited for drapery stackback, a top treatment used by itself can give the window a finished look without a great deal of effort.

Fabric has a lot to do with the look. The same style can be made in moire or linen; the moire will be elegant for a tailored look, and the linen will be more casual for a country look. A straight valance or cornice is usually more tailored than one that is gathered, but in a formal fabric a gathered one can be just as elegant.

Valances are simply short curtains, draperies, or soft shades used at the top of a window. A valance may be mounted on a separate curtain rod or on a mounting board inside or outside the window frame. Mounting boards are cut from 1" (2.5 cm) lumber; the depth may be 2" to 5" (5 to 12.5 cm), or more, depending on the return of the underdrapery, curtain, or shade. Valances are generally "soft," as opposed to a "hard" cornice constructed of plywood.

Swags are soft drapes of fabric across the top of the window. They are usually attached to a mounting board, although a more informal look is to drape a swag over a wooden or decorative pole. They usually have an attached side drape of fabric, called either a *jabot* or a *cascade*. Jabots may be pleated, gathered, or casually draped.

Cornices are custom-built boxes without backs that cover the top of the window. They may be stained, painted, or upholstered to match a window treatment. The lower edge of a cornice may be cut straight or cut into a decorative shape.

Measuring for a Top Treatment

There are few hard and fast rules for top treatments, because they are an excellent opportunity to express creativity. In general, the length of the valance should be in proportion to the total length of the window or window treatment. This length is usually about one-fifth of the window treatment. To add visual height to a room, a top treatment may be mounted at the ceiling, or at least several inches (centimeters) above the window.

For shaped treatments such as swags, the shortest point should come 4" (10 cm) below the top of the window glass and cover 6" to 8" (15 to 20.5 cm) of an underdrapery heading.

If a valance or cornice is not mounted at the ceiling, allow at least 4" (10 cm) of clearance between the top of the drapery and the valance for the mounting brackets.

For mounting a top treatment over draperies, add 4" (10 cm) to the width, and 2" to 3" (5 to 7.5 cm) to the depth on each side, to allow for clearance at the return. For example, if using a valance with an underdrapery, use a 5½" (14 cm) valance return over a standard 3½" (9 cm) underdrapery return.

Mock Cornices

Top treatments that resemble cornices can be made without carpentry or upholstery techniques. Mock cornices are mounted on flat curtain rods that measure 4½" (11.5 cm) wide. Fusible fleece applied inside the rod pocket gives the treatment a padded look. The top and bottom of the rod pocket are accented with fabric-covered welting or twisted welting. For added flair, a pleated or gathered skirt is sewn below the rod pocket.

These versatile top treatments can be used to dress up windows that have existing treatments, such as vertical or horizontal blinds, pleated shades, or curtains. In some cases, they may provide a totally new look, using existing wide flat rods.

For best results, select a lightweight fabric that can be successfully railroaded (page 206). This will eliminate the need for seams in the rod pocket. The skirt can be seamed in the center, hiding the seam in a pleat or gathers. Two skirts lengths and both rod-pocket pieces can be cut from one width of 54" (137 cm) decorator fabric, provided the skirt length does not exceed 16" (40.5 cm).

✂ Cutting Directions

Determine the desired finished width of the valance, the depth of the returns, and the desired finished length of the skirt. Preshrink decorator fabric and lining by steaming.

Cut a strip of decorator fabric for the front of the rod pocket, 6" (15 cm) wide, with the length equal to the desired finished width of the valance, including returns, plus 1" (2.5 cm) for end seams plus ½" (1.3 cm) for ease. Cut a strip of decorator fabric for the back of the rod pocket, 6" (15 cm) wide, with the length equal to the cut length of the front rod-pocket strip plus 1" (2.5 cm). Cut a strip of lining fabric for the front rod-pocket facing, with the same length and width as the front rod-pocket strip.

Cut the decorator fabric for the skirt, with the length equal to the desired finished length plus 4½" (11.5 cm). If making a gathered skirt, the cut width of the skirt is equal to twice the desired finished width, including returns, plus 1" (2.5 cm). If making a pleated skirt, determine the cut width by making a pattern as on page 252, steps 1 to 3. Cut the lining for the skirt, with the length equal to the finished length of the skirt plus ½" (1.3 cm) and the cut width equal to the cut width of the decorator fabric.

Cut bias fabric strips, if making fabric-covered welting, as on page 270.

Cut a strip of fusible fleece, 5" (12.5 cm) wide, with the length equal to the finished width of the valance, including returns, plus ½" (1.3 cm) for ease.

YOU WILL NEED

Decorator fabric.

Lining fabric.

Fusible fleece.

Fabric-covered welting, twisted welting, or 5/32" **(3.8 mm) cord and fabric,** for making fabric-covered welting.

Flat curtain rod, 4½" (11.5 cm) wide, with adjustable mounting brackets to obtain necessary projection.

Self-adhesive hook and loop tape.

Knife-pleated skirt and twisted welting create a crisp, tailored mock cornice.

How to Sew a Mock Cornice with a Gathered Skirt

1) **Center** fusible fleece strip on the wrong side of the front rod-pocket strip; fuse in place, following manufacturer's instructions.

2) **Make** fabric-covered welting as on pages 270 and 271, steps 1 to 3, and attach it to upper and lower edges of front rod-pocket strip, if desired; begin and end welting 1/2" (1.3 cm) from ends of strip. Or attach purchased welting.

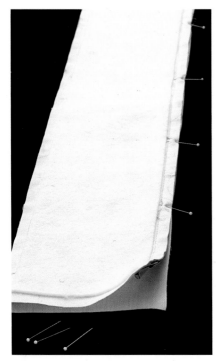

3) **Place** front rod pocket over the front rod-pocket facing strip, right sides together, aligning edges; pin along lower edge and ends.

4) **Stitch** 1/2" (1.3 cm) seam along lower edge and ends, using zipper foot and stitching with facing side down. Crowd cording by stitching just inside previous stitches.

5) **Clip** lower corners diagonally; turn front rod pocket right side out, and press. Baste upper edges together within 1/2" (1.3 cm) seam allowance.

6) Seam fabric for skirt, if necessary; repeat for skirt lining. Pin skirt and lining, right sides together, along lower edge. Stitch 2" (5 cm) from raw edges.

7) Press 2" (5 cm) hem allowance away from lining. Pin skirt to lining, right sides together, along sides, aligning upper edges; skirt will form fold even with lower edge of hem allowance. Stitch ½" (1.3 cm) side seams.

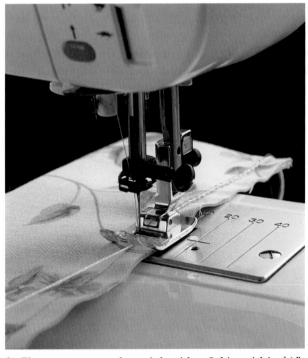

8) Clip lower corners diagonally. Press the lining side seam allowances toward lining. Turn skirt right side out, realigning upper edges; press. Baste the upper edges together.

9) Zigzag over a cord on right side of skirt within ½" (1.3 cm) seam allowance of upper edge.

(Continued on next page)

10) Divide skirt into eighths; pin-mark. Divide lower edge of back rod pocket into eighths, beginning and ending 1" (2.5 cm) from ends. Pin wrong side of skirt to right side of back rod pocket along lower edge, matching pin marks and raw edges.

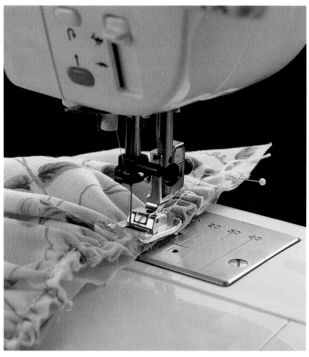

11) Pull gathering cord on skirt to fit lower edge of back rod pocket; pin in place. Stitch ½" (1.3 cm) from raw edges. Press seam allowances toward back rod pocket.

12) Pin back rod pocket to front rod pocket along upper edge, right sides together; ends of back rod pocket extend 1" (2.5 cm) beyond ends of front rod pocket. With the front rod pocket on top, stitch ½" (1.3 cm) seam, using zipper foot; crowd cording.

13) Press seam allowances toward back rod pocket. Turn under ends of back rod-pocket strip ½" (1.3 cm) twice, encasing ends of seam allowances; stitch.

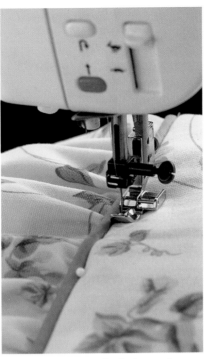

14) Turn skirt and back rod pocket down behind rod pocket. From the right side, pin skirt in place along the seamline at lower edge of rod pocket, just above welting.

15) Stitch in the ditch from the right side by stitching in the well of the seam above the welting, using a zipper foot.

16) Insert the curtain rod into rod pocket. Mount rod on bracket. Pull taut toward returns; secure returns to the sides of brackets, using self-adhesive hook and loop tape.

How to Sew a Mock Cornice with a Pleated Skirt

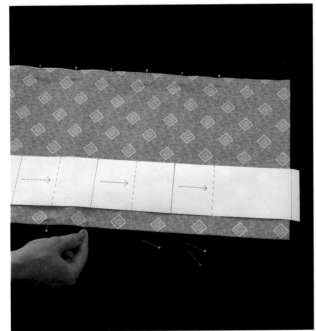

1) Make a pattern for the pleated skirt, as on page 252, steps 1 to 3. Follow steps 1 to 8 on pages 242 and 243. Lay the skirt faceup on flat surface; lay pattern over upper edge of skirt, aligning the marked seamlines to seamed outer edges. Transfer pattern markings to skirt. Repeat along lower edge.

2) Pin pleats in place along upper and lower edges of skirt; press. Baste along upper edge. Pin wrong side of skirt to right side of back rod pocket along lower edge; stitch. Press seam allowances toward the rod pocket. Complete mock cornice, following steps 12 to 16, opposite and above.

Overlapping Triangle Valances

An overlapping triangle valance is a simple lined treatment made from two panels attached to a mounting board. Welting accents the diagonal edge of the panels.

Mount the valance on a 1 × 3 board no longer than 50½" (128.3 cm) or a 1 × 4 board no longer than 49½" (126.3 cm). The standard-size boards actually measure about ¾" × 2½" (2 × 6.5 cm) and ¾" × 3½" (2 × 9 cm), respectively. The lengths given are the maximum for which the panels can be constructed using a single width of 54" (137 cm) fabric.

The mounting board can be mounted either at the top of the window frame or on the wall above the window. The finished width of the valance should be at least 2" (5 cm) wider than the outside measurement of the window frame or 2" (5 cm) wider than the width of an undertreatment. The finished length at the side of the valance and the depth, or projection, of the mounting board determine the angle of the panels and the depth of the overlap at the center.

Tape a length of string at the upper corners of the window and experiment with different side lengths to help determine the desired finished length.

✂ Cutting Directions

Cut two rectangles each from outer fabric and lining. The cut width of the rectangles is equal to the length of the mounting board plus the depth, or projection, of the mounting board for one return plus 1" (2.5 cm) for seam allowances. The cut length of the rectangles is equal to the finished length of the valance plus the depth of the mounting board plus ½" (1.3 cm) for seam allowance. The rectangles are cut to size on page 248, steps 1 to 3.

YOU WILL NEED

Decorator fabric; two coordinating fabrics may be used.	**Mounting board.**
	Heavy-duty stapler; staples.
Lining fabric.	
Purchased welting.	**Angle irons;** pan-head screws or molly bolts.

How to Sew an Overlapping Triangle Valance

1) **Place** one piece each of fabric and lining wrong sides together. On right side of fabric, ½" (1.3 cm) from side edge, measure from upper edge, the width of the mounting board plus ½" (1.3 cm); mark point.

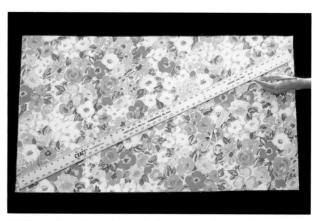

2) **Draw** line from lower left corner through point at upper right to mark lower edge of left valance panel and lining. Cut on marked line; discard excess fabric.

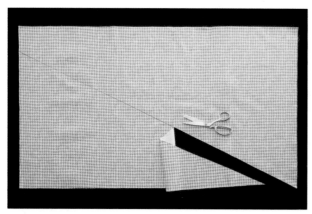

3) **Repeat** steps 1 and 2 to cut the right valance panel and lining; mark and cut diagonal lower edge at angle opposite that of left panel. Set aside lining panels until step 7.

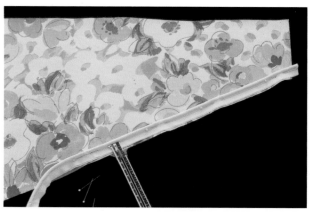

4) **Pin** welting to right side of the outer fabric along diagonal lower edge; position stitching line of welting ½" (1.3 cm) from raw edge of fabric. Trim ends of welting even with edges of fabric.

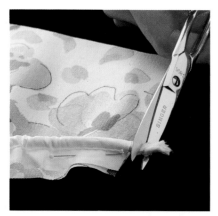

5) **Pull** the cording at each end and trim away about ⅝" (1.5 cm), to reduce bulk in the seam allowance. Smooth welting in place.

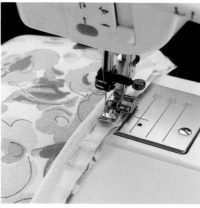

6) **Baste** welting to valance, using a zipper foot and ½" (1.3 cm) seam allowance.

7) **Pin** lining to the outer fabric, with right sides together and raw edges even. With outer fabric up, stitch around sides and lower edges in ½" (1.3 cm) seam; at diagonal edge, stitch just inside previous stitching.

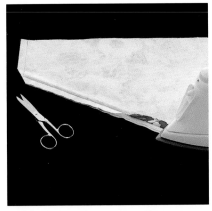

8) Trim corners diagonally; trim seam allowances at lower point. Press seam allowances open.

9) Turn valance right side out; press. Smooth layers flat; pin upper edges together. Finish upper edge, using overlock or zigzag stitch.

10) Measure from the side edge of panel the width of mounting board; fold to lining side. Lightly press to crease return. Repeat for remaining panel.

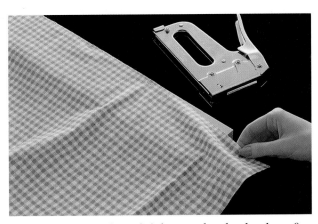

11) Align upper edge of right panel to back edge of the board, and position fold of return at right edge of the board; staple to within 6" (15 cm) of right edge of the board.

12) Make diagonal fold at the corner to fold in excess fullness; staple.

13) Repeat steps 11 and 12 to staple the left panel to the mounting board.

14) Secure angle irons to the bottom of mounting board, near ends, using pan-head screws. Secure angle irons to top of window frame or into wall studs, using pan-head screws; if securing to drywall or plaster, use molly bolts.

Pleated Valances

Pleated valances offer a wide range of design possibilities, from crisply pressed tailoring to softly folded elegance. Knife pleats and box pleats are the two basic styles, with inverted box pleats offering a third alternative. Unlimited variations in pleat sizes and arrangements make it possible to design unique valances to suit any decorating scheme.

Knife pleats are commonly arranged as a series of sharp pleats of equal size and spacing, usually 1" to 2" (2.5 to 5 cm), and all turned in the same direction. For symmetry, knife-pleated valances are usually divided visually in the center, with pleats turned toward the outer edges. Pleats may be arranged continuously from the center outward, or in clusters of three or more pleats separated by spaces.

A box pleat has the appearance of two abutting knife pleats turned toward each other. Box pleats are generally deeper than knife pleats and are separated by wider spaces. A valance may be designed with continuous box pleats of equal size and spacing, with a pleat centered at each front corner. To vary the look, fewer box pleats may be placed farther apart, perhaps accenting existing structural divisions of the window.

For inverted box pleats, the excess fabric of the pleat is folded to the outside. This style is especially appealing when the folds are left unpressed for a softer look. If desired, a decorative trim may be applied to the lower edge of a valance with unpressed pleats.

Careful consideration must be given to the fabric for pleated valances. Pleating will obviously distort the pattern of the fabric, so smaller, all-over prints are more desirable than large prints. Striped and plaid fabrics can work very well for pleated valances as long as the pleat sizes and arrangements are planned to coincide with the fabric pattern.

A diagram of the valance will help to determine finished width and length. It is necessary to make a paper pattern of the valance, following steps 1 to 3 on page 252. The pattern will help determine pleat size, spacing, and placement of seams, allowing for adjustments before the fabric is cut. Any seams must be hidden in the folds of the pleats. If possible, the fabric may be railroaded (page 206), eliminating the need for seams.

To prevent excess bulk at the hem, pleated valances may be self-lined or lined with a lightweight fabric in an accent color. If white or off-white lining is preferred, a flat bias edging, 1/2" (1.3 cm) wide, may be sewn into the lower seam, preventing the lining from peeking out at the lower edge. Self-lined valances may be interlined with lightweight drapery lining, if necessary, to prevent the pattern on the back from showing through to the front.

Knife pleats in the top valance were planned to play off the plaid pattern in the fabric. Unpressed inverted box pleats (above) are edged with a tassel fringe trim.

How to Make a Pattern for the Valance

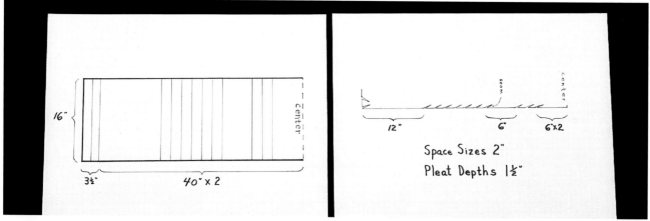

1) Diagram valance to scale on graph paper, indicating finished length, width, return depth, and desired placement of pleats. Returns of 3½" (9 cm) or more can accommodate two or more knife pleats or half of a box pleat. Avoid pleats on smaller returns. Draw an aerial view of the valance, indicating pleat depths,

space sizes, and any seam placements. When planning pleat sizes and placement, avoid excess bulk of overlapping pleats. For striped or plaid valance, follow fabric pattern to determine pleat and space sizes. Check to see that space measurements add up to finished width.

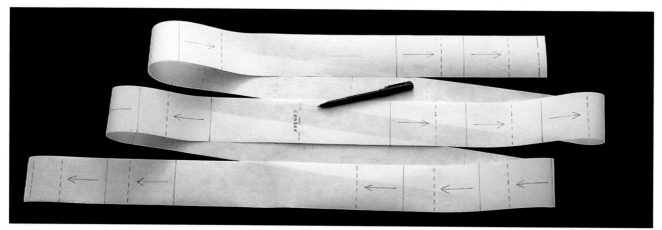

2) Unroll adding machine paper on flat surface. Mark ½" (1.3 cm) side seam allowance at end. Measure and mark all spaces and pleats as determined in step 1. Mark folds with solid lines; mark

placement lines with dotted lines. Indicate direction of folds with arrows. Mark pattern for entire width of valance, ending with ½" (1.3 cm) seam allowance for opposite end; cut paper.

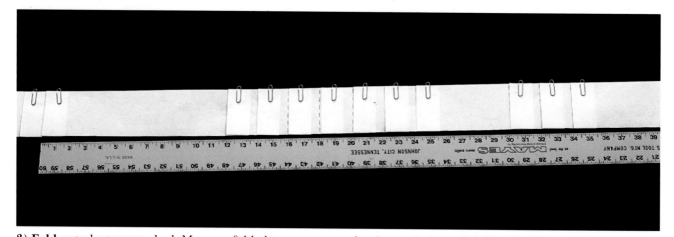

3) Fold out pleats as marked. Measure folded pattern to see that it equals desired finished width, including returns; adjust a few pleats, if necessary.

Graph paper.

Roll of paper, such as adding machine paper.

Decorator fabric.

Lightweight decorator fabric in accent color, for lining; or drapery lining, if valance is not self-lined.

Lightweight decorator fabric, for flat bias edging on valance lined with drapery lining.

Lightweight drapery lining, for interlining on self-lined valance, optional.

Heavy paper, for pressing pleats.

Decorative trim, for valance with unpressed pleats, optional.

Mounting board, cut to necessary length.

Angle irons with flat-head screws; length of angle iron should be more than one-half the projection of board.

8 × 2½" (6.5 cm) flat-head screws, for installing valance into wall studs; or molly bolts or toggle anchors, for installing into drywall or plaster.

Staple gun and staples.

✂ Cutting Directions

Cut the fabric for a self-lined valance with the length equal to twice the desired finished length plus 3" (7.5 cm).

Cut the fabric for a lined valance with the length equal to the desired finished length plus 2" (5 cm).

Determine the approximate cut width by measuring the total width of the pattern, opposite; allow excess width for placing seams in the folds of pleats. Cut the valance fabric to the necessary width in step 1, below.

Cut the interlining for an interlined valance with the length equal to the desired finished length of the valance plus 1½" (3.8 cm), and the width equal to the cut width of the valance fabric.

Cut the lining for a lined valance with the same length and width as the valance fabric.

Cut bias fabric strips 2" (5 cm) wide, if making a lined valance with a flat bias edging.

How to Sew a Self-lined Pleated Valance

1) Seam fabric widths as necessary. Trim the seam allowances to ¼" (6 mm); press open. Lay valance pattern over seamed fabric, aligning seams to points in pattern where they will be hidden in pleats; cut fabric to width of pattern.

2) Pin interlining, if desired, to wrong side of the valance, matching upper edges and ends. Fold end of valance in half lengthwise, right sides together. Sew ½" (1.3 cm) seam on outer edge of the return. Repeat for opposite end of valance.

(Continued on next page)

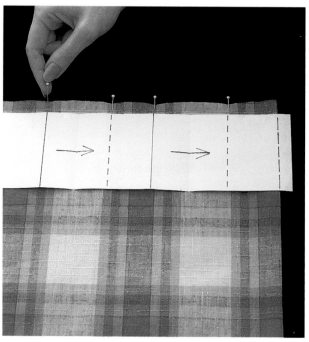

3) Turn valance right side out; press. Match upper raw edges. The lower edge of interlining, if used, extends to lower fold of the valance. Machine-baste layers together, ½" (1.3 cm) from upper raw edges. For valance with unpressed pleats, apply trim to the lower edge, if desired.

4) Lay valance faceup on flat surface; lay pattern over upper edge of valance, aligning end seamlines to seamed outer edges. Transfer pattern markings to valance. Repeat along lower edge.

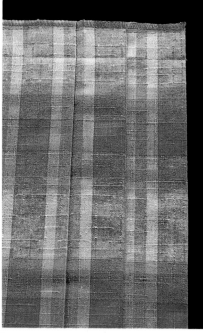

5) Pin pleats in place along upper and lower edges and center of the valance. Measure the valance width; adjust if necessary, distributing the adjustment among several pleats. If unpressed pleats are desired, omit step 6.

6) Press pleats on face of valance, removing pins from one pleat at a time; insert heavy paper under each pleat as it is pressed, to avoid imprinting. Replace pins along upper edge.

7) Stitch pleats in place across the valance, 1½" (3.8 cm) from the upper edge; remove pins. Finish the upper edge, using overlock or zigzag stitch.

8) Cover the mounting board with fabric. Position valance on mounting board, using stitching line as guide to extend upper edge 1½" (3.8 cm) onto top of board; position end pleats at front corners of the board. Staple valance in place at returns. Clip fabric at corner pleats close to stitching line to control the excess bulk. Staple valance in place; ease or stretch valance slightly to fit board, if necessary. Mount the valance.

How to Sew a Lined Pleated Valance

1) Follow step 1 on page 253. Cut lining to same width as valance fabric. Make flat bias edging and attach it to lower edge of the valance, if desired; begin and end edging ½" (1.3 cm) from side edges.

2) Place valance and lining right sides together, matching raw edges; pin along sides and lower edge. Stitch ½" (1.3 cm) seams on sides and lower edge. Complete valance as in steps 3 to 8, opposite and above.

Tapered Valance

The graceful curve of a tapered valance frames a window in soft folds of fabric. This valance is often used over mini-blinds and pleated shades to soften severe lines, or with short cafe curtains for a comfortable, casual look.

Tapered valances are usually lined when print fabrics are used, because you see the wrong side of the fabric as it cascades down the side of the window. If the lower edge has a ruffled finish, however, it does not have to be lined because the fall of the ruffle hides the wrong side of the fabric. Lightweight or sheer fabrics are also good choices for a ruffled valance, and do not require a lining.

The side length can be to the sill or apron, but it should be no less than one-third the length of the window. To determine the finished length at center of valance, see Measuring for a Top Treatment, page 240. To check the curve, you may wish to make a paper pattern or mock-up with old sheets or lining fabric.

✂ Cutting Directions

Cut fabric and lining 2 times the width of the rod. To estimate length, measure at longest point and add amount for rod pocket and heading plus 1" (2.5 cm) for seam allowance and turn-under. To determine cut length at center of valance, add allowance for rod pocket and heading plus ½" (1.3 cm) for turn-under to desired finished length at center.

For unlined valance with ruffle, use 2½ times fullness for valance. Subtract width of ruffle from finished length. Cut ruffle 2 times the length of the curve and finished width plus 1" (2.5 cm); seam fabric as necessary. Measure the curve after cutting the valance; or make a test muslin, and measure.

YOU WILL NEED

Decorator fabric for valance.

Lining for valance.

Flat curtain rod or Continental® rod.

How to Sew a Tapered Valance

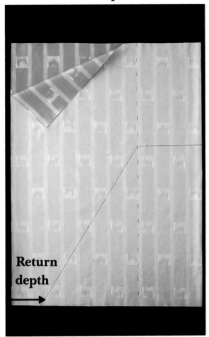

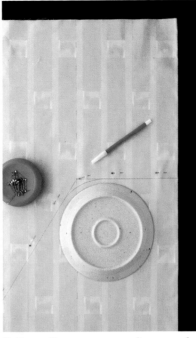

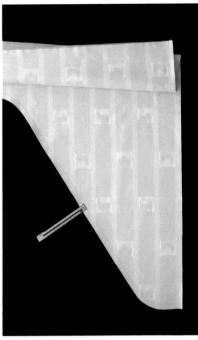

1) Seam fabric widths as necessary. Divide and mark fabric vertically into thirds. Fold in half. At center, mark cut length. At side, mark depth of return. Draw a straight line from return mark to nearest one-third marking at finished length in center.

2) Round upper corner into gentle curve; repeat for lower corner at return. Pin fabric layers together, and cut both layers as one. Center third is straight. Cut lining, using valance as pattern.

3) Place right side of lining and valance fabric together. Stitch ½" (1.3 cm) seam around valance, leaving upper edge open.

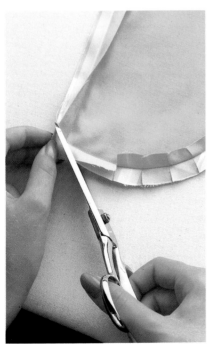

4) Press lining seam allowance toward lining. Clip curve. Diagonally trim corners.

5) Turn right side out. Turn under and stitch rod pocket and heading. Insert curtain rod in pocket.

Unlined valance with ruffle. Stitch 1" (2.5 cm) double side hems on valance. Turn under and stitch rod pocket and heading. Make and attach ruffle.

Swags & Jabots

A classic *swag* is a draping of soft folds used as a top treatment with pleated or gathered side panels. The side panels of the treatment are the *jabots* or *cascades*.

Window width and personal preference determine the number of swags. Each swag should generally be no wider than 40" (102 cm). This size can be adapted to any window size by increasing or decreasing the overlap on adjoining swags. The length of a swag is usually from 15" to 20" (38 to 51 cm) at the longest point in the center. Shallower swags may be used on narrow windows.

The jabot length should be about one-third of the drapery or window length, or should fall to a point of interest, such as the sill or floor. Its shortest point should be lower than the center of the swag. Jabots are 9" to 11" (23 to 28 cm) wide. Pleated jabots are more formal than gathered jabots, which are less controlled. Instructions are given here for the pleated jabot, but cutting and sewing techniques are basically the same for a gathered jabot. To gather the jabot, zigzag over a cord and pull the cord up to the desired fullness.

For outside mounting, attach swags and jabots to a cornice or mounting board placed 4" (10 cm) above the molding if used alone, or about 4" (10 cm) above the drapery rod if they are used over draperies. The cornice return must be deep enough to clear the underdrapery. Jabot returns are the same width as the cornice or mounting board. In homes with beautiful moldings the swags may be mounted inside the window on a board that fits inside the frame, and there are no returns.

Make a test swag to use as a pattern for cutting the decorator fabric. Use muslin or an old sheet that will drape softly. The test swag provides an opportunity to experiment and determine the appearance you want. Do not hesitate to drape the muslin and pin it at different positions until you find the look you like.

For each jabot, you will need one width of decorator fabric and lining the length of the jabot plus 1" (2.5 cm). For each swag, you will need 1 yd. (.95 m) of decorator fabric and lining if draped tape measurement, left, is less than the fabric width; you will need 2 yd. (1.85 m) if draped measurement is more than the fabric width.

YOU WILL NEED

Muslin or an old sheet for test swag.

Decorator fabric and lining for swags and jabots.

Wide twill tape, width of the mounting board plus 2 times the return.

Mounting board or cornice; heavy-duty stapler.

How to Estimate the Size of a Swag

Drape a tape measure or string to simulate the planned shape of each swag. For double swags, drape two tape measures.

How to Cut Jabots and Swags

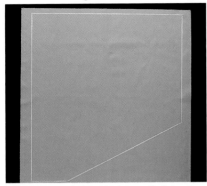

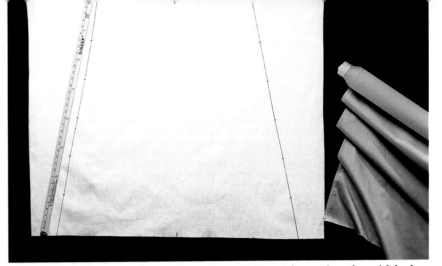

Jabots. Cut jabot 3 times finished width plus return and 1" (2.5 cm) seam allowance. On one side, mark shortest point plus 1" (2.5 cm). On the other side, mark longest point plus 1" (2.5 cm). From longest point, measure the width of return plus ½" (1.3 cm). Connect marks.

Swag. Cut muslin for the test swag 36" (91.5 cm) long. Cut the width the measurement from draped tape measure (left) plus 2" (5 cm) on each side for final adjustments. Mark width of window, centering marks at top of fabric. At lower edge, mark width from tape measure; connect the marks, forming diagonal guidelines. Divide each guideline equally into one more space than the number of folds; mark. For example, for five folds, divide into six spaces.

How to Make a Test Swag for Pattern

1) Fold muslin on first mark of diagonal line, and pull fold to the mark for upper corner; pin to ironing board. Continue pinning marked folds to corners, alternating sides and keeping upper edge straight.

2) Check the drape, and adjust pins and pleats as necessary. When folds are adjusted as desired, trim excess fabric 1" (2.5 cm) from outer edges and along the curved bottom edge about 3" (7.5 cm) from last fold.

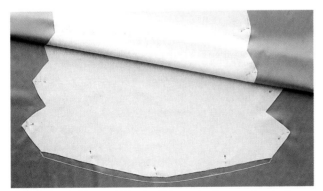

3) Unpin folds. Fold in half lengthwise to check that it is balanced and even; adjust cutting lines. Use as a pattern for cutting swag and lining. Add ½" (1.3 cm) seam allowances on upper and lower edges. This swag is not finished on ends and is mounted under jabot.

Alternative style. Fold muslin at first marks, and bring fold up to mounting board about 5" (12.5 cm) from ends. Drape smoothly, and continue folding, pulling each fold up and out slightly, toward end of board. The swag is finished at ends and can be mounted on top of or under jabot.

259

1) Pin lining to swag, right sides together, along lower curved edge. Stitch curved edge in ½" (1.3 cm) seam. Press lining seam allowance toward lining. Turn right side out; press stitched edge.

2) Pin swag front and lining together at remaining three sides. Overlock or zigzag raw edges together.

3) Pin pleats in place. The outside edge of each notch is the fold point.

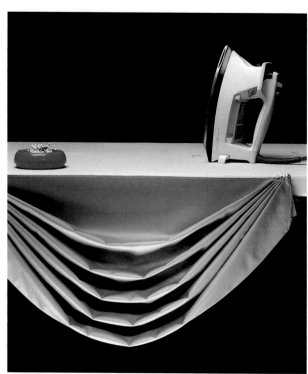

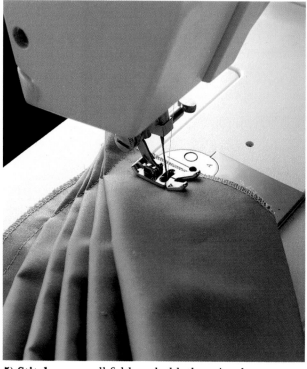

4) Check drape of swag again by pinning swag to the side of ironing board or mounting board. Make minor adjustments as desired.

5) Stitch across all folds to hold pleats in place.

How to Sew Jabots

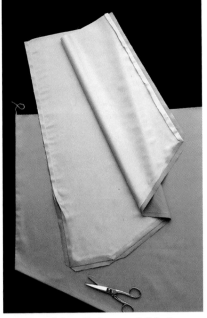

1) Place jabot lining and fabric, right sides together; stitch ½" (1.3 cm) seam on sides and bottom. Press lining seam allowance toward lining. Clip corners, and turn right side out. Press stitched edges. Stitch upper edges together in ½" (1.3 cm) seam. Zigzag or overlock raw edges.

2) Lay jabot, wrong side up, on large flat surface. On sides, fold under return and press in place. Turn jabot right side up.

3) Fold into evenly spaced pleats, starting on the outer edge; steam in position. Pleat other jabot in opposite direction. Check pleats by hanging jabot over edge of ironing board. Stitch ⅜" (1 cm) from upper edge to hold pleats in place.

How to Attach Swag and Jabots to a Mounting Board

1) Center swag on mounting board or cornice with edge of swag ½" (1.3 cm) from edge of board. Staple swag to board at 6" (15 cm) intervals.

2) Place top of one jabot at end of mounting board, with pressed fold at corner. Staple return in place. Position pleats on mounting board, overlapping swag. Fold under excess fabric at corner, and staple.

3) Cover fabric edges with wide twill tape. Staple tape along both edges, mitering at corners.

Padded Cornices

A cornice is a painted or fabric-covered wooden frame used as a tailored top treatment. When fabric-covered, the frame is padded with foam or bonded polyester to round the corners and give it a soft, upholstered look.

A cornice not only frames and finishes a window treatment by hiding the hardware, but also provides good insulation and energy-saving efficiency, because it encloses the top of the treatment and prevents cold air from escaping into the room.

Cornices are usually custom-built to fit the window. With simple carpentry skills you can build a cornice from plywood or pine boards. Any imperfections in the carpentry are covered with padding and fabric.

Measure the outside frame of the window after the drapery hardware is in place. The cornice should clear the curtain or drapery heading by 2" to 3" (5 to 7.5 cm), and it should extend at least 2" (5 cm) beyond the end of the drapery on each side. The measurements are the cornice *inside* measurements. Allow for the thickness of the wood when cutting.

The cornice should completely cover the drapery headings and hardware. Generally, apply the same guidelines for height as for any other top treatment. The cornice should be about one-fifth the height of the window treatment.

Use contrasting welting around the top and bottom edges to set the cornice apart when it is covered with the same fabric as the drapery.

When estimating fabric, railroad the fabric on a cornice to eliminate seams on plain fabrics. If the fabric cannot be railroaded because of a directional print, place the seams inconspicuously, never in the center. Prints should be centered or balanced.

✂ Cutting Directions

For face piece, cut decorator fabric 6" (15 cm) wider than front plus sides, and the height of cornice plus 3" (7.5 cm). Cut a 4" (10 cm) inner lining strip from decorator fabric, the same width as the face piece. Cut a strip of lining fabric the same width as the face piece and the same height as the cornice.

Cut a strip of batting or foam to cover the front and sides of the cornice.

Cover cording, pages 270 and 271, steps 1 to 3, to make welting slightly longer than the distance around the lower edge.

YOU WILL NEED

Decorator fabric and lining to cover cornice; optional coordinating or contrasting fabric for welting.

To build the cornice, ½" (1.3 cm) plywood for the front, top, and sides; carpenter's glue; sixpenny finishing nails.

To pad the cornice, 1" (2.5 cm) bonded polyester upholstery batting or ½" (1.3 cm) foam. If not available in local stores, you may be able to obtain through an upholsterer or upholstery supply.

⁵/₃₂" cording slightly longer than the distance to be corded.

Cardboard upholsterer's stripping to cover lower edge and sides; heavy-duty stapler, ½" (1.3 cm) and ¼" (6 mm) staples; spray foam adhesive; angle irons for mounting.

How to Build a Cornice

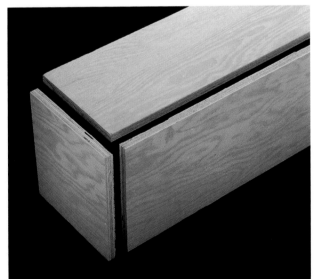

1) Measure and cut top to correspond to inside measurements for clearance. Cut front same width as top, and desired height. Cut sides same height as cornice and depth of top piece plus thickness of plywood.

2) Glue the top in place to front of board first. Remember which edges abut. Nail to secure. Then attach sides, first gluing in place to hold and then securing with nails.

How to Pad and Cover a Cornice

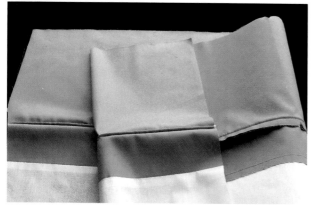

1) Stitch welting on right side of face piece in ½" (1.3 cm) seam, raw edges even. Sew welted edge to inner lining strip; sew free edge of inner strip to lining. Fold face piece in half to mark center at top and bottom.

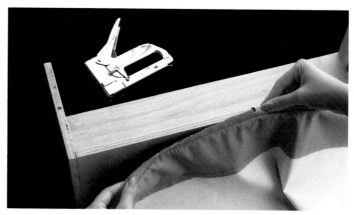

2) Mark center of cornice at top and bottom. Place *wrong* side of face fabric on outside of cornice, with welting seam on front edge of cornice; match center markings. Tack.

5) Fold lining to inside. Fold under raw edge, and staple at inside where top and face meet; at lower corners, miter fabric and staple close to corner. Tuck excess fabric into upper corners, and staple.

6) Rip excess welting seam back to end of cornice; trim welting to 1" (2.5 cm). Trim cord even with cornice edge. Staple lining to wall end of cornice; trim excess lining. Staple welting to wall end.

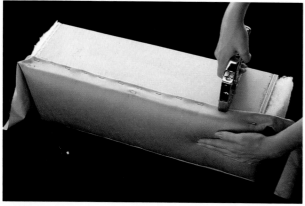

9) Tack at center and ends, removing slack. Do not stretch too tightly. Starting at center, turn under raw edge and staple to each end, placing staples 1½" (3.8 cm) apart, smoothing fabric as you go.

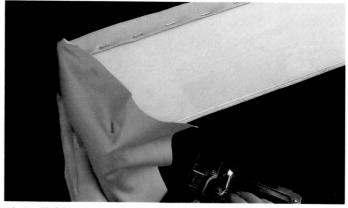

10) Pull fabric around corner to top back corner, removing slack; tack. Fold side fabric to back edge; staple. Trim excess fabric at back edge.

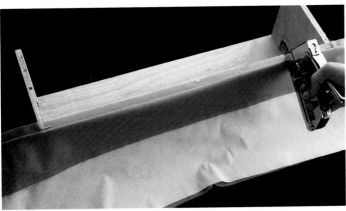

3) Pull seam taut to corners, and tack. Staple every 4" (10 cm) from center to ends. Flip lining back to check that welting is straight.

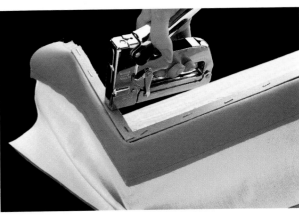

4) Place cardboard stripping tight against welting seam. Staple every 1" to 1½" (2.5 to 3.8 cm). Cut and overlap stripping at corners.

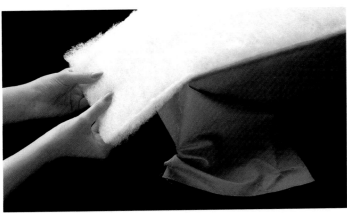

7) Turn cornice face up. Apply adhesive to front and sides. Place padding over glued surface, and stretch it slightly toward each end. Allow glue to set.

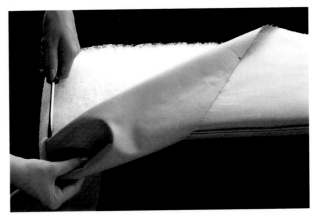

8) Fold face fabric over the front of cornice. Use a screwdriver to hold padding in place at corners. Gently smooth fabric toward top of cornice.

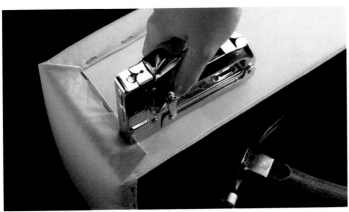

11) Fold fabric diagonally at corner to form a miter. Staple at corner and across ends. If fabric is bulky, tap staple with hammer. Repeat on both corners.

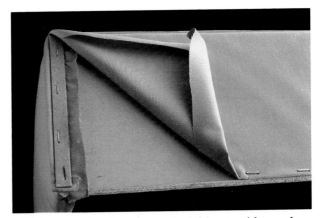

Welting at upper edge. Staple welting to sides and front, with seam at edge. On cornice front, place fabric over welting, with right sides together and raw edges even. Staple cardboard stripping at front and side edges as in step 4, above. Pull fabric to top of cornice, and fold under at sides and back; staple next to folds.

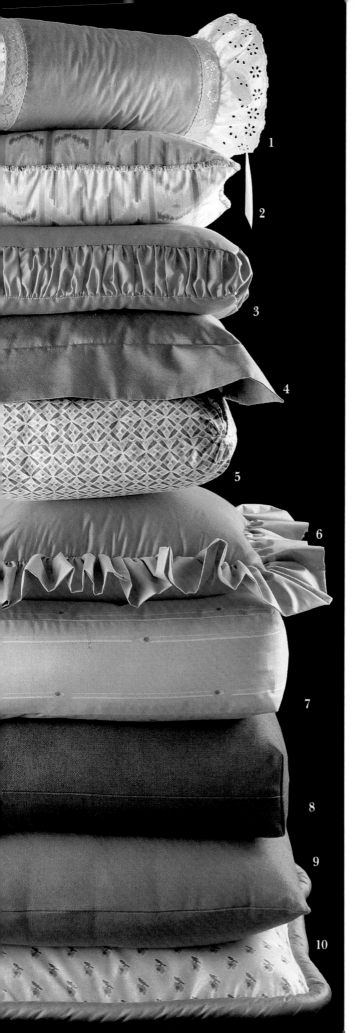

Pillows

Pillow styles range from simple to elaborate. Choice of technique affects your sewing time. Choose a simple knife-edge pillow, or invest more time in tailoring a box pillow complete with cording and a zipper.

1) Neckrolls are small round bolsters that are often trimmed with lace or ruffles. Sleeping bag pillows are the simplest neckroll bolsters to make. They are made with a drawstring closure at each end of a one-piece tube.

2) Shirred corded pillow is made by inserting gathered cording in the seam around the pillow. Cording is gathered using a technique, known as shirring, to gather the bias strip that covers the cord. Make cording in matching or contrasting fabric to add a decorative finish to a pillow.

3) Shirred box pillow uses shirring to gather both edges of the boxing strip. This makes the pillow softer than the traditional box pillow.

4) Flange pillow has a single or double, flat self-border, usually 2" (5 cm) wide, around a plump knife-edge pillow.

5) Mock box pillow is a variation of the knife-edge pillow, with shaped corners to add depth. Corners made using *gathered* style are tied inside the pillow.

6) Ruffled pillow features gathered lace or ruffles made in single or double layers. Pillow tops framed by ruffles in matching or contrasting fabric make attractive showcases for needlepoint, quilting, embroidery or candlewicking.

7) Box pillow has the added depth of a straight or shirred boxing strip. It can be soft for a scatter pillow, or firm for a chair cushion or floor pillow.

8) Mock box pillow can be made with *mitered* corners to create a tailored box shape.

9) Knife-edge pillow is the easiest pillow to make. It consists of two pieces of fabric sewn together, turned right side out and stuffed.

10) Corded pillow is a knife-edge pillow with matching or contrasting cording sewn in the seams. Use purchased cording or make your own. Or finish the pillow with a mock corded edge for a corded look without extra sewing time or fabric. Corded pillows are often called piped pillows.

To choose the right fabric for your pillow, consider how the pillow will be used and where it will be placed in your home. For a pillow that will receive hard wear, select a sturdy, firmly woven fabric that will retain its shape.

Pillows get their shape from forms or loose fillings. Depending on their washability, loose fillings may be stuffed directly into the pillow covering or encased in a separate liner for easy removal. For ease in laundering or dry cleaning, make a separate inner covering or liner for the stuffing, using lightweight muslin or lining fabric, or use purchased pillow forms. Make the liner as you would a knife-edge pillow (pages 268 and 269), fill it with stuffing, and machine-stitch it closed. Choose from several kinds of forms and fillings.

Standard polyester forms are square, round and rectangular for knife-edge pillows in sizes from 10" to 30" (25.5 to 76 cm). These forms are nonallergenic, washable, do not bunch, and may have muslin or polyester outer coverings. Choose muslin-covered forms for pillows with hook and loop tape closings. The loose muslin fibers do not catch on the rough side of the tape.

Polyurethane foam is available in sheets ½" to 5" (1.3 to 12.5 cm) thick for firm pillows and cushions. Some stores carry a high-density foam, 4" (10 cm) thick, for extra firm cushions. Since cutting the foam is difficult, ask the salesperson to cut a piece to the size of your pillow. If you must cut your own foam, use an electric or serrated knife with silicone lubricant sprayed on the blade. Polyurethane foam is also available shredded.

Polyester fiberfill is washable, nonallergenic filling for pillows or pillow liners. Fiberfill comes in loose-pack bags or pressed into batting sheets of varying densities. For a smooth pillow, sew an inner liner of batting, then stuff with loose fill. Soften the hard edges of polyurethane foam by wrapping the form with batting.

Kapok is vegetable fiber filling, favored by some decorators because of its softness. However, kapok is messy to work with and becomes matted with use.

Down is washed, quill-less feathers from the breasts of geese and ducks. Down makes the most luxurious pillows, but it is expensive and not readily available.

Knife-edge
Pillow or Liner

Knife-edge pillows are plump in the center and flat around the edges. These simple pillows can be made in half an hour.

Use the knife-edge pillow directions to make removable pillow liners. Sew liners from muslin, sheeting, cotton sateen, or similar fabrics.

✂ Cutting Directions

Cut front and back 1" (2.5 cm) larger than finished pillow or liner. For hook and loop tape or zipper closure, add 1½" (3.8 cm) to back width; for overlap closure, add 5½" (14 cm).

YOU WILL NEED

Decorator fabric for pillow front and back.

Lining fabric for pillow liner, front, and back.

Pillow form or polyester fiberfill. Use 8 to 12 oz. (227 to 360 g) fiberfill for a 14" (35.5 cm) pillow, depending on desired firmness.

Zipper or other closure (optional) may be inserted (pages 282 to 285).

How to Make a Knife-edge Pillow or Liner

1) Fold front into fourths. Mark a point halfway between the corner and the fold on each open side. At corner, mark a point ½" (1.3 cm) from each raw edge.

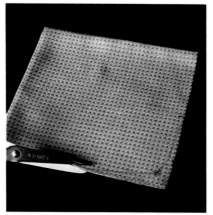

2) Trim from center mark to corner, gradually tapering from the edge to the ½" (1.3 cm) mark. Taper from ½" (1.3 cm) mark to center mark on opposite edge.

3) Unfold front and use it as a pattern for trimming back so that all corners are slightly rounded. This will eliminate dog-ears on the corners of the finished pillow.

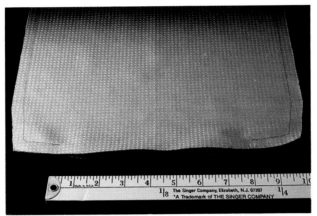

4) Pin front to back, right sides together. Stitch ½" (1.3 cm) seam, leaving opening on one side for turning and stuffing. Backstitch at the beginning and end of seam.

5) Trim corners diagonally, ⅛" (3 mm) from stitching. On pillows with curved edges or round corners, clip seam allowance to stitching at intervals along curves.

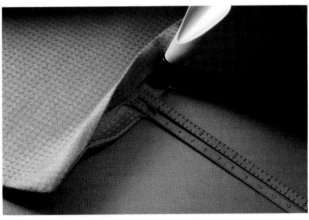

6) Turn pillow right side out, pulling out corners. Press the seams. Press under the seam allowances in the opening.

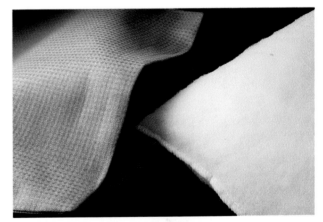

7a) Insert a purchased pillow form into the pillow, or stuff the pillow with polyester fiberfill as in step 7b, below. Use a removable form or liner in pillows that will be drycleaned or laundered.

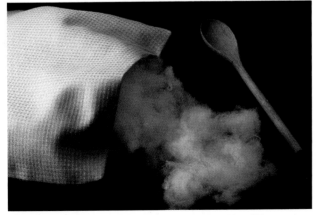

7b) Stuff pillow or liner with polyester fiberfill, gently pulling pieces apart to fluff and separate fibers. Work filling into corners, using long, blunt tool such as a spoon handle.

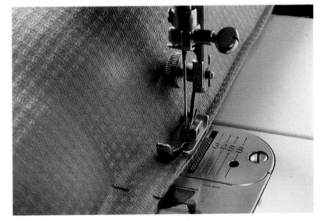

8) Pin opening closed and edgestitch close to folded edge, backstitching at beginning and end of the stitching. Or slipstitch opening closed.

Corded Knife-edge Pillow

Cording adds stability to pillows and gives them a more tailored look. Cording is made by covering cord with bias strips.

✄ Cutting Directions
Cut pillow front and back 1" (2.5 cm) larger than finished pillow. For hook and loop tape or zipper closure, add 1½" (3.8 cm) to back width; for overlap closure, add 5½" (14 cm). Cut bias strips for cording as in step 1, below.

YOU WILL NEED

Decorator fabric for pillow front, back, and cording.

Cord (twisted white cotton or polyester cable), 3" (7.5 cm) longer than distance around pillow.

Pillow form or knife-edge liner.

Zipper or other closure (optional) may be inserted (pages 282 to 285).

How to Make a Corded Knife-edge Pillow

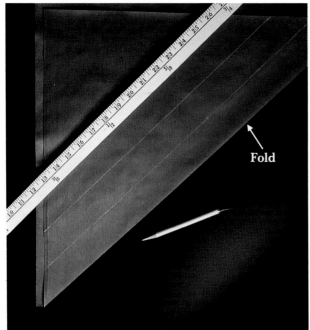

1) Cut bias strips. Determine bias grainline by folding fabric diagonally so selvage aligns with crosswise cut. For ¼" (6 mm) cord, mark and cut 1⅝" (4.2 cm) strips parallel to bias grainline. Cut wider strips for thicker cord.

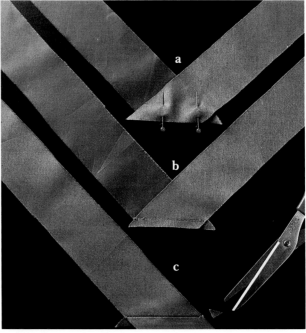

2) Pin strips at right angles, right sides together, offset slightly **(a)**. Stitch ¼" (6 mm) seams **(b)**, and press open, making one continuous strip equal in length to perimeter of pillow plus 3" (7.5 cm). Trim seam allowances even with edges **(c)**.

3) Center cord on wrong side of bias strip. Fold strip over cord, aligning raw edges. Using zipper foot on right side of needle, stitch close to cord, gently stretching bias to help cording lie smoothly around pillow.

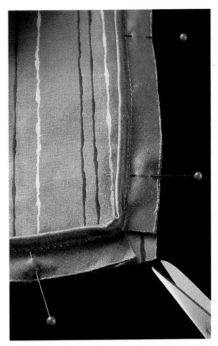

4) Pin the cording to the right side of the pillow front, with raw edges aligned. To ease corners, clip seam allowances to stitching at corners.

5) Stitch, crowding the cord; stop stitching 2" (5 cm) from the point where ends of cording will meet. Leave needle in fabric. Cut off one end of cording so it overlaps the other end by 1" (2.5 cm).

6) Take out 1" (2.5 cm) of stitching from each end of cording. Trim cord ends so they just meet.

7) Fold under ½" (1.3 cm) of overlapping bias strip. Lap it around the other end and finish stitching. Pin pillow front to back, right sides together.

8) Stitch inside stitching line, using zipper foot; crowd stitching against cord. Leave opening. Finish as for knife-edge pillow, page 269, steps 5 to 7b. Slipstitch opening closed.

271

Mock Box Pillow

Mock box pillows are variations of knife-edge pillows and can be made in three styles. Corners on gathered styles are tied inside the pillow. Mitered styles have a short seam across each corner to create a tailored box shape. Pleated styles have neat tucks at each corner. Pillows with gathers or pleats are sometimes called Turkish pillows.

YOU WILL NEED

Knife-edge pillow form. Or, make a mock box pillow liner using the directions below.

Decorator fabric for pillow front and back.

Zipper or other closure (optional) may be inserted (pages 282 to 285).

How to Make a Mock Box Pillow with Mitered Corners

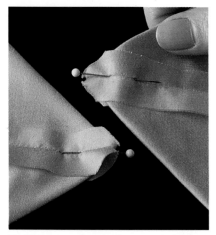

1) Stitch as directed on page 269, step 4. Press seams open. Separate front and back at corners. Center seams on each side of corner, on top of each other. Pin through seam.

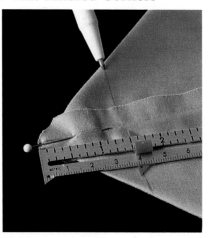

2) Measure on side seam from corner to half the finished depth; for example, for pillow 3" (7.5 cm) deep, measure 1½" (3.8 cm) from corner. Draw a line perpendicular to the seam.

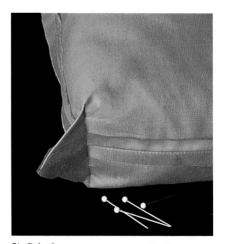

3) Stitch across corner of pillow on marked line; backstitch at beginning and end. Do not trim seam. Finish pillow as for knife-edge pillow, page 269, steps 6 to 7b. Slipstitch opening closed.

How to Make a Mock Box Pillow with Gathered Corners

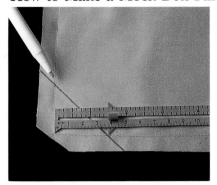

1) Stitch pillow front to pillow back as for knife-edge pillow, page 269, steps 4 and 5. Measure on each seamline from corner to finished pillow depth. Draw diagonal line across the corner.

2) Hand-baste on diagonal line with topstitching and buttonhole twist or doubled thread. Pull up thread to gather.

3) Wrap thread several times around corner; secure with knot. Do not trim corner. Repeat for each corner. Finish as for knife-edge pillow, page 269, steps 6 to 7b. Slipstitch opening closed.

How to Make a Mock Box Pillow with Pleated Corners

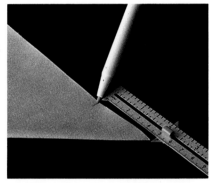

1) Fold corner in half diagonally. On raw edge, measure from the corner to half the finished pillow depth plus ½" (1.3 cm); for example, for pillow 3" (7.5 cm) deep, measure 2" (5 cm) from the corner.

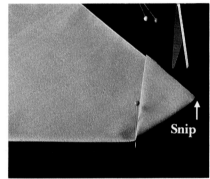

Snip

2) Mark measured point with ¼" (6 mm) snips through both seam allowances. Fold corner back at snips to form triangle. Mark fold with pin. Press triangle in place.

3) Spread corner flat, right side up. Fold fabric from snip to pin; bring fold to pressed center mark, forming pleat. Pin pleat in place. Repeat for other side.

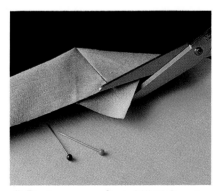

4) Baste across pleat, ½" (1.3 cm) from raw edge, removing pins as you stitch. Trim triangle-shaped piece from corner. Repeat for each corner of front and back.

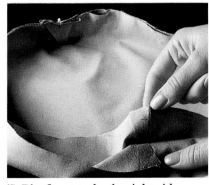

5) Pin front to back, right sides together, with front tucked into back to form a "basket." Match pleated corners precisely.

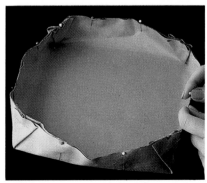

6) Stitch ½" (1.3 cm) seam, leaving opening on one side. Finish as for knife-edge pillow, page 269, steps 6 to 7b. Slipstitch opening closed.

Mock Corded Pillow

Mock corded pillows are corded *after* the pillow is assembled.

✂ Cutting Directions

Cut pillow front 1" (2.5 cm) larger than the finished pillow. Cut back the same length as front. For hook and loop tape or zipper closure, add 1½" (3.8 cm) to back width; for overlap closure, add 5½" (14 cm).

YOU WILL NEED

Decorator fabric for pillow front and back.

Hook and loop tape or zipper, 2" (5 cm) shorter than length of pillow.

Cord, ½" to 1" (1.3 to 2.5 cm), equal in length to distance around the pillow.

Pillow form or knife-edge liner.

How to Make a Mock Corded Pillow

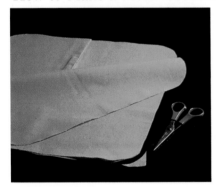

1) Trim corners of front and back into gentle curves. Insert hook and loop tape or other closure in center of pillow back (pages 282 to 285).

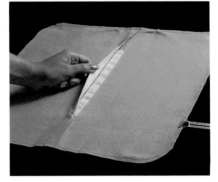

2) Pin front to back, right sides together. Stitch ¼" (6 mm) seam around entire pillow. Turn pillow right side out.

3) Pin cord inside pillow, as tightly as possible against seam. Ends of cord should just meet.

4) Stitch cord from right side, crowding stitching against cord, using zipper foot. Leave 3" (7.5 cm) opening where cord ends meet.

5) Pull out cord about 4" (10 cm) at each end to gather. Adjust gathers. Cut cord so ends just meet. Tack ends together.

6) Topstitch opening closed, using zipper foot. Start and end stitching on previous stitching lines. Insert pillow form or liner.

Box Pillow

Box pillows can be used for cushions as well as for casual pillows. They are firm because of the boxing strip that is sewn between the pillow front and back.

✄ Cutting Directions

Cut pillow front and back 1" (2.5 cm) larger than finished pillow. Cut the boxing strip with length equal to distance around pillow plus 1" (2.5 cm) for seams, width equal to depth of pillow plus 1" (2.5 cm).

YOU WILL NEED

Decorator fabric for pillow front, back and boxing strip.

Polyurethane foam wrapped in batting. Or make a box pillow liner, using directions below.

How to Make a Box Pillow

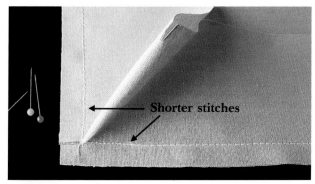

1) Stitch short ends of boxing strip, right sides together, to form continuous loop. Fold loop into fourths and mark each fold with ⅜" (1 cm) clip on both edges.

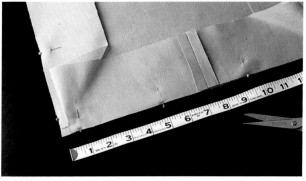

2) Pin boxing strip to pillow front, right sides together, raw edges even, matching clipped points on strip to pillow corners.

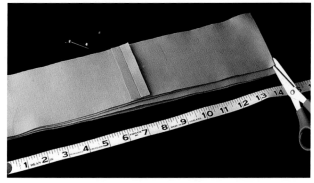

Shorter stitches

3) Stitch ½" (1.3 cm) seam, shortening stitches for 1" (2.5 cm) on each side of corner; take one or two stitches diagonally across each corner instead of sharp pivot.

4) Pin boxing strip to pillow back, right sides together; match clips to corners. Stitch seam as in step 3, leaving one side open. Press seams, turning under seam allowances at opening. Insert form or liner; slipstitch opening closed.

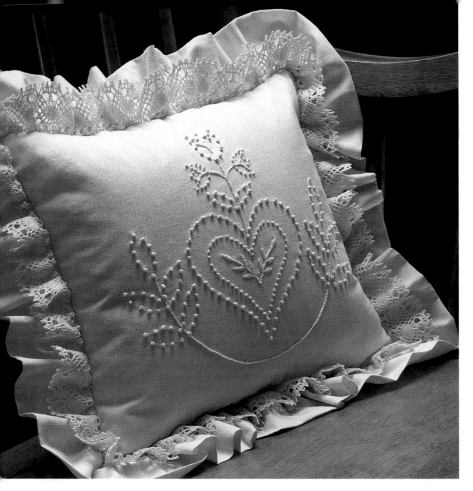

Ruffled Pillow

Ruffles add interest to a pillow or enhance needlework pillows. Make ruffles from matching or contrasting fabric, or purchase lace or eyelet ruffling.

✂ Cutting Directions

Cut pillow front and back 1" (2.5 cm) larger than finished pillow. Cut ruffle strips twice the desired width plus 1" (2.5 cm) for seam, length two to three times the distance around pillow. Ruffles are usually about 3" (7.5 cm) wide.

YOU WILL NEED

Decorator fabric for pillow front and back and double ruffle.

Purchased ruffling (optional), equal in length to distance around pillow plus 1" (2.5 cm).

Cord, (string, crochet cotton or dental floss) for gathering.

Pillow form or knife-edge liner.

How to Make a Ruffled Pillow

1) Stitch short ends of ruffle strip with ½" (1.3 cm) seam, right sides together, to form a loop. Fold strip in half lengthwise, wrong sides together; fold into fourths. Mark each fold with a ⅜" (1 cm) clip.

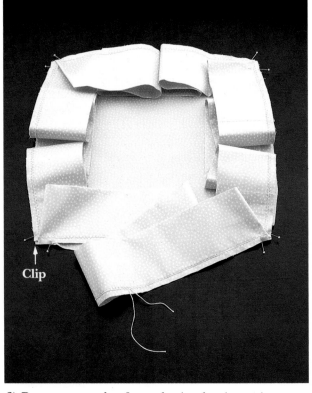

Clip

2) Prepare raw edge for gathering by zigzagging over a cord (page 296). For square pillows, match clips on ruffles to corners of pillow front, right sides together and raw edges even; for rectangular pillow, match clips to center of sides, right sides together and raw edges even. Pin.

3) Pull up the gathering cord until ruffle fits each side of the pillow front. Distribute gathers, allowing extra fullness at corners so ruffle will lie flat in finished pillow. Pin ruffle in place.

4) Machine-baste ruffle to pillow front, stitching just inside gathering row.

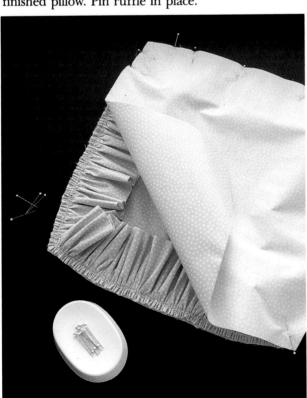

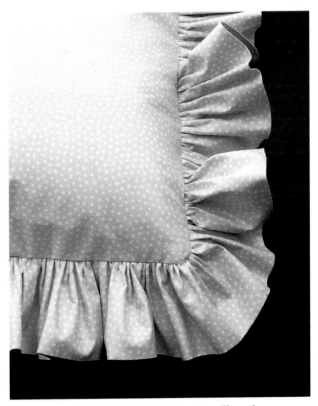

5) Pin pillow back to front, right sides together, with ruffle between pieces. Stitch ½" (1.3 cm) seam, leaving 8" (20.5 cm) opening on one side for turning.

6) Turn pillow right side out. Insert pillow form or knife-edge liner; slipstitch opening closed.

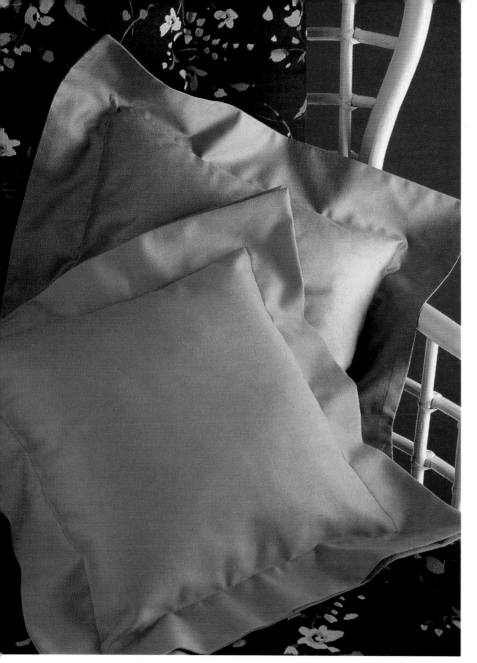

Flange Pillows

A *flange* is a flat border around a plump knife-edge pillow. Flanges may be single or double, and are usually about 2" (5 cm) wide. The double-flange pillow is made with a closure; the single-flange pillow is sewn closed.

✄ Cutting Directions

For single flange, cut pillow front and back 5" (12.5 cm) larger than stuffed inner area. This allows for 2" (5 cm) flange and ½" (1.3 cm) seam on each side.

For double flange, cut pillow front 9" (23 cm) larger than pillow form. This allows for a 2" (5 cm) flange and ½" (1.3 cm) seam on each side. For hook and loop tape or zipper closure, add 1½" (3.8 cm) to back width; for overlap closure, add 5½" (14 cm).

YOU WILL NEED

Decorator fabric for pillow front and back.

Polyester fiberfill for single-flange pillow, about 6 oz. (170 g) for 12" (30.5 cm) pillow.

Pillow form or knife-edge liner for double-flange pillow, to fit inner area.

Zipper or alternate closure for double-flange pillow, 2" (5 cm) shorter than the length of stuffed inner area (pages 282 to 285).

How to Make a Single-Flange Pillow

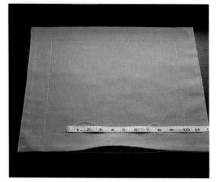

1) Pin pillow front to back, right sides together. Stitch ½" (1.3 cm) seam, leaving 8" (20.5 cm) opening. Turn right side out. Press. Topstitch 2" (5 cm) from edge, beginning and ending at opening.

2) Stuff inner area with polyester fiberfill. Work filling into corners, using long blunt tool such as spoon handle. Do not stuff the flange.

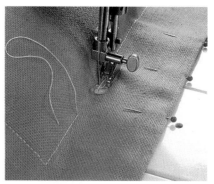

3) Topstitch inner area closed, using zipper foot, starting and ending at first stitching line. Slipstitch flange opening, or edgestitch around entire pillow.

How to Make a Double-Flange Pillow with Mitered Corners

1) Insert zipper (page 284), hook and loop tape, or snap tape (page 283) in pillow back.

2) Press under 2½" (6.5 cm) on each side of front and back. Place front and back together to make sure corners match; adjust pressed folds, if necessary.

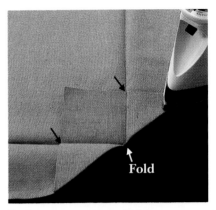

3) Open out corner. Fold corner diagonally so pressed folds match (arrows). Press diagonal fold.

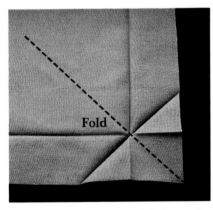

4) Open out corner. Fold through center of corner (dotted line), right sides together.

5) Pin on diagonal fold line, raw edges even. Stitch on fold line at right angle to corner fold.

6) Trim seam to ⅜" (1 cm). Press seam open.

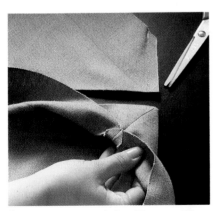

7) Turn corner right side out. Use point turner to get a sharp point. Press edges. Repeat with other corners, front and back.

8) Pin pillow front to back, wrong sides together, matching mitered corners carefully.

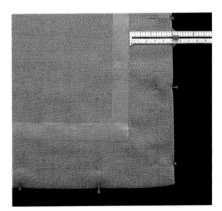

9) Measure 2" (5 cm) from edge for flange; mark stitching line with transparent tape. Insert pillow form or liner. Topstitch through all thicknesses along edge of tape.

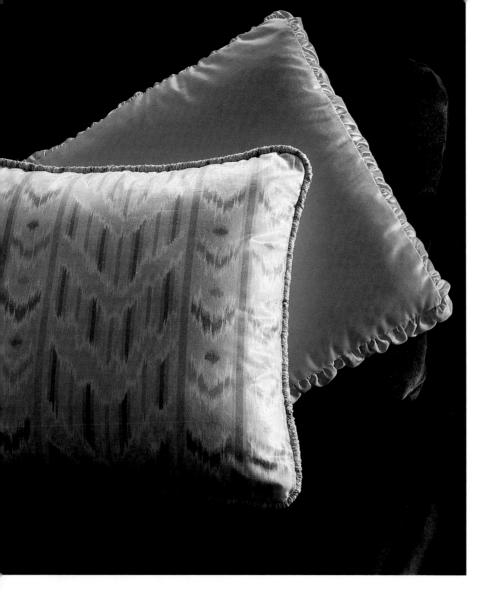

Shirred Pillows

Shirred cording or boxing strips give pillows a formal look.

✂ Cutting Directions

For shirred box pillow, cut pillow front and back 1" (2.5 cm) larger than finished pillow. Cut boxing strip 1" (2.5 cm) wider than depth of form and two to three times longer than distance around form.

For shirred corded pillow, cut pillow front and back 1" (2.5 cm) larger than finished pillow. For cording, cut fabric strips on the crosswise grain, wide enough to cover cord plus 1" (2.5 cm) for seam. The combined length of the strips should be two to three times the distance around pillow.

YOU WILL NEED

Decorator fabric for pillow front and back and for cording or boxing strips.

Cord (twisted white cotton or polyester cable, if making shirred cording). Cut 3" (7.5 cm) longer than distance around pillow.

Gathering cord (string, crochet cotton or dental floss).

Pillow form wrapped in polyester batting, or liner.

How to Make a Shirred Box Pillow

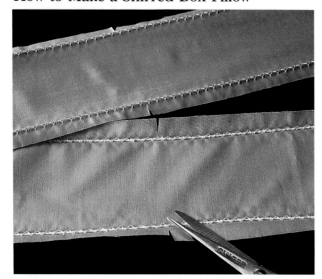

1) Join short ends of boxing strip with ½" (1.3 cm) seam. Prepare raw edges for gathering by zigzagging over cord (page 296) or by stitching two rows of bastestitching. Fold strip into fourths and mark both edges of folds with ⅜" (1 cm) clips.

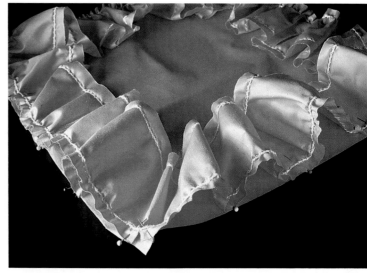

2) Pin boxing strip to pillow front, right sides together, raw edges even, matching clips on boxing strip to pillow corners. Pull up the gathering cord to fit each side of the pillow.

How to Make Shirred Cording

1) Join ends of cording strips using ¼" (6 mm) seams. Press the seams open. Stitch one end of the cord to the wrong side of the cording strip, ⅜" (1 cm) from the end of the strip.

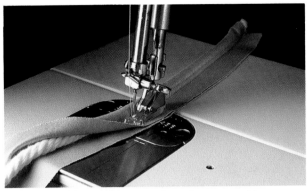

2) Fold cording strip around cord, wrong sides together, matching raw edges. Using zipper foot, machine-baste for 6" (15 cm), close to but not crowding cord. Stop stitching with needle in fabric.

3) Raise presser foot. While gently pulling cord, push cording strip back to end of cord until fabric behind needle is tightly shirred. Continue stitching in 6" (15 cm) intervals until all cording is shirred.

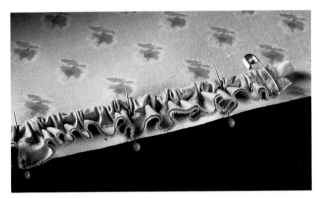

4) Insert pin through strip and cord at end to secure cord. Distribute gathers evenly. Attach shirred cording to pillow front and join ends of cord, page 271, steps 4 to 8.

3) Distribute gathers evenly, pinning as necessary. Stitch all four sides inside gathering row, stitching corners as directed on page 275, step 3.

4) Pin the lower edge of the boxing strip to pillow back. Repeat steps 2 and 3, except stitch only three sides, leaving one side open to insert the pillow form.

5) Finish as for knife-edge pillow, page 269, steps 6 and 7a, inserting a pillow form wrapped in polyester batting. Slipstitch opening closed.

Pillow Closures

A simple overlap closure is a technique for pillow shams (page 292) as well as an easy and inexpensive closure method for any pillow.

Snap tape and hook and loop tape are easy to handle and give closures a flat, smooth finish. Snap tape allows some give on closures and is suitable for pillows that are very soft. Because closure seam allowances are ¾" (2 cm) wide, use ⅝" (1.5 cm) tape.

Overlap closures are placed in the center back of a pillow. Zippers, hook and loop tape, or snap tape can be inserted in the center back or side seam. Except for pillows with overlap closures, cut pillows allowing for ¾" (2 cm) seam allowances on closure seam.

How to Sew an Overlap Closure

1) Cut pillow back 5½" (14 cm) wider than front to allow 3" (7.5 cm) overlap. Cut back in half, cutting *across* widened dimension.

2) Press under ¼" (6 mm), then 1" (2.5 cm) for double-fold hem on each center edge of pillow back. Edgestitch or blindstitch the hems in place.

3) Pin pillow front to back with raw edges even and hemmed edges overlapping in center. Stitch ½" (1.3 cm) seams. Turn right side out and insert pillow form or liner.

How to Sew a Side Seam Closure with Hook and Loop or Snap Tape

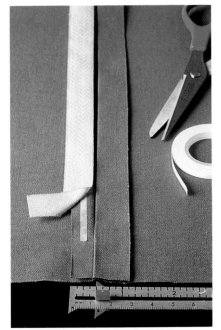

1) Prepare seam, page 285, steps 1 and 2. Cut tape 1" (2.5 cm) longer than opening. Trim one seam allowance to ½" (1.3 cm). Place hook side of tape along fold of trimmed seam allowance; ends extend ½" (1.3 cm) beyond opening. Secure with basting tape or pins.

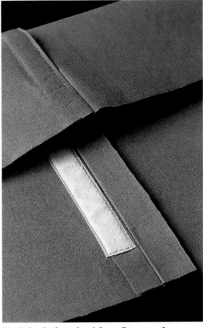

2) Stitch hook side of tape close to edges on all four sides, stitching through pillow back and seam allowance. Stitches show on right side of pillow.

3) Stitch loop side of tape to wrong side of opposite seam allowance, overlapping tape ⅛" (3 mm) on seam allowance, and extending tape ½" (1.3 cm) beyond opening at each end.

4) Turn loop side of tape to right side of seam allowance and stitch to seam allowance on remaining three sides.

5) Place hook side of tape on loop side of tape. Pin pillow front to back along three sides, right sides together. Stitch ½" (1.3 cm) seams. Turn pillow right side out and insert pillow form or liner.

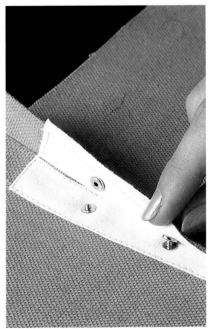

6) Snap tape. Apply as directed in steps 1 to 5 making sure balls and sockets are aligned for smooth closure. Use zipper foot to stitch close to snaps.

How to Insert a Centered Zipper in a Pillow Back

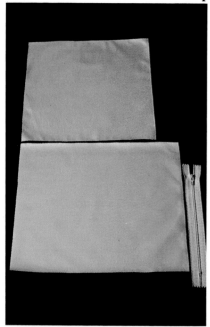

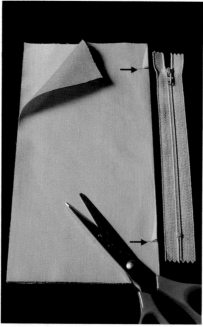

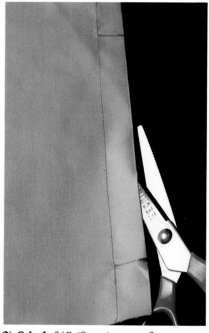

1) Cut pillow back 1½" (3.8 cm) wider than front to allow for a ¾" (2 cm) seam allowance at center back. Use zipper 2" (5 cm) shorter than length of finished pillow back.

2) Fold the pillow back in half lengthwise, right sides together. Press. Center zipper along fold. Snip into fold to mark ends of zipper coil (arrows).

3) Stitch ¾" (2 cm) seam from pillow edge to first snip; backstitch. Machine-baste to ½" (1.3 cm) past second snip. Shorten stitch length; backstitch. Stitch to edge. Cut on fold; press seam open.

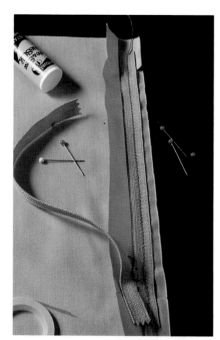

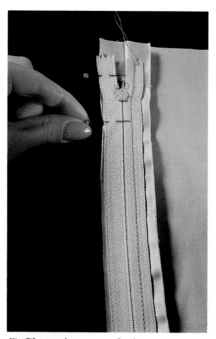

4) Open zipper and center it face down between snips with coil on seamline. Pin, or use glue stick or basting tape to hold right side of zipper tape on the right seam allowance. Machine-baste in place.

5) Close zipper, and pin or use glue stick or basting tape to hold the left side of tape to the left seam allowance. Machine-baste in place.

6) Spread pillow flat, right side up. Mark top and bottom of zipper coil with pins. Center ½" (1.3 cm) transparent tape over the seam; topstitch along edges of tape. Tie threads on wrong side of pillow; remove basting.

How to Insert a Lapped Zipper in a Pillow Seam

1) Use zipper 2" (5 cm) shorter than length of finished pillow. Pin pillow front to back along one side, right sides together. Position zipper along pinned seam, leaving equal distance at each edge. Mark ends of zipper coil on seam.

2) Stitch ¾" (2 cm) seam at each end of zipper opening; backstitch at marks. Press under ¾" (2 cm) seam allowances.

3) Open zipper. Place one side face down on seam allowance of pillow front, with zipper coil on seamline. Secure with pins, glue stick or basting tape. Using zipper foot, stitch tape to seam allowance only.

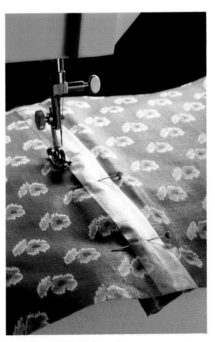

4) Close zipper. Spread pillow flat, right side up. Pin the zipper in place from right side, catching the zipper tape underneath.

5) Place ½" (1.3 cm) transparent tape along seamline as stitching guide. Starting at seamline, stitch across bottom of zipper. Pivot and continue stitching. At top of zipper, pivot and stitch to seamline. Pull threads to wrong side and tie.

6) Open zipper. Turn pillow wrong side out and pin front to back on remaining three sides. Stitch ½" (1.3 cm) seam. Turn pillow right side out, and insert pillow form or liner.

Cushions

A cushion is usually shaped to fit a chair or bench. It has a firm inner core, and is anchored to furniture with a tie or tab. Follow directions for any of the basic knife-edge or box pillows to make a cushion.

Because a cushion needs body, use a 1" (2.5 cm) thick piece of polyurethane wrapped with polyester batting to soften the edges, as a core for the cushion.

✂ Cutting Directions

For knife-edge cushion, cut front and back same size as area to be covered adding half the cushion depth and ½" (1.3 cm) for seams to each of the dimensions.

For box cushion, cut boxing strip desired width plus 1" (2.5 cm); cut front and back same size as area to be covered, adding 1" (2.5 cm) to each dimension for cushion fullness and ½" (1.3 cm) for seams.

How to Cut Fabric for Cushions

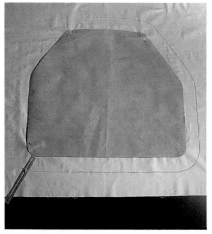

1) Measure length and width of area to be covered by cushion. For a square or rectangular cushion, use these dimensions to cut fabric. For a cushion with unusual shape, prepare a paper pattern.

2) Cut paper pattern in same shape as area to be covered. Mark the paper pattern to show where ties or tabs should be attached.

3) Use paper pattern to cut fabric for cushion, adding amount for depth and seams for cushion style. Transfer tie or tab markings to edge of right side of fabric.

Tufted Cushion

Add button tufting to chair or bench cushions to prevent filling from shifting inside the cover. Tufting is done after the cushion is finished. Tufted cushion covers are usually not removed, so zippers or other closures are not necessary.

Use covered flat buttons with a shank. Buttons for covering are available in kits, complete with a button front and back, and tools that simplify covering the button. Dampen the button fabric just before beginning. As the fabric dries around the button, it will shrink slightly to fit smoothly.

YOU WILL NEED

Long needle, with large eye.

Strong thread such as button and carpet thread or buttonhole twist.

Flat dressmaker buttons with shanks, two for each tuft.

How to Tuft a Cushion

1) Thread a long needle with extra-strong button and carpet thread or several strands of buttonhole twist. Thread strands through button shank; tie ends to shank with double knot.

2) Push needle through cushion, pulling button tight against pillow to create a "dimple." Clip thread near needle.

3) Thread second button on one strand of thread. Tie single knot with both strands and pull until button is tight against bottom of cushion. Wrap thread two or three times around button shank. Tie double knot. Trim threads.

Cushion Ties

Attach cushions to chairs with traditional fabric ties. Ties prevent cushions from sliding, and add a decorative accent to chairs.

Make ties to suit the style of the chair and cushion. Experiment with different sized fabric strips tied around the chair posts, to determine the appropriate length and width of the ties. Trim the fabric strip to desired size to use as a pattern.

✄ Cutting Directions

Cut each tie 1½" (3.8 cm) longer and 1" (2.5 cm) wider than the fabric pattern, allowing ½" (1.3 cm) for seam end and 1" (2.5 cm) for knotting the finished end. Cut two ties for each post where the ties will be attached.

How to Make Cushion Ties

1) Make two ties for each post where ties will be attached. Press under ¼" (6 mm) on long edges of each tie. Press tie in half lengthwise, wrong sides together, pressed edges even; pin.

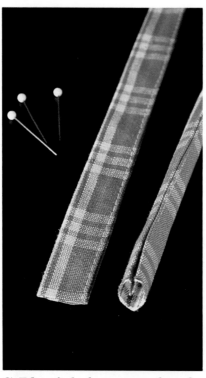

2) Edgestitch along open edge of ties. Leave both ends of tie open. Tie a single knot at one end of tie, enclosing the raw edges in the knot.

3) Pin unfinished ends of ties to right side of cushion front at marks. Pin cushion front to back, right sides together. Stitch, backstitching over ties. Finish cushion and tie to chair post.

Hook & Loop Tabs

Hook and loop tape tabs make a cushion extremely easy to attach and remove, and because they are small and inconspicuous they blend in well with furniture.

The length of the tab depends on the size of the rung or post that the tab goes around. Measure accurately because the tabs must fit snugly. Tabs may be hand-stitched to existing cushions because they do not need to be stitched in a seam.

✄ Cutting Directions

Cut tabs just long enough to go around chair post and overlap by 1" to 1½" (2.5 to 3.8 cm), plus ½" (1.3 cm) for seam; twice the finished width, plus ½" (1.3 cm).

Cut hook and loop tape 1" to 1½" (2.5 to 3.8 cm) long for each tab.

How to Make Cushion Ties with Hook and Loop Tape

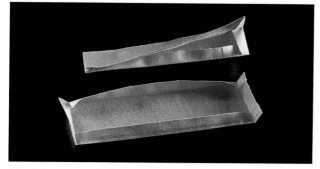

1) Make one tab for each corner. Press under ¼" (6 mm) on each edge of tab. Press tab in half lengthwise, wrong sides together. Edgestitch all four sides of tab.

2) Cut hook and loop tape for each tab. Separate hook and loop sides. Attach opposite sides of tape to opposite sides of tab. Stitch around all four sides of hook and loop tape.

3) Stitch pillow front to back. Before stuffing, pin center of tab to seam at cushion corners. Place all tabs in same direction; stitch and backstitch.

4) Finish cushion. Attach cushion to chair or bench by fastening hook and loop tabs around posts, overlapping ends to secure.

Bed Coverings

Sewing for the bedroom is a good area to start, because these projects use easy-to-handle fabric and consist of seams and hems. Measure the bed with the blankets and sheets that are normally on the bed. Comforters, coverlets, and duvets reach 3" to 4" (7.5 to 10 cm) below the mattress on both sides and at the foot. For dust ruffle length, measure from the top of the box spring to the floor. These measurements give you the finished length.

Duvet Cover

To use the decorative border on a sheet, conceal the zippered opening under the border on the right side of the cover. Or add a decorative border to a plain sheet, using lace or ribbon trims.

✂ Cutting Directions
Measure the down or fiberfill duvet. For snug fit, make the finished duvet cover 2" (5 cm) shorter and 2" (5 cm) narrower than duvet measurements.

For back of cover, cut or tear a sheet 1" (2.5 cm) wider and 1" (2.5 cm) longer than finished size.

For front, cut or tear bordered sheet 1" (2.5 cm) wider than finished size; for bordered zipper flap, right, fold sheet in half lengthwise and mark a line 20" (51 cm) from edge of sheet; for zipper strip, mark second line 3" (7.5 cm) from first line. Cut on both lines. To determine the length to cut the

remaining front section, use chart at right. Line up sheet section with edge of table, and use a T-square to square lower edge.

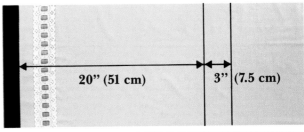

20" (51 cm)   3" (7.5 cm)

Cut Length of Duvet Cover Front	in. (cm)
1) Finished length of cover	
2) Bordered zipper flap, 20" (51 cm)	−
3) Width of border	+
4) 1" (2.5 cm) seam allowance	+
5) Front cut length	=

YOU WILL NEED

Flat sheets with decorative border.
Two zippers, 22" (56 cm) long.

How to a Sew a Duvet Cover from Sheets

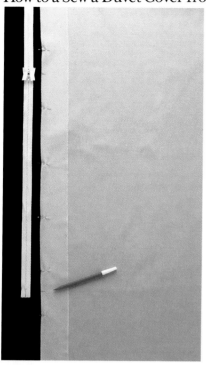

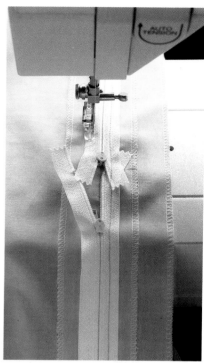

1) Zigzag or overedge raw edges of zipper strip and upper edge of front. Pin zipper strip to upper edge, right sides together. Mark zipper opening 22" (56 cm) in both directions from center.

2) Stitch 1"(2.5 cm) zipper seam, starting at one side. At zipper marking, backstitch, and then machine-baste across zipper opening; backstitch and continue to other edge. Press seam open.

3) Center open zippers face down on seam allowance, with teeth on basted seam and tab ends meeting in center. Using zipper foot, stitch on one side of teeth. Close zippers; stitch other side. Remove basting.

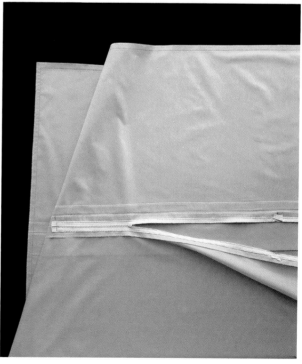

4) Pin decorative border section over zipper, right side up, with zipper seam 1" (2.5 cm) from inner edge of border. Stitch on edge of border through all layers. Open zippers.

5) Pin front to back, with right sides together and back side up. Stitch ½" (1.3 cm) from raw edge. To finish, serge or zigzag raw edges. Turn right side out; insert duvet.

Pillow Shams

Pillow shams can be plain, ruffled or trimmed with a flange or banding. A sham has an overlap, or flap pocket closure, on the back to make it easy to slip a pillow into it. The easiest sham to make is cut in one piece with the ends turned under and hemmed so that the overlap is part of the fold.

To add a ruffle or coordinating flange, cut the front, back and overlap pieces separately so that there will be a seam completely around the pillow. Seams on shams should be finished. Use French seams on one-piece shams and pillowcase shams; zigzag the seams on ruffled shams. Flanged shams have enclosed seams.

✂ Cutting Directions

For one-piece sham, cut fabric same width as pillow plus 1" (2.5 cm); length equal to two times the length of pillow plus 11" (28 cm).

For ruffled sham, cut front and back 1" (2.5 cm) larger than pillow. Cut overlap 10" (25.5 cm) wide, length equal to width of pillow plus 1" (2.5 cm). Cut ruffle two times desired width plus 1" (2.5 cm), and length equal to two times the distance around pillow, plus 1" (2.5 cm).

For flanged pillow sham, cut front 5" (12.5 cm) wider and 5" (12.5 cm) longer than pillow. Cut back 5" (12.5 cm) wider and 2" (5 cm) longer than pillow. Cut overlap 5" (12.5 cm) wider than pillow and 13" (33 cm) long. This allows for ½" (1.3 cm) seams and 2" (5 cm) flange. Cut banding or trimming desired width and long enough to go around entire pillow.

For ruffled pillowcase sham, cut fabric same width as pillow plus 1" (2.5 cm); length equal to two times the length of pillow plus 1" (2.5 cm). Cut ruffle two times desired width plus 1" (2.5 cm), and length four times width of pillow. Cut facing strip 3" (7.5 cm) wide; length equal to two times the width of pillow plus 1" (2.5 cm).

How to Sew a One-piece Sham

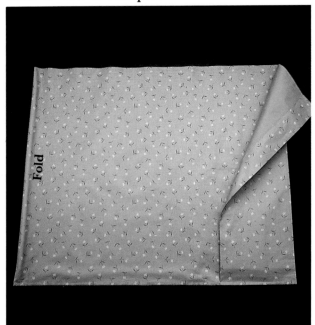

1) Stitch ½" (1.3 cm) double-fold hem on one short end of sham back. Turn under ½" (1.3 cm), then 2" (5 cm) hem on one long edge of overlap; stitch. Prepare and attach ruffle to right side of sham front, as for ruffled pillow, pages 276 and 277, steps 1 to 4.

2) Stitch ¼" (6 mm) seam on two long sides. Trim seams to ⅛" (3 mm). Turn sham wrong side out. Press seam edges. Stitch ¼" (6 mm) from the edges for French seams. Turn the sham right side out. Insert the pillow.

How to Sew a Ruffled Sham

1) Stitch ½" (1.3 cm) double-fold hem on one short end of sham back. Turn under ½" (1.3 cm), then 2" (5 cm) hem on one long edge of overlap; stitch. Prepare and attach ruffle to right side of sham front, as for ruffled pillow, pages 286 and 287, steps 1 to 4.

2) Pin unfinished edge of overlap to one end of front, right sides together, with ruffle between two layers. Pin back to front, positioning back and overlap as shown. Stitch ½" (1.3 cm) seam around sham. Trim corners; finish seam allowances. Turn right side out and insert pillow.

How to Sew a Flanged Pillow Sham

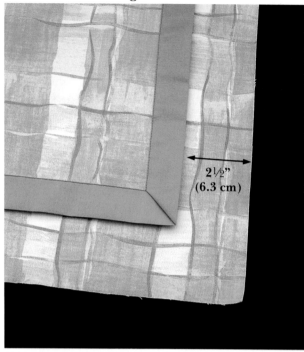

1) Position banding to front of pillow sham 2½" (6.3 cm) from edge. Miter corners, as for placemats with mitered ribbon trimming, page 313. Stitch *inner* edge of band only.

2) Make sham following instructions for ruffled sham (page 293), omitting ruffle; finish seams. Turn sham right side out and topstitch along outer edge of banding. Insert pillow.

How to Sew a Ruffled Pillowcase Sham

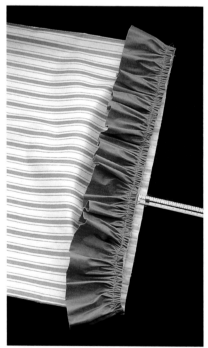

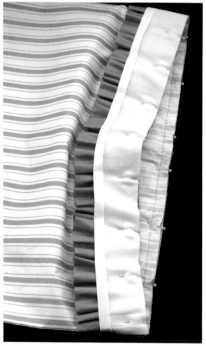

1) Fold sham crosswise, wrong sides together; stitch French seams (page 214). Prepare and attach the ruffle to right side of open end of sham, as directed, pages 276 and 277, steps 1 to 4.

2) Press under ½" (1.3 cm) on one long side of facing strip. Join short ends of strip. Pin right side of strip to right side of pillow sham with ruffle between two fabric layers. Stitch ½" (1.3 cm) seam.

3) Press seam toward pillow sham. Edgestitch or slipstitch along pressed fold of facing strip. (Facing strip is shown in contrasting color to make it more visible.)

Dust Ruffles & Bed Skirts

Dust ruffles and bed skirts are designed to hide the box spring and legs of a bed. They can be made to coordinate with a comforter or quilt. Gathered dust ruffles give a soft effect; pleated bed skirts are more tailored. Dust ruffles and bed skirts are gathered or pleated around only three sides of the bed.

Gathered dust ruffles can be made with either one or two layers of gathered fabric. When making a two-layered dust ruffle, gather the two layers as one piece. The type of fabric you choose determines the fullness of a gathered dust ruffle. Allow three times the fullness for lightweight fabrics; allow two to three times the fullness for mediumweight fabrics.

The directions that follow are for a gathered dust ruffle with split corners; the dust ruffle is attached to a fitted sheet. This open-cornered style, which is made in three sections, is suitable for a bed with a footboard. Dust ruffles may also be made in one continuous piece for beds without footboards.

Pleated bed skirts have deep pleats and they are made from medium to heavyweight fabrics. The directions that follow allow for a 6" (15 cm) pleat at each end corner and the center of each side. A 1" (2.5 cm) double-fold hem is used at the lower edge and sides of the skirt. The pleated bed skirt is for a bed without a footboard; the skirt is attached to a deck. The deck can be made from muslin or from broadcloth or a flat sheet in a color that matches the bed skirt.

✄ Cutting Directions

For gathered dust ruffle length, cut two pieces each the length of the box spring times the desired fullness, plus 4" (10 cm) for 1" (2.5 cm) double-fold side hems; cut one piece the width of the box spring times the desired fullness, plus 4" (10 cm) for 1" (2.5 cm) double-fold side hems. Dust ruffle depth is equal to distance from top of box spring to floor, plus 4" (10 cm).

For pleated bed skirt, cut deck 1" (2.5 cm) wider and 1" (2.5 cm) longer than box spring. Cut bed skirt on lengthwise grain of fabric. Cut two pieces the length of the box spring plus 18" (46 cm). Cut one piece the width of the box spring plus 18" (46 cm). Bed skirt depth equals distance from top of box spring to floor minus ¼" (6 mm) for clearance, plus 2½" (6.5 cm) for seam and hem.

YOU WILL NEED

Decorator fabric for dust ruffle or bed skirt.

Fitted sheet for deck of gathered dust ruffle.

Broadcloth, flat sheet or muslin for deck of pleated bed skirt.

How to Sew a Gathered Dust Ruffle with Open Corners

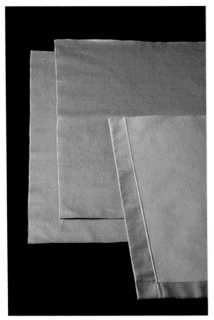

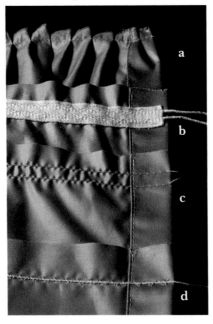

1) Stitch 1" (2.5 cm) double-fold hem along lower edges of the three dust ruffle pieces, then turn under and stitch 1" (2.5 cm) double-fold hem on both ends of each of the pieces.

2) Gather 1" (2.5 cm) from upper edge with ruffler attachment (**a**), two-string shirring tape (**b**), two rows of bastestitching (**c**), or zigzag stitching over a cord (**d**).

3) Place fitted sheet on box spring. On sheet, mark upper edge of box spring. Mark every 12" (30.5 cm) along this line. Mark upper edge of dust ruffle every 24" (61 cm) for double fullness, every 36" (91.5 cm) for triple fullness.

How to Sew a Pleated Bed Skirt

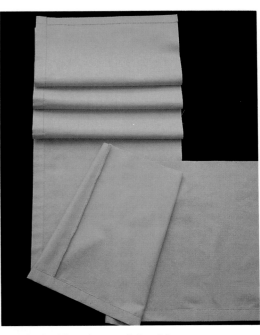

1) Fold deck in half lengthwise, then crosswise so corners are together. Using saucer as a guide, cut to curve corners gently.

2) Fold curved corners in half to determine centers; mark fold with ¼" (6 mm) clips. Also, mark center of each side with clip.

3) Stitch skirt pieces, right sides together, on narrow ends, with shorter piece in center. Stitch 1" (2.5 cm) double-fold hem on lower edge of skirt and on unstitched narrow ends of skirt pieces.

4) Pin right sides of dust ruffle pieces along three sides of sheet, raw edges on marked line and hems overlapping at corners. Match markings on dust ruffle pieces to markings on sheet. Pull up gathering cord to fit.

5) Remove sheet from box spring, keeping dust ruffle pinned in place. Stitch on gathering line, 1" (2.5 cm) from raw edge of dust ruffle.

6) Turn dust ruffle down over lower edge of sheet. If desired, topstitch ½" (1.3 cm) from seam, stitching through dust ruffle and sheet.

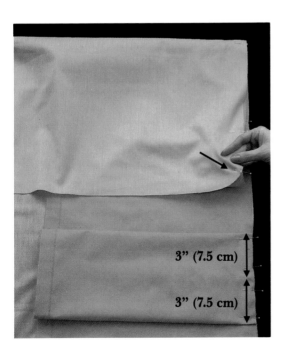

3" (7.5 cm)

3" (7.5 cm)

4) Pin skirt to deck, right sides together, with stitching of side hem at clip on one end of deck (arrow). Form 6" (15 cm) pleats at clips on sides and corners of deck. Seams will fall inside pleats.

5) Remove skirt and machine-baste pleats. Reposition skirt on deck. Pin, right sides together. Clip center of corner pleats. Stitch ½" (1.3 cm) seam.

6) Press seam allowance toward deck. Press ¼" (6 mm) double-fold hem at open end of deck; stitch hem. Topstitch the skirt seam allowance to deck. Press pleats.

Circular Ruffle Bed Skirt

The circular ruffle bed skirt has soft draping. Its simple style complements a tailored decor, but also works well for a room that is elaborately decorated, without detracting from other furnishings.

The circular ruffle bed skirt is easy to sew and requires less time than most bed skirts, because there are no gathers or pleats. To prevent the bed skirt from shifting out of position, the upper edge of the skirt is attached to a fitted sheet. If the bed does not have a footboard, the bed skirt is attached as one continuous strip. For a bed with a footboard, a split-corner bed skirt can be attached to the sheet in three sections.

✂ Cutting Directions

Determine the number of circular pieces required, as indicated in the chart, opposite. To make it easier

to cut the circles, cut fabric squares the size of the circle diameter; then cut the circular pieces, opposite.

The calculations given in the chart are based on a 15½" (39.3 cm) cut length. This gives an adequate amount of ruffling for any cut length up to at least 15½" (39.3 cm); you may have excess ruffling, which can easily be cut off during construction. The actual length of ruffling per circle is equal to the circumference of the inner circle minus 1" (2.5 cm) for seams and side hems.

YOU WILL NEED

Decorator fabric, in the yardage amount indicated in the chart, opposite.

Fitted sheet.

How to Cut Circles

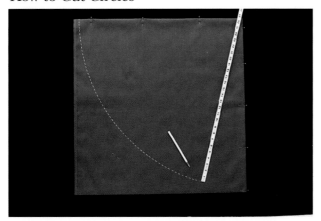

1) Fold the fabric square in half lengthwise, then crosswise, right sides together. Using straightedge and pencil, mark an arc on fabric, measuring from the folded center of fabric, a distance equal to the radius. Cut on marked line through all layers.

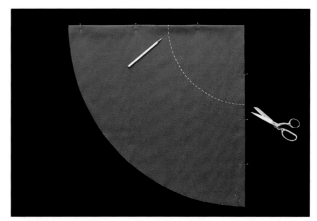

2) Add 1" (2.5 cm) to the drop length of bed skirt; measure and mark this distance away from arc. Draw second arc at this distance. Cut on marked line through all layers. Circumference of inner circle minus 1" (2.5 cm) determines length of ruffling per circle.

How to Cut Half-circles

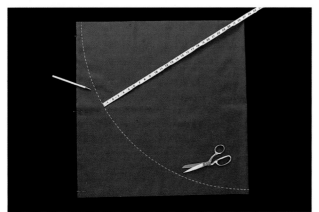

1) Cut rectangle across the width of fabric, with short sides equal to one-half the width of the fabric. Fold fabric in half, matching short sides. Using straightedge and pencil, mark an arc on fabric, measuring from the lengthwise fold, a distance equal to the radius. Cut on marked line through both layers.

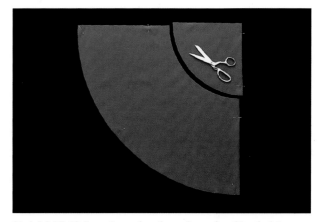

2) Add 1" (2.5 cm) to the drop length of bed skirt; measure and mark this distance away from arc. Draw second arc at this distance. Cut on marked line through both layers.

Determining the Circular Pieces Needed

Diameter of Circles	Ruffling Length per Circle	Twin		Full		Queen		King	
		Circles Needed	Yardage Needed	Circles Needed	Yardage Needed	Circles Needed	Yardage Needed	Circles Needed	Yardage Needed
45" (115 cm)	47" (120 cm)	4	5 yd. (4.6 m)	4½	5⅝ yd. (5.15 m)	5	6¼ yd. (5.75 m)	5½	6⅞ yd. (6.3 m)
48" (122 cm)	58" (147 cm)	3½	4⅔ yd. (4.33 m)	3½	4⅔ yd. (4.33 m)	4	5⅓ yd. (4.92 m)	4½	6 yd. (5.5 m)
54" (137 cm)	76" (193 cm)	2½	3¾ yd. (3.45 m)	3	4½ yd. (4.15 m)	3	4½ yd. (4.15 m)	3½	5¼ yd. (4.8 m)
60" (153 cm)	95" (242 cm)	2	3⅓ yd. (3.07 m)	2½	4¼ yd. (3.9 m)	2½	4¼ yd. (3.9 m)	3	5 yd. (4.6 m)

How to Sew a Circular Ruffle Bed Skirt

1) **Cut** circles for bed skirt (pages 298 and 299). Slash each piece from outer to inner edges on crosswise grain. Staystitch ½" (1.3 cm) from inner edge.

2) **Stitch** circles together in a long strip, right sides together; finish seam allowances. Clip up to the staystitching at 2" (5 cm) intervals; space the clips evenly so bed skirt will hang in even folds.

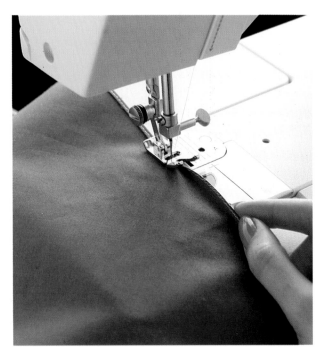

3) **Machine-stitch** ¼" (6 mm) from hem edge. Turn edge to wrong side on stitching line; press fold. Stitch close to fold. Trim excess fabric close to stitching. Turn hem edge to wrong side a scant ¼" (6 mm), enclosing raw edge. Edgestitch.

4) **Place** fitted sheet over box spring; mark sheet along upper edge of box spring, using water-soluble marking pen or chalk.

5) Lay circular ruffle on top of box spring; pin ruffle to sheet, right sides together, matching staystitching to marked line. Ruffle may extend around corners at head of bed, if desired; extend raw edge ½" (1.3 cm) beyond desired endpoint to allow for side hem.

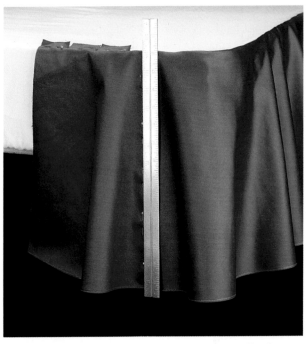

6) Mark side hems at head of bed perpendicular to floor, allowing ½" (1.3 cm) for double ¼" (6 mm) hem.

7) Remove fitted sheet and ruffle from bed. Cut off any excess ruffle at sides; stitch side hems. Stitch ruffle to fitted sheet, stitching just beyond staystitching.

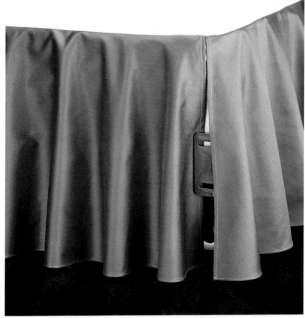

Split corners. Follow steps 1 to 4. Cut ruffle into three sections, each section long enough to fit on one side of the bed plus 1" (2.5 cm) for side hems. Lay section for foot of bed on top of box spring; pin to sheet, right sides together, matching staystitching to marked line. Mark side hems at corner, as in step 6. Pin side sections to sheet, overlapping hem allowances at corners. Complete bed skirt, as in steps 6 and 7.

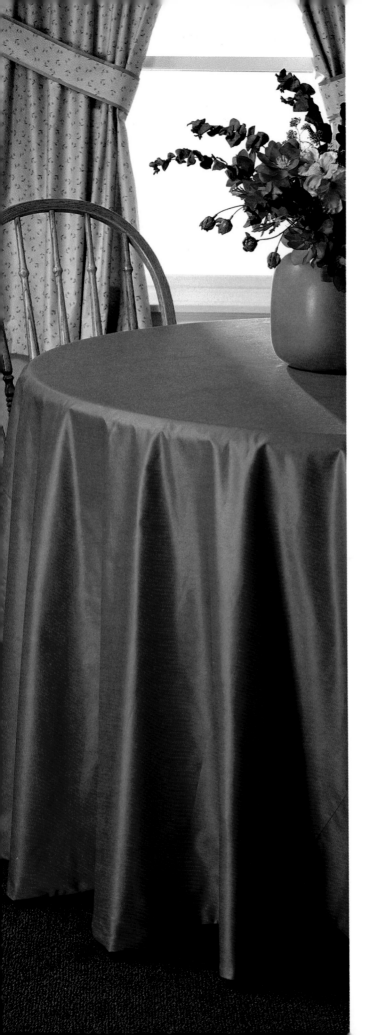

Table Coverings

Customized tabletop fashions are a simple way to change the look of a room without spending too much time or money. These easy projects make good home sewing sense for several reasons.

Home-sewn table fashions, unlike purchased ones, are not limited to a small selection of standard sizes. Design a tablecloth yourself, and scale it to the exact size and shape of your table. Choose from an abundant supply of fabric colors, patterns and textures to complement the decor of your room.

Because most tablecloths are wider than one fabric width, you must seam fabric widths together to make the tablecloth the width you need. Avoid a center seam by using a full fabric width in the center and stitching narrower side panels to it.

Use selvage edges in seams to eliminate seam finishing. If the selvage tends to pucker, clip it at regular intervals of 1" to 6" (2.5 to 15 cm). If selvages are not used in seams, finish with French or overedge seams. Use plain seams for reversible tablecloths.

Placemats, napkins and table runners give you an opportunity to experiment with finishing techniques you may be reluctant to try on larger projects.

Selecting Fabrics

When you design tabletop fashions, look for durable, stain-resistant fabrics that have been treated to repel soil and water. Permanent press fabrics offer easy care. Drape the fabric over your arm to see how it hangs.

For everyday use, lightweight cotton is appropriate; use a lightweight tablecloth with a table pad to protect fine wood tables. For an elegant look, use a sheer lace or eyelet tablecloth over a heavier cloth.

Small random prints are easier to work with than prints that may need matching. Avoid heavily napped fabrics or fabrics with difficult-to-match design motifs such as printed plaids or stripes, diagonals or one-way patterns.

Measuring the Table

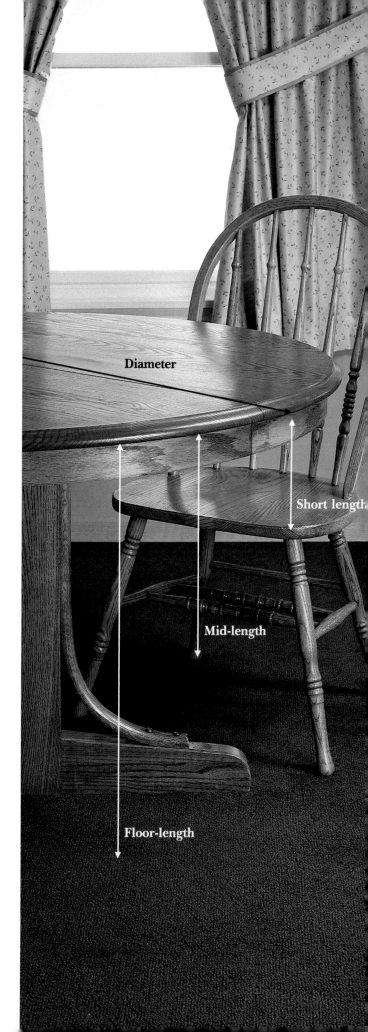

The length of the tablecloth from the edge of the table to the bottom of the cloth is the *drop*. Always include the drop length in your tablecloth measurements.

There are three common drop lengths: short, 10" to 12" (25.5 to 30.5 cm); mid-length, 16" to 24" (40.5 to 61 cm); and floor-length, 28" to 29" (71 to 73.5 cm). Short cloths end at about chair seat height and are good tablecloths for everyday use. Mid-length cloths are more formal. Elegant floor-length coverings are used for buffet and decorator tables.

Round tablecloth. Measure the diameter of the table, then determine the drop length of the cloth. The size of the tablecloth is the diameter of the table plus twice the drop length plus 1" (2.5 cm) for a narrow hem allowance. A narrow hem is the easiest way to finish the curved edge of a round tablecloth.

Square tablecloth. Measure the width of the tabletop; then determine the drop length of the cloth. Add twice the drop length plus 1" (2.5 cm) for a narrow hem allowance or 2½" (6.5 cm) for a wide hem allowance.

Rectangular tablecloth. Measure the length and width of the tabletop, then determine the drop length of the cloth. The size of the finished tablecloth is the width of the tabletop plus twice the drop length, and the length of the tabletop plus twice the drop length. Add 1" (2.5 cm) for a narrow hem or 2½" (6.5 cm) for a wide hem.

Oval tablecloth. Measure the length and width of the tabletop, then determine the drop length of the cloth. Join fabric widths as necessary to make a rectangular cloth the length of the tabletop plus twice the drop length, and the width of the tabletop plus twice the drop length; add 1" (2.5 cm) to each dimension for a narrow hem allowance. Put a narrow hem in an oval tablecloth because it is the simplest way to finish the curved edge. Because oval tables vary in shape, mark the finished size with the fabric on the table. Place weights on the table to hold fabric in place, then use a hem marker or cardboard gauge to mark the drop length evenly.

Round Tablecloths

To determine the yardage for a tablecloth without a flounce, divide tablecloth diameter by fabric width less 1" (2.5 cm). Count fractions as one width. This is the number of widths. Then multiply number of widths by diameter and divide by 36" (100 cm) to find the total yards (meters).

For center of flounced-edge tablecloth, subtract two times the finished depth of the flounce from the finished length of the tablecloth. Determine yardage for center as for tablecloth above.

Determine the flounce length by multiplying diameter of center by 3½; double this figure. For number of strips, divide flounce length by fabric width. Then multiply number of strips by cut depth and divide by 36 for total yards (meters).

✂ Cutting Directions

For tablecloth without a flounce, cut center panel with length equal to tablecloth diameter plus hems. Add partial panels to form square.

For tablecloth with flounce, cut center panel with length equal to the diameter of center plus seam allowances. Add partial panels to form square. Cut strips for flounce the depth of flounce, plus hem and seam allowances and length as determined above.

How to Cut a Round Tablecloth

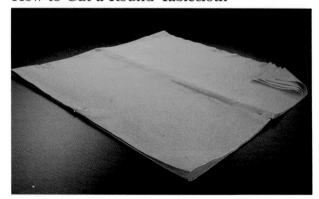

1) Join fabric panels, right sides together, with ½" (1.3 cm) seams to form square. Fold square into fourths. Pin layers together to prevent slipping.

2) Measure a string the length of the radius of the cloth. Tie one end of string around a marking pencil; pin other end at center folded corner of cloth. Mark outer edge of circle, using string and pencil as compass. Cut on marked line; remove pins.

How to Sew Narrow and Flounced Hems

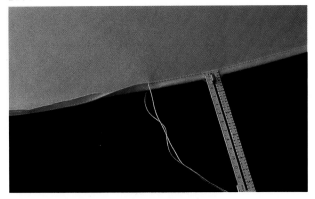

Narrow hem. Stitch around tablecloth ¼" (6 mm) from edge. Press under on stitching line. Press under ¼" (6 mm) again, easing fullness around curves. Edgestitch close to folded edge. Or, use narrow hemmer.

Flounced edge. Seam strips of flounce, right sides together, to form loop. Hem lower edge. Zigzag over cord to make ruffles (page 296). Attach flounce to tablecloth.

How to Sew a Corded Hem

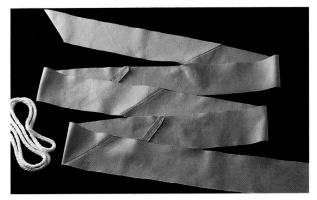

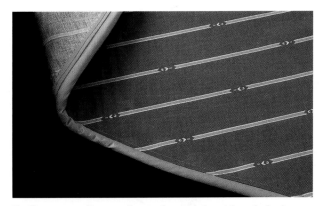

1) Multiply diameter of the tablecloth by 3½ to determine length of cording needed. Cut and join bias strips, right sides together, to cover cording (page 270).

2) Cover cording and attach to right side of cloth as for corded pillow, page 271, steps 3 to 7. Zigzag seam and press to back of tablecloth. Topstitch ¼" (6 mm) from cording seam.

How to Sew a Reversible Round Tablecloth

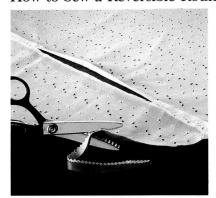

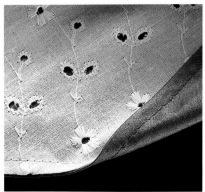

1) Join lining panels, leaving 12" (30.5 cm) opening in one seam for turning. Stitch the lining to the outer tablecloth, wrong sides together, ½" (1.3 cm) from edge. Trim seam or clip curves.

2) Turn tablecloth right side out by pulling outer fabric through opening in lining seam. Slipstitch opening closed.

3) Topstitch ¼" (6 mm) from edge. If lining is contrasting color, match upper thread to outer fabric, bobbin thread to lining.

Balloon Table Topper

To give basic round tablecloths a custom look, layer them in pairs. Make the bottom cloth floor length, and the top cloth shorter. Although the length of the top cloth is not critical, cutting it one-third or two-thirds of floor length creates a pleasing proportion. For a standard table 30" (76 cm) high, the top cloth should end either 10" (25.5 cm) or 20" (51 cm) from the floor.

Shirr the upper cloth into graceful swags for a balloon topper. To decide the number of swags and the depth to shirr the edge, layer the cloths on the table and pin some test swags in place.

For the fastest hem finish, use an overlock machine to satin stitch the edges or to make a rolled hem. On a conventional machine, apply bias binding or use a hemming foot to sew a narrow hem.

YOU WILL NEED

Decorator fabric for table topper.

Strips of bias tricot or bias tape, equal to number of swags, each as long as the area to be shirred.

Narrow cords such as soutache braid or shade cord, cut twice as long as the area to be shirred plus 1" (2.5 cm). Number should equal the number of swags.

How to Sew a Balloon Table Topper

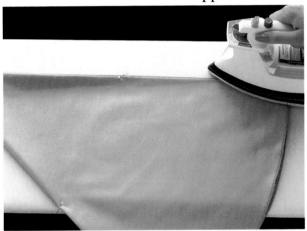

1) Fold hemmed round cloth into quarters, sixths, or eighths, depending on the number of swags. Press crease at each fold to mark desired depth of shirring.

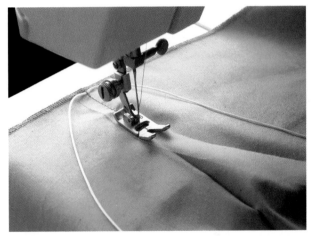

2) Pin doubled cord at hem at each crease. Center bias tricot or bias tape over crease, and pin. Stitch through center of tape, catching cord in stitching at hem edge.

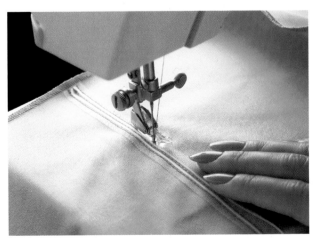

3) Bring cord next to stitching at center of tape. Using zipper foot, stitch along both outer edges of tape to encase cord.

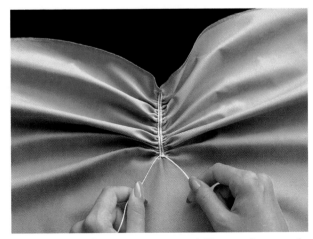

4) Pull up cords to create swags. Adjust gathers, and tie ends of cords securely. Tuck ends of cord into swag; do not cut. Swags can be released for laundry or storage.

Square & Rectangular Tablecloths

Make tablecloths the desired width by joining fabric widths as necessary, using full widths on the lengthwise edges. Straighten the crosswise ends of fabric (page 212) to square the corners. Use French or overedge seams, or use selvage edges to eliminate seam finishing.

Select the width and finish of the hem to complement the weight and texture of the fabric. Mitering is the neatest way to square corners because it covers raw edges and eliminates bulk.

Determine the amount of fabric needed for the tablecloth by dividing the total width of the tablecloth by the width of your fabric, less 1" (2.5 cm). Multiply this figure, which is the number of panels needed, by the total length of the tablecloth. Divide this number by 36" (100 cm) to get the total yards (meters) required.

Wide and Narrow Hems

1) Wide hem. Press under ¼" to ½" (6 mm to 1.3 cm), then press under 1" or 2" (2.5 or 5 cm) hem on all sides.

2) Open out corner, leaving first fold turned under. Miter corners as for double-flange pillow, page 279, steps 3 to 7. Blindstitch or straight-stitch hem.

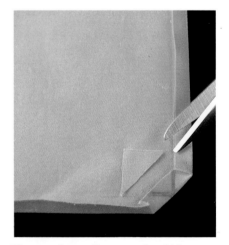

Narrow hem. Press under ½" (1.3 cm) on each side. Open corner; fold diagonally so pressed folds match. Press; trim corner. Fold raw edge under ¼" (6 mm). Fold again on first fold line; press. Stitch hem.

Quilted Table Covers

Quilting adds body to table coverings and provides additional protection for table surfaces. The thickness and slight puffiness of quilted table accessories also adds visual appeal. Use quilted fabrics for placemats, table runners and table mats. Finish edges with bias binding.

Prequilted fabrics are available, but quilting your own fabric provides the luxury of coordinating colors and prints, and the economy of making only the amount of quilted fabric needed for a project. The quilting guide foot with the attached guide bar makes the channel-quilting process easy. Lengthen the stitch length and loosen the pressure for even quilting. Begin by stitching the center quilting row, and work toward the sides.

Use polyester fleece or needle-punched batting for tabletop fashions. It will retain its shape and body when laundered.

How to Machine Quilt Fabric Using a Quilter Bar

1) Cut fabric, fleece and lining slightly larger than finished size of item. Place fleece between wrong sides of fabric and lining. Pin or baste all three layers together.

2) Mark first quilting line in center of fabric with yardstick and chalk pencil. (If not using quilter bar, mark every quilting row an equal distance apart.)

3) Stitch center line. Determine the distance to next quilting line. Adjust quilter bar to follow the previous row of stitching as you stitch the next row.

Placemats, Table Runners & Table Mats

Placemats, table runners and table mats protect tabletops and add color and style to table settings. Use them over tablecloths, or alone to show off the beauty of wood and glass tables. The sewing techniques for placemats, table runners and table mats are very similar.

Select fabric for mats and runners according to the general guidelines for choosing tablecloth fabrics. Fabric may be machine-quilted using the procedure described on page 309.

Finish edges of tabletop projects with wide banding (pages 312 and 313) or bias binding. To make bias binding, cut and join bias strips (page 270). Fold strip in half lengthwise, wrong sides together, and press. Open binding and press cut edges toward center.

Tips for Binding Placemat Edges

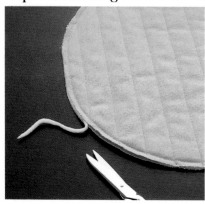

Quilted fabrics. Before applying binding, stitch placemat ¼" (6 mm) from edge. Trim batting from hem area to reduce bulk in bound edge.

Slipstitched edges. Open out bias binding. Pin right side of binding to front of mat, raw edges even. Stitch on foldline. Turn binding to back of mat and slipstitch.

Topstitched edges. Open out bias binding. Pin right side of binding to back of mat, raw edges even. Stitch on foldline. Turn binding to front of mat and topstitch.

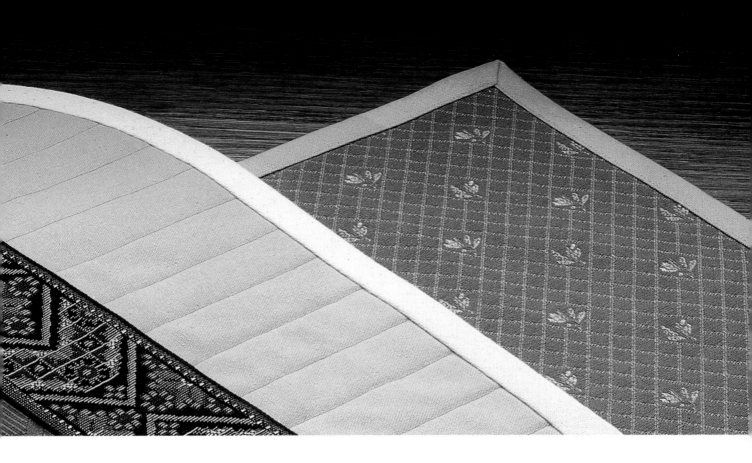

Placemats can be lined, underlined with fusible interfacing, made of quilted fabric, or sewn double for extra body. Two common finished sizes of placemats are 18" × 12" (46 × 30.5 cm) and 16" × 14" (40.5 × 35.5 cm). Choose the best size for your table and place settings.

Table runners are usually 12" to 18" (30.5 to 46 cm) wide; make them wider if they will be used as

placemats. Drop lengths vary from 8" to 12" (20.5 to 30.5 cm). Table runners may be cut on either the lengthwise or the crosswise grain of the fabric, but less piecing of fabric is required if they are cut on lengthwise grain.

Table mats protect the surface of a table without hiding the legs or base. Cut and sew a mat to the exact size of the tabletop and finish the edges.

Corners. Sandwich the fabric in binding, starting binding at center of one side. Baste binding and topstitch to corner, catching all layers. At corner, fold diagonally; baste and topstitch next side. Finish ends, right.

Oval mats. Shape corners of mat using a dinner plate as a guide. Before applying bias binding, shape binding to curves with a steam iron.

Finishing ends. Cut bias binding 1" (2.5 cm) beyond the end. Turn under ½" (1.3 cm); finish stitching to end of binding. Slipstitch.

Banded Placemats

Wide double banding creates reversible placemat.

✄ Cutting Directions

Determine size of finished mat (page 310) and desired width of finished banding. Cut placemat center the size of finished mat minus two times the width of finished banding, plus ½" (1.3 cm). For each mat, cut two centers. Stitch centers, wrong sides together, a scant ¼" (6 mm) from raw edge.

Cut banding twice the finished width plus ½" (1.3 cm); length the distance around outer edge of *finished* mat plus ½" (1.3 cm). Use ¼" (6 mm) seams. Press in half lengthwise, wrong sides together. Press under ¼" (6 mm) on lengthwise edges.

How to Sew Banded Placemats with Mitered Corners

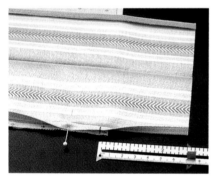

1) Mark beginning stitching point on band the width of finished band plus ¼" (6 mm). Place mark ¼" (6 mm) from corner of mat, raw edges even and right sides together.

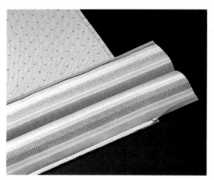

2) Mark and pin band at adjacent corner ¼" (6 mm) from edge. Pin between corners. Stitch on foldline from mark to mark; backstitch at ends to secure.

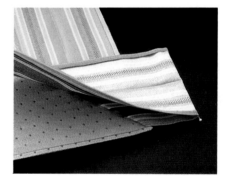

3) Fold band from mat diagonally. Mark out from corner stitching the width of finished band. Fold at mark, right sides together. Mark ¼" (6 mm) from corner of mat.

4) Repeat steps 2 and 3, above, for next two corners.

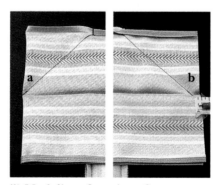

5) Mark lines for miters from previous stitching to foldline; end lines at folded edge **(a)** or ¼" (6 mm) from raw edge **(b)**; stitch. Trim excess fabric. Press seams open.

6) Turn band to finished position. Fold miters on underside of band; pin folded edge of band to seamline. Slipstitch miters and edges of band.

Trimmed Placemats

Trimmed placemats have banding stitched to one side. Purchase finished trim or cut trim from fabric. The same method may also be used to stitch banding on tablecloths.

✂ Cutting Directions

Cut the placemat 1" (2.5 cm) larger than desired finished size (page 310). Press ½" (1.3 cm) seam allowance to right side of placemat on all edges. Cut trimming long enough to go around edge of placemat, plus 1" (2.5 cm). You will need approximately 61" (155 cm) for each placemat. If making your own banding from fabric, allow ¼" (6 mm) on each side for finishing. Press under ¼" (6 mm) on long sides of banding.

How to Sew Placemats with Mitered Ribbon Trimming

1) Position short end of band ½" (1.3 cm) beyond edge of mat, aligning lengthwise edge of band with folded outer edge of the placemat; pin.

2) Fold trimming straight back at corner so fold is even with edge of mat. Fold trimming diagonally to form right angle; press and pin. Repeat at next two corners.

3) Fold end diagonally at first corner to form right angle; press. Remove pins. Baste on diagonal foldlines, using pins or glue stick.

4) Stitch each corner of trim on diagonal foldline, stitching on wrong side and beginning at inner edge. Backstitch at beginning and end of seam to secure.

5) Adjust mat size or miters if necessary. Trim seam allowances of miters to ¼" (6 mm); press seams open. Press under seam allowance that extends at one corner.

6) Baste trim to mat, with outer edges even. Stitch outer edge, beginning at one side and pivoting at corners; backstitch. Stitch inner edge.

Six Ways to Make and Hem Napkins

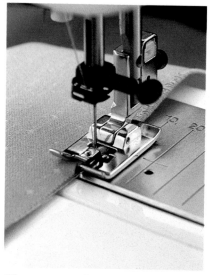

Satin stitch. Turn under ½" (1.3 cm) on all sides. Miter corners (page 308). Edgestitch along raw edge to use as guide. Use wide, closely spaced zigzag to stitch from right side over edgestitching.

Zigzag overedge. Trim loose threads from napkin edges. Stitch over raw edge, using wide, closely spaced zigzag. Use overedge foot or special-purpose foot to maintain zigzag width.

Decorative stitch. Press under ¼" (6 mm) and stitch. From right side, stitch with a decorative stitch, using straight stitching as the guideline. Blanket stitch (shown above) gives a hemstitched look.

Napkins

Coordinating napkins are the finishing touch to your tabletop fashions. Standard finished napkins are 14" or 17" (35.5 or 43 cm) square. Before cutting the fabric, square the ends, using a carpenter's square. For fringed napkins, square the ends by pulling a thread.

Napkin hems can be decorative. Experiment with some of the decorative stitches on your sewing machine. The hemming techniques shown here can also be used on tablecloths and placemats.

✄ Cutting Directions
Cut napkins 1" (2.5 cm) larger than finished size. One yard (meter) of 36" (91.5 cm) wide fabric yields four 17" (43 cm) napkins. A piece of fabric 45" (115 cm) square yields nine 14" (35.5 cm) napkins.

Narrow hem. Press under ¼" (6 mm) double-fold hem on opposite sides of all napkins. Edgestitch from one napkin to the next using continuous stitching. Repeat for remaining sides.

Double-fold hem. Turn under ¼" (6 mm) on all edges and press. Turn under another ¼" (6 mm). Miter corners as directed for narrow hem (page 308). Edgestitch close to folded edge.

Fringe. Cut napkins on a pulled thread to straighten edges. Stitch ½" (1.3 cm) from raw edges with short straight stitches or narrow, closely spaced zigzag. Pull out threads up to the stitching line.

Index

Creative Publishing international, Inc.
offers a variety of how-to books. For
information write:
  Creative Publishing international, Inc.
  Subscriber Books
  5900 Green Oak Drive
  Minnetonka, MN 55343